t

Exam Ref MS-101 Microsoft 365 Mobility and Security

Brian Svidergol
Bob Clements

Exam Ref MS-101 Microsoft 365 Mobility and Security

Published with the authorization of Microsoft Corporation by:
Pearson Education, Inc.

Copyright © 2019 by Pearson Education

ISBN-978-0-13-557489-8
ISBN-0-13-557489-7

Library of Congress Control Number: 2019941779

1   2019

Trademarks

Warning and Disclaimer

Special Sales

For information about buying this title in bulk quantities, or for special sales opportunities (which may include electronic versions; custom cover designs; and content particular to your business, training goals, marketing focus, or branding interests), please contact our corporate sales department at corpsales@pearsoned.com or (800) 382-3419.

For government sales inquiries, please contact governmentsales@pearsoned.com.

For questions about sales outside the U.S., please contact intlcs@pearson.com.

Editor-in-Chief	Brett Bartow
Executive Editor	Loretta Yates
Sponsoring Editor	Charvi Arora
Development Editor	Troy Mott
Managing Editor	Sandra Schroeder
Senior Project Editor	Tracey Croom
Editorial Production	Backstop Media
Copy Editor	Liv Bainbridge
Indexer	MAP Systems
Proofreader	Jana Gardner
Technical Editor	Santos Martinez
Cover Designer	Twist Creative, Seattle

Contents at a glance

Contents

Chapter 3   Manage Microsoft 365 governance and compliance   205

Acknowledgments

Brian Svidergol I would like to acknowledge my wife Lindsay, my son Jack, and my daughter Leah – thanks for being supportive of my endeavors. And thanks for providing me good times and great memories that enable me to maintain a high level of motivation. I love you! I would also like to thank the people working hard on the backend of the project – Loretta Yates (executive editor), Santos Martinez (technical reviewer), Charvi Arora (assistant sponsoring editor), and Troy Mott. I would like to dedicate this book to all the IT professionals taking the time to explore, learn, experiment, and test their skills with certification exams. Keep up the good work and good luck!

Bob Clements I would like to acknowledge my amazing family for all their love, support, and laughter. To my wife Diane, who enables me to work on fun projects like these. To my daughter Abigail, who surprises me every day with her kindness and creativity. And to my son Samuel, who consistently finds ways to make me laugh out loud. Thank you! I would like to dedicate this book to my wife Diane. Your encouragement and support are invaluable. Thank you for all that you do!

About the Authors

BRIAN SVIDERGOL designs and builds infrastructure, cloud, and hybrid solutions. He holds many industry certifications including the Microsoft Certified Solutions Expert (MCSE) – Cloud Platform and Infrastructure. Brian is the author of several books covering everything from on-premises infrastructure technologies to hybrid cloud environments. He has extensive real-world experience from startup organizations to large Fortune 500 companies on design, implementation, and migration projects.

BOB CLEMENTS specializes in enterprise device management. He holds industry certifications around client manageability and administration for Windows, Mac, and Linux. Bob has an extensive background in designing, implementing, and supporting device management solutions for private and public sector companies. In his free time he enjoys spending time with his family, writing, and exploring new technologies.

Introduction

The MS-101 exam focuses on common tasks and concepts that an administrator needs to understand to deploy and manage infrastructure in Microsoft Azure. Managing Azure subscriptions and resources is a key topic on the exam, which includes configure cost center quotas, tagging, subscription level policies, as well as resource organization using resource groups. Another topic covered is implementing and managing storage; which includes creating and configuring storage accounts, implementing Azure backup, as well as configuring Azure files and understanding the services for importing and exporting data to Azure. A significant portion of the exam is focused on deploying and managing virtual machines, which includes configuring of networking, storage and monitoring, automated deployments and managing VM backups. Configuring, managing, and monitoring virtual networks is part of the exam, as-is configuring load balancing. This book covers the creation and managing of virtual networks, DNS, connectivity between virtual networks, and configuring network security groups. The final topic is managing identities, which includes topics on managing Azure Active Directory (AD) when creating users, groups, and devices. You will also find the configuring of hybrid identity using Azure AD Connect, multi-factor authentication, as well as configuring services such as identity protection and self-service password resets.

This book is geared toward Azure administrators who manage cloud services that span storage, security, networking and compute. It explains how to configure and deploy services across a broad range of related Azure services to help you prepare for the exam.

This book covers every major topic area found on the exam, but it does not cover every exam question. Only the Microsoft exam team has access to the exam questions, and Microsoft regularly adds new questions to the exam, making it impossible to cover specific questions. You should consider this book a supplement to your relevant real-world experience and other study materials. If you encounter a topic in this book that you do not feel completely comfortable with, use the "Need more review?" links you'll find in the text to find more information and take the time to research and study the topic. Great information is available on MSDN, TechNet, and in blogs and forums.

Organization of this book

This book is organized by the "Skills measured" list published for the exam. The "Skills measured" list is available for each exam on the Microsoft Learning website: *https://aka.ms/examlist*. Each chapter in this book corresponds to a major topic area in the list, and the technical tasks in each topic area determine a chapter's organization. If an exam covers six major topic areas, for example, the book will contain six chapters.

Microsoft certifications

Microsoft certifications distinguish you by proving your command of a broad set of skills and experience with current Microsoft products and technologies. The exams and corresponding certifications are developed to validate your mastery of critical competencies as you design and develop, or implement and support, solutions with Microsoft products and technologies both on-premises and in the cloud. Certification brings a variety of benefits to the individual and to employers and organizations.

> **MORE INFO**   **ALL MICROSOFT CERTIFICATIONS**
>
> For information about Microsoft certifications, including a full list of available certifications, go to *http://www.microsoft.com/learn*.

Quick access to online references

Throughout this book are addresses to webpages that the author has recommended you visit for more information. Some of these addresses (also known as URLs) can be painstaking to type into a web browser, so we've compiled all of them into a single list that readers of the print edition can refer to while they read.

Download the list at *MicrosoftPressStore.com/ExamRefMS101/downloads*

The URLs are organized by chapter and heading. Every time you come across a URL in the book, find the hyperlink in the list to go directly to the webpage.

Errata, updates, & book support

We've made every effort to ensure the accuracy of this book and its companion content. You can access updates to this book—in the form of a list of submitted errata and their related corrections—at:

MicrosoftPressStore.com/ExamRefMS101/errata

If you discover an error that is not already listed, please submit it to us at the same page.

For additional book support and information, please visit *MicrosoftPressStore.com/Support*.

Please note that product support for Microsoft software and hardware is not offered through the previous addresses. For help with Microsoft software or hardware, go to *http://support.microsoft.com*.

Stay in touch

Let's keep the conversation going! We're on Twitter: *http://twitter.com/MicrosoftPress*.

Important: How to use this book to study for the exam

Certification exams validate your on-the-job experience and product knowledge. To gauge your readiness to take an exam, use this Exam Ref to help you check your understanding of the skills tested by the exam. Determine the topics you know well and the areas in which you need more experience. To help you refresh your skills in specific areas, we have also provided "Need more review?" pointers, which direct you to more in-depth information outside the book.

The Exam Ref is not a substitute for hands-on experience. This book is *not* designed to teach you new skills.

We recommend that you round out your exam preparation by using a combination of available study materials and courses. Learn more about available classroom training and find free online courses and live events at *https://microsoft.com/learn*. Microsoft Official Practice Tests are available for many exams at *https://aka.ms/practicetests*.

This book is organized by the "Skills measured" list published for the exam. The "Skills measured" list for each exam is available on the Microsoft Learn website: *http://aka.ms/examlist*.

Note that this Exam Ref is based on this publicly available information and the author's experience. To safeguard the integrity of the exam, authors do not have access to the exam questions.

CHAPTER 1

Implement modern device services

In this chapter we are working with cloud-based services within Microsoft 365 that are designed to deploy, secure, and manage devices in the enterprise. Throughout this book we will be working with various Microsoft technologies such as Azure, Microsoft Intune, Office 365, and System Center Configuration Manager (ConfigMgr). Along the way there will be several walkthroughs and examples that illustrate how to manage these tools. For these demonstrations we do recommend that you follow along in your own lab. Here are a few links to help get you started:

> **IMPORTANT**
>
> **Have you read page xvii?**
>
> It contains valuable information regarding the skills you need to pass the exam.

- **Enterprise Mobility + Security 90-day trial (includes Azure Active Directory Premium P2)** *https://www.microsoft.com/cloud-platform/enterprise-mobility-security-trial*
- **Office 365 Business Premium 30-day trial**: *https://products.office.com/business/office-365-business-premium*
- **System Center Configuration Manager Current Branch 90-day technical preview** *https://www.microsoft.com/evalcenter/evaluate-system-center-configuration-manager-and-endpoint-protection-technical-preview*

Skills in this chapter:

- Implement Mobile Device Management
- Manage device compliance
- Plan for devices and apps
- Plan Windows 10 deployment

Skill 1.1: Implement Mobile Device Management

There are a variety of mobile device management (MDM) solutions available in the market for managing corporate devices and applications. Microsoft Intune is an MDM solution designed around modern device management and built within the Microsoft 365 umbrella.

Without a functional MDM solution, the devices that are meant to provide value and productivity to your workforce, can also introduce security threats, IT support inefficiencies, and an overall inconsistent user experience.

When considering how to manage devices in the enterprise, you need to consider answers to questions such as: is on-premises data protected when accessed from an unmanaged device? Are users able to work in a consistent and effective manner when moving between devices? Can you support a bring-your-own-device (BYOD) program? MDM helps solve these problems by providing a centrally managed service that delivers a secure and productive experience to your organization. In this skill section we will review the process for implementing MDM, including planning considerations, configuration of the MDM, and device enrollment.

This section covers the following topics:

- Plan for MDM
- Configure MDM integration with Azure AD
- Set an MDM authority
- Set device enrollment limit for users

Plan for MDM

In this section we will cover planning considerations for MDM. For the exam you will need to be familiar with the different MDM services that are available from Microsoft, what those services support, and which service to choose if given a scenario with specific requirements. Other considerations that we will cover include prerequisites for your environment, such as network security and capacity planning, as well as pre-existing Group Policy Objects that may overlap with future MDM policies.

The planning stage for MDM is all about knowing what your options are, what the needs of the organization are, and how these two points intersect.

Choose an MDM solution

Microsoft offers a combination of MDM solutions to their customers. These offerings have changed over the years, with heavy investments into cloud services and integration with Azure. The introduction of Windows 10 has also influenced the way you manage devices with a set of native MDM protocols within the operating system, eliminating the need to install another agent on your endpoints. Knowing which solution to choose depends on your organization's deployment goals and objectives. Here is a breakdown of these cloud-based services and some examples on why you might choose one over the other:

- **Microsoft Intune** This solution works best for customers that require modern management capabilities for Windows 10 devices, but also need to limit their on-premises server infrastructure. Microsoft Intune is a cloud-based management solution that does not require additional server infrastructure. Platform support for Intune includes management capabilities for Windows 10 and macOS. You also have access to features like Autopilot, which can help reduce traditional operating system deployment requirements.

- **Co-management between Microsoft Intune and ConfigMgr**   This solution bridges Microsoft Intune and ConfigMgr, enabling customers to co-manage devices based on their requirements. ConfigMgr is an on-premises management solution that includes additional platform support, such as Windows Server. It also includes a unique set of technologies, such as task sequences and image deployment. Environments with co-management can take workloads for their Windows 10 devices and mobile devices and move them to the cloud, while still supporting traditional infrastructure.

- **MDM for Office 365**   This MDM solution works best for customers that rely heavily on Office 365 and have a requirement to manage iOS and Android mobile devices. MDM for Office 365 is a cloud-based management solution that does not require additional server infrastructure, but has the smallest footprint when it comes to MDM capabilities.

There is a fourth solution that is not listed here, and that is Microsoft Intune Hybrid. This configuration was an earlier capability that enabled integration between ConfigMgr and Intune in order to maximize platform support and enable administrators to manage devices from a single pane of glass. With the rapid release of new capabilities in Intune, Microsoft reworked how these products were integrated. Intune Hybrid has now been deprecated and will be reaching the end of its support in September 2019.

MORE INFO   **TRANSITION FROM HYBRID MDM**

For more information about the transition from hybrid MDM to co-management, visit: *https://techcommunity.microsoft.com/t5/Intune-Customer-Success/Move-from-Hybrid-Mobile-Device-Management-to-Intune-on-Azure/ba-p/280150*. ConfigMgr plays an important role in bridging traditional device management with cloud-based MDM, and co-management is the technology that makes this happen. This is not to be confused with Intune Hybrid. Co-management is a feature available in the ConfigMgr management console starting with ConfigMgr 1710 and supports Windows 10 1709 and later. Setup will require a licensed Intune account to initiate the connection. Once enabled, an administrator can decide which workloads remain managed by ConfigMgr and which workloads move to Intune. For example, Windows Update policies is a workload that can be moved to Intune.

Table 1-1 breaks down each MDM solution in additional detail, along with the list of supported operating systems. From an exam perspective, plan for questions that describe a company's requirements for MDM. You should be familiar with the capabilities and supported operating systems for each solution.

TABLE 1-1 Available MDM solutions and capabilities

Management Platform	Capabilities	Supported Operating Systems
Microsoft Intune	All the capabilities of MDM for Office 365 Mobile device inventory and reporting Certificate management Application management Conditional Access Manage Windows 10 devices	iOS, Android, Surface Hub, Windows 10 Mobile, Windows 10, Windows Holographic for Business
MDM for Office 365	Secure access to Office 365 email and documents, security policies to enforce settings such as PIN lock, selective wipe of company data	iOS, Android, Windows mobile

EXAM TIP

The MS-101 exam is focused on Microsoft 365 mobility and security. This covers modern cloud-based technologies and solutions that help customers move to the cloud. As you prepare for the exam keep an eye on new features and capabilities, such as co-management and how it fits in with modern MDM management. In Skill 1.3 we cover co-management in detail.

Plan your infrastructure

Cloud-based MDM services can help reduce or eliminate the need for on-premises server infrastructure, but there are other infrastructure components to consider, such as external network communication and bandwidth requirements.

Devices that are enrolled in MDM for Office 365 or Microsoft Intune will require regular communication with these cloud services. Communication is standardized across HTTP (80) and HTTPS (443). Microsoft maintains a published list of domains and IP addresses that should be reviewed and implemented into your existing firewall exceptions to ensure that devices can reach the corresponding cloud service. For the exam, you are not expected to memorize this list, but you should know what ports the service communicates over.

Moving from an on-premises management solution to the cloud will impact Internet bandwidth. Your organization's Internet connection must be scaled accordingly to accommodate the increase in traffic. For example, depending on the policies you define, a device enrolled with Intune will check in daily for policy changes, updates, and malware definitions. Other activities like software updates or software distribution can have a substantial impact if they are not accounted for. At a minimum, Microsoft recommends that managed devices remain connected to the Internet for at least one hour each day. The following technologies can be implemented to help reduce network bandwidth impact:

- **Proxy server** A caching proxy server can be used to cache certain types of content, reducing the impact of redundant downloads from multiple devices. For example, a Windows 10 feature update can be multiple gigabytes in size. Caching this content can dramatically reduce Internet bandwidth usage.

- **Delivery Optimization**   Delivery Optimization is a cloud-managed solution that helps reduce bandwidth consumption by leveraging peer-caching technology, sharing package contents between devices on a per-deployment basis. This technology is available for Windows 10 devices. Because it is a cloud-managed service, devices must have access to the Internet to leverage its capabilities.

> **MORE INFO** **INTUNE NETWORK REQUIREMENTS AND DELIVERY OPTIMIZATION**
>
> To learn more about the types of Intune communication, frequency and network requirements, visit: *https://docs.microsoft.com/en-us/intune/network-bandwidth-use*. To learn more about Delivery Optimization and the available configurations, visit: *https://docs.microsoft.com/en-us/windows/deployment/update/waas-delivery-optimization*.

Plan your device policies

This section covers the planning considerations for device policies when implementing MDM for Office 365 or Microsoft Intune. In a traditional Active Directory domain, Group Policy serves multiple roles. Administrative templates in Group Policy enable you to define various custom configuration changes for the operating system and your business applications. Enrolling devices in MDM will present two challenges to plan for:

1. **Policy conflicts**   Once a device is enrolled in MDM, you create and assign a series of new policies to manage the device. Some of these policies may overlap with configurations that exist in Group Policy, or possibly other management tools, such as Config-Mgr. One example could be Windows Update settings, because these options can be configured in Group Policy, ConfigMgr, and MDM. Considering this challenge as part of the planning phase can save countless hours troubleshooting policy conflicts following enrollment.

2. **Unified management**   The policies available in MDM for Office 365 and Microsoft Intune continue to evolve, providing additional controls for device management. There are, however, policy settings that are not yet available. In these situations, consider the impact of eliminating the policy setting altogether, or continuing to support traditional on-premises controls until they can be fully managed by MDM or are no longer needed.

Now that you know some of the challenges with policy management, let's look at two possible solutions that can help you address these challenges as you plan for MDM. First, in Windows 10 1803 Microsoft introduced a new Intune policy called ControlPolicyConflict. When applied, this MDM policy ensures that when a conflict occurs between MDM and Group Policy, the MDM policy will always win. Figure 1-1 shows the Intune portal with the custom policy setting defined for ControlPolicyConflict. You can create this policy by following these steps:

1. Sign-in to the Microsoft Azure portal at *https://portal.azure.com/*.
2. Click **All services**.
3. Search for **Intune** and select it.
4. Under Manage, click **Device configuration**.

5. On the Device Configuration blade, under Manage, click **Profiles**.

6. Click **Create profile**.

7. On the Create Profile blade, fill in the following:

   A. **Name** ControlPolicyConflict

   B. **Platform** Windows 10 and later

   C. **Profile type** Custom

8. On the Custom OMA-URI Settings blade, click **Add**.

9. On the Add Row blade, fill in the following and click **OK**.

   D. **Name** ControlPolicyConflict

   E. **OMA-URI** ./Device/Vendor/MSFT/Policy/Config/ControlPolicyConflict/MDMWin-sOverGP

   F. **Data type** Integer

   G. **Value** 1

10. On the Custom OMA-URI Settings blade, click **OK**.

11. On the Create profile blade, click **Create**.

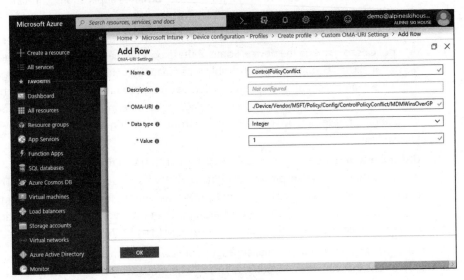

FIGURE 1-1 Custom Intune policy for ControlPolicyConflict

The second solution helps you identify Group Policy settings in your domain that are not supported by MDM. This solution is the MDM Migration Analysis Tool (MMAT). When executed, MMAT will scan the policies in your domain and compare them against a list of supported MDM policies. Once complete, the tool will generate an XML and HTML report that can assist administrators in determining potential conflicts.

In Figure 1-2 you can see an example of the HTML report generated by MMAT. In this example the tool has identified settings in the default domain policy that are not compatible with MDM and will need to be addressed. The following requirements need to be met before running MMAT in your environment:

1. The latest version of the Remote Server Administration Tools (RSAT) must be installed on the system you will be running MMAT from.

2. Execution is supported on Windows 7, Windows 8, Windows 8.1, and Windows 10.

3. The Invoke-MdmMigrationAnalysisTool.ps1 script needs to be executed from an elevated PowerShell window.

4. The PowerShell execution policy needs to be temporarily bypassed to run the script.

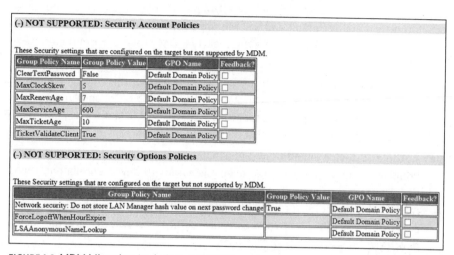

(-) NOT SUPPORTED: Security Account Policies

These Security settings that are configured on the target but not supported by MDM.

Group Policy Name	Group Policy Value	GPO Name	Feedback?
ClearTextPassword	False	Default Domain Policy	☐
MaxClockSkew	5	Default Domain Policy	☐
MaxRenewAge	7	Default Domain Policy	☐
MaxServiceAge	600	Default Domain Policy	☐
MaxTicketAge	10	Default Domain Policy	☐
TicketValidateClient	True	Default Domain Policy	☐

(-) NOT SUPPORTED: Security Options Policies

These Security settings that are configured on the target but not supported by MDM.

Group Policy Name	Group Policy Value	GPO Name	Feedback?
Network security: Do not store LAN Manager hash value on next password change	True	Default Domain Policy	☐
ForceLogoffWhenHourExpire		Default Domain Policy	☐
LSAAnonymousNameLookup		Default Domain Policy	☐

FIGURE 1-2 MDM Migration Analysis Tool (MMAT) results

MORE INFO **MMAT DOCUMENTATION**

At the time of this writing MMAT is still in active development and available on GitHub. For more information about the tool, including where to download it, prerequisites and runtime instructions, visit: *https://github.com/WindowsDeviceManagement/MMAT.*

Configure MDM integration with Azure AD

This section covers how to configure MDM integration with Azure Active Directory (Azure AD). This integration enables you to enroll Windows 10 devices, and is not associated with other platforms, such as iOS and Android. Microsoft has developed a series of protocols in the Windows 10 operating system that are designed to communicate with Azure AD and cloud-based MDM solutions. Furthermore, they have developed an open framework for third-party MDM providers to integrate their solutions with Azure AD. With these components interlinked, administrators can integrate MDM, whether it be Intune or a third-party solution, with Azure AD in an efficient manner. The outcome provides a consistent experience for administrators and end-users.

Plan for MDM integration

Organizations that are starting to take steps toward cloud-based modern management are going to have some new challenges to undertake. In many cases the first obstacle will be an existing on-premises Active Directory domain, with several business applications and processes that have interlinking dependencies. Over the next three sections we will look at steps to help address these early obstacles.

The integration between MDM and Azure AD has a few key prerequisites that you should be familiar with before implementation.

- **Active MDM subscription with a supported provider**   During the configuration of MDM, you can select which MDM provider you are going to configure. Intune is there by default and will require a supported subscription to enable. You also have the option to select a third-party MDM provider from the Azure AD app gallery.

- **Configure MDM settings**   Once you have obtained a subscription for Intune or an alternative MDM provider, you can start configuring you MDM enrollment settings. These settings include the URLs for MDM terms of use, MDM discovery, MDM compliance, and the scope of devices that will use automatic enrollment.

- **Automatic device enrollment**   At a minimum you will need an active Azure AD Premium P1 subscription in order to enable automatic device enrollment. This is an important prerequisite, as most organizations are going to want to leverage automatic enrollment for some portion of their organization. For information about Azure AD pricing, you can visit *https://azure.microsoft.com/en-us/pricing/details/active-directory/*.

- **Configure devices for automatic hybrid domain join with Azure AD and enrollment with Intune**   For modern management of devices in MDM, they need to be domain joined with Azure AD. If you have an on-premises Active Directory environment, you can accomplish this by configuring the hybrid Azure AD domain join.

Now that we have reviewed some of the planning considerations prior to configuring MDM integration, let's explore the Azure portal and see where these configurations are located.

1. Sign-in to the Microsoft Azure portal at *https://portal.azure.com/*.

2. Click **All Services**.

3. Search for **Azure Active Directory** and select it.

4. Locate **Mobility (MDM and MAM)** and select it.

5. On the Mobility (MDM and MAM) blade, click **Add Application**. Figure 1-3 shows an example of the third-party MDM applications that are available in the Azure AD app gallery at the time of this writing. Notice there is an option available for an on-premises MDM. This option enables administrators to setup and MDM provider that is not hosted on an Azure tenant.

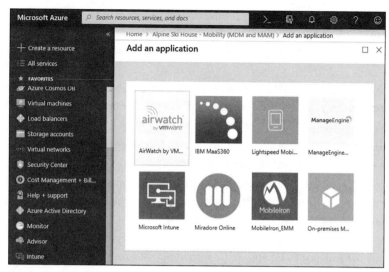

FIGURE 1-3 Azure AD App Gallery for MDM applications

6. Return to the Mobility (MDM and MAM) blade by clicking the navigation link above the **Add An Application** blade.

7. On the Mobility (MDM and MAM) blade, click the **Microsoft Intune** application. If your subscription includes an active Azure AD Premium license then you will reach the MDM and MAM configuration page, as shown in Figure 1-4. Otherwise, you will be presented with the option to sign up for a premium subscription.

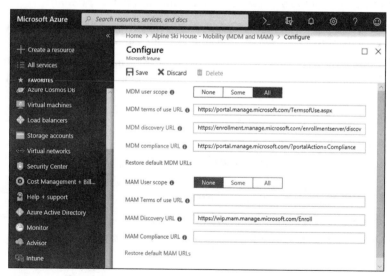

FIGURE 1-4 Azure AD MDM and MAM configuration page

From the configuration page you can define the following MDM settings.

- **MDM user scope** The user scope setting defines the list of users that will be enabled for automatic MDM enrollment. This setting is dependent on the device being joined to Azure AD. You have the option to enable this setting for all users or specify multiple groups.
- **MDM terms of use URL** The terms of use URL is used during manual device enrollment and displays your organization's terms of use to users before a device can be enrolled. The default URL is configured for Microsoft Intune.
- **MDM discovery URL** The discovery URL is used for device enrollment to the MDM. The default URL is configured for Microsoft Intune.
- **MDM compliance URL** The compliance URL is used when a device is found to be non-compliant. This URL displays the compliance issue to the user for further action. The default URL is configured for Microsoft Intune.

At this stage the settings we have reviewed deal primarily with setting up your MDM provider in Azure AD and modifying automatic enrollment for Azure AD joined devices. In the next section we will look at how to setup automatic enrollment using Group Policy or ConfigMgr, but before introducing those options you need to understand some basics about hybrid Azure AD join.

Administrators that manage an on-premises Active Directory domain can leverage configurations in Group Policy or ConfigMgr to enable hybrid Azure AD join and MDM enrollment. Hybrid Azure AD join is a foundational technology for migrating to the cloud. Organizations that have an on-premises domain will use this as a stepping stone to meet future goals and objectives. Before configuring hybrid Azure AD join or device enrollment, there are a few prerequisites to be aware of. For this exam you should be familiar with the following:

- **Azure AD Connect** Azure AD Connect is an application that synchronizes users, groups and computer objects in your on-premises domain with Azure AD.
- **Registration URLs** For hybrid Azure AD join to work, devices in your organization will require communication with Microsoft Azure. The following URLs must be accessible by the devices on your network that will be enrolling:
    - *https://enterpriseregistration.windows.net*
    - *https://login.microsoftonline.com*
    - *https://device.login.microsoftonline.com*

> **MORE INFO   HYBRID AZURE AD JOIN IN-DEPTH**
>
> For more information about planning your hybrid Azure AD join implementation, visit: *https://docs.microsoft.com/azure/active-directory/devices/hybrid-azuread-join-plan.*

Setup MDM integration using Group Policy

Earlier in this chapter we discussed policy management between Group Policy and MDM. In that scenario we covered two methods for identifying and preventing Group Policy conflicts when MDM is introduced into an environment. Here we review two Group Policy settings that will assist you in configuring devices for MDM enrollment.

The first policy setting enables administrators to configure automatic hybrid Azure AD join for domain joined devices. This setting is supported on Windows 10 1607 and later. Use the following steps to locate and enable this setting.

> **NOTE GROUP POLICY PREREQUISITES**
>
> In these examples use the group policy templates for Windows 10 1803. Earlier versions of the templates may not support these settings. You will also need the Group Policy management console installed on your device before proceeding.

1. Open the **Group Policy Management Editor**.
2. Create a new Group Policy Object (GPO) and name it "Azure AD Join."
3. Right-click the new GPO and select **Edit**.
4. Under Computer Configuration, expand **Policies**.
5. Expand Administrative Templates.
6. Expand Windows Components.
7. Locate and select **Device Registration**.
8. Locate and edit the policy: Register Domain Joined Computers As Devices.
9. Select the radio button next to **Enabled**, as shown in Figure 1-5.

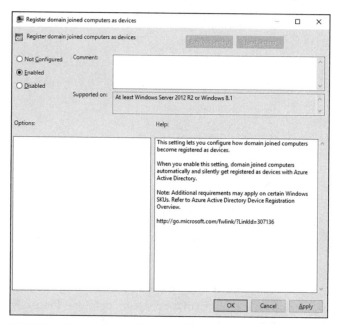

FIGURE 1-5 Group Policy preference editor

10. Click **OK**.

Once configured, you can link this GPO to a domain, site, or Organizational Unit (OU) to enforce hybrid Azure AD join. With the previous prerequisites complete, the targeted devices will join Azure AD. The following setting controls automatic enrollment into MDM. This setting is supported on Windows 10 1709 and later. Use the following steps to locate and enable this setting.

1. Open the **Group Policy Management Editor**.

2. Create a new Group Policy Object (GPO) and call it "Intune MDM Enrollment."

3. Right-click the new GPO and select **Edit**.

4. Under Computer Configuration, expand **Policies**.

5. Expand **Administrative Templates**.

6. Expand **Windows Components**.

7. Locate and select **MDM**.

8. Locate and edit the policy: Enable Automatic MDM Enrollment Using Default Azure AD Credentials.

9. Select the radio button next to Enabled, as shown in Figure 1-6.

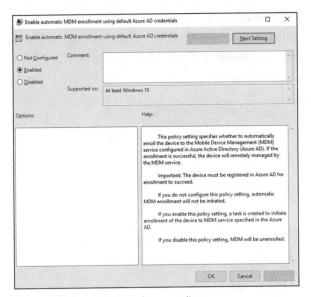

FIGURE 1-6 Group Policy preference editor

10. Click **OK**.

After applying this GPO, supported Windows 10 devices will begin enrolling into the MDM provider that you previously configured at the start of the chapter. For Intune, these devices should start appearing in the Devices blade of the Intune Azure portal.

Setup MDM integration using ConfigMgr

The policy settings described in the previous section can also be applied with ConfigMgr. The effect on the managed device is often the same, but ConfigMgr offers some additional flexibility for administrators. For example, if you want to test these settings on a small ring of devices, you can explicitly target those devices in ConfigMgr, as opposed to creating a new OU.

ConfigMgr is now releasing major product updates every four months. The features introduced with these updates will account for new features found in the Windows 10 operating system. For example, when MDM automatic enrollment was introduced with Windows 10 1709, support was introduced with ConfigMgr 1710

Here you will see how to enable the comparable settings for hybrid Azure AD join and MDM enrollment with ConfigMgr. This walkthrough assumes you already have a current version of ConfigMgr running in your environment. First, let's examine enabling hybrid Azure AD join.

> **NOTE   CONFIGMGR VERSION**
>
> These examples use ConfigMgr 1806. Earlier versions of ConfigMgr may not have these options available.

1. Click Start, search for **Configuration Manager Console** and select it.
2. In the Configuration Manager Console, click the **Administration Workspace**.
3. Under Overview, click **Client Settings**.
4. In the ribbon, click **Create Custom Client Device Settings**.
5. On the Create Custom Client Device Settings window, enter **Azure AD join**.
6. Select the **Cloud Services** checkbox and click Cloud Services in the navigation pane.
7. Under Device Settings, choose **Yes** from the dropdown next To **Automatically Register New Windows 10 Domain Joined Devices With Azure Active Directory**, as shown in Figure 1-7.

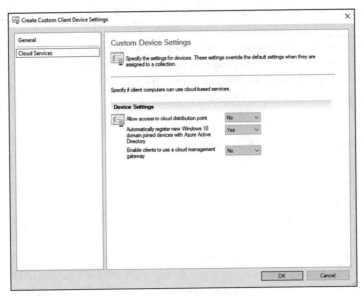

FIGURE 1-7 ConfigMgr custom client device settings

8. Click **OK**.

Before deploying these custom client device settings, be aware that you may need to increase the priority value in comparison to other device settings that are deployed. This will ensure these settings take priority over any conflicting deployments. Next, you can create a device collection with the devices you need to target, followed by a deployment for the custom client device settings.

Automatic MDM enrollment with ConfigMgr is the last configuration setting we will be reviewing in this section. This setting is controlled in the properties for Co-Management, a feature that was first introduced in the 1710 release of ConfigMgr. Because of this, you will need to have Co-Management enabled before you can configure this setting. We will go into more detail on Co-Management in Chapter 3, "Plan for devices and apps." For now, let's examine how automatic MDM enrollment is managed in ConfigMgr.

1. Click Start, search for **Configuration Manager Console** and select it.

2. Click the **Administration Workspace**.

3. Under Overview, expand **Cloud Services**.

4. Click **Co-Management**.

5. Right-click the Co-Management policy and select **Properties** (requires prior configuration of Co-Management).

6. On the Properties window, on the Enablement tab, review the available options in the dropdown for Automatic enrollment in Intune. The following options are available:

    ■ **None**   Selecting this option will disable automatic enrollment. This option is preferred if you are not ready to enable automatic enrollment or you are managing it through another solution, such as Group Policy.

- **Pilot** Selecting this option will enable automatic enrollment for the devices contained in a pilot collection, which you define on the Staging tab of the properties window. This option is preferred if you need to enable automatic enrollment on a select list of devices. If you choose this option, be sure to have your pilot collection created and ready for targeting.

- **All** Selecting this option will enable automatic enrollment for all supported devices managed by ConfigMgr.

7. Select Pilot from the dropdown list. Refer to Figure 1-8 for an example of this setting configuration.

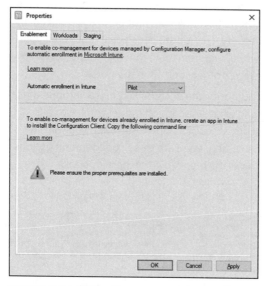

FIGURE 1-8 ConfigMgr Co-management properties

8. Click the **Staging** tab.

9. Under Pilot Collection, click **Browse** and select a device collection that you want to enable automatic enrollment for. This device collection should be closely monitored and only contain devices that you need to enroll.

10. Click **OK**.

EXAM TIP

MDM integration settings in ConfigMgr are not configured from the same location in the management console. Be prepared for questions that test your knowledge of the interface. For example, you are provided with a list of six steps to enable automatic MDM enrollment for Windows 10. You are asked to select the three steps required to accomplish the task and put them in the correct order. Client device settings and Co-Management are both listed as available options and you need to know which interface is the correct one.

Set an MDM authority

For the exam you will need to understand what role the MDM authority plays relative to your overall goals and objectives for device management. As the MDM administrator, you can't enroll any devices until the MDM authority is configured, which highlights this as an important prerequisite. In its simplest form, the MDM authority that you assign determines which interface you will be administering devices from. Microsoft has a few configuration options available, and we will be reviewing each of these in greater detail.

Choose the MDM authority

Previously we discussed the steps for configuring MDM integration. Among those steps we discussed the need for Azure AD join and automatic enrollment, but before you can enable device enrollment you must assign an MDM authority. This is both a technical requirement, associating devices with the solution, but also a literal requirement in that the Intune portal requires an MDM authority defined before you can access other controls in the portal.

When it comes to choosing an MDM authority, the decision is centered around the products you are using in your environment and what subscription model you have chosen. For example, if you have a pre-existing subscription, such as Office 365, then you will have access to MDM for Office 365. At the time of this writing, there are three configuration options for assigning an MDM authority. Table 1-2 shows the breakdown of these options.

TABLE 1-2 Available MDM authorities

MDM Authority	Capabilities	Key Points
Microsoft Intune	Standalone cloud-based MDM No on-premises server requirements Support for all Intune management capabilities	Requires an Intune or EMS subscription Support for Windows 10, Mac OS X, iOS and Android No server management Migration support from on-premises to the cloud using Co-management
Microsoft Intune Hybrid	Integration with on-premises ConfigMgr environment Supports a limited set of Intune capabilities Extended capabilities through ConfigMgr Single pane of glass for managing modern and legacy operating systems	Requires an Intune or EMS subscription Solution is deprecated as of August 2018, support ending September 2019 Limited set of Intune capabilities New capabilities tied to support with ConfigMgr
MDM for Office 365	Cloud-based MDM Integration with Intune Support for a limited set of Intune capabilities	Requires an Office 365 subscription Limited set of Intune capabilities Support for iOS and Android Configured from the Office 365 Admin Center

As mentioned in Table 1-2, at the time of this writing, the Microsoft Intune Hybrid solution is still available to customers. Support, however, will be ending in September 2019. Customers that are using the hybrid MDM solution today will need to start working on a retirement strategy.

Set the MDM authority

Next, we will walk through setting the MDM authority for standalone Intune and MDM for Office 365. While Intune Hybrid is still supported, do not expect to see any exam questions related to setup. The next two sections will include screenshots for the most important elements of the interface, but it is recommended that you follow along in your own lab. These exams will test your knowledge of the management interface.

STANDALONE INTUNE

In this first section we are working with standalone Intune. For this example, we are working in an environment where the MDM authority has not been configured yet.

1. Sign-in to the Microsoft Azure portal at *https://portal.azure.com/*.

2. Click **All Services**.

3. Search for **Intune** and select it.

4. Under manage, click **Device Enrollment**. Review the Device enrollment blade in Figure 1-9. Notice that the MDM authority field is blank, and the account status is active. Without an MDM authority assigned, the Choose MDM Authority blade will open automatically.

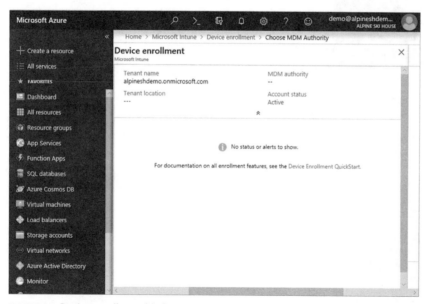

FIGURE 1-9 Device enrollment blade

5. On the Choose MDM Authority blade, select the radio button next to Intune MDM Authority, as shown in Figure 1-10.

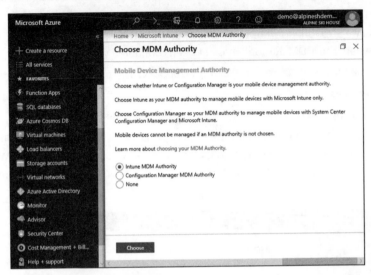

FIGURE 1-10 Choose MDM Authority blade

6. Click **Choose** to complete the configuration.

7. Review the Azure portal notifications to confirm that the MDM Authority was successfully chosen (see Figure 1-11).

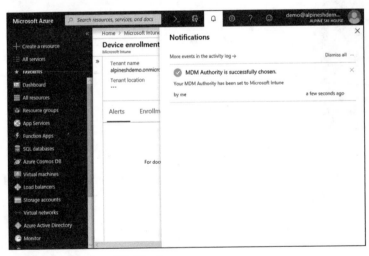

FIGURE 1-11 Azure Portal Notifications

1. Unlike standalone Intune, the MDM for Office 365 configuration change is done through the Microsoft 365 admin center. Sign-in to the Microsoft 365 admin center at *https://admin.microsoft.com/*.

2. On the Home page, type **mobile device management** in the search field and select it from the list of available options.

3. On the Set up Mobile Device Management for Office 365 page, review the list of available features, as shown in Figure 1-12. Click **Let's Get Started**. This will start the setup process and can take a few hours to complete.

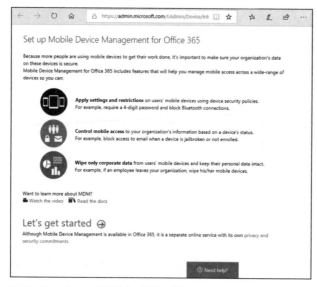

FIGURE 1-12 Set up MDM for Office 365

4. Once setup is complete, click **Manage Devices** or navigate to *https://admin.microsoft.com/adminportal/home#/MifoDevices*. All device management tasks will take place from the Microsoft 365 admin center.

5. To verify your MDM authority is set, sign-in to the Microsoft Azure portal at *https://portal.azure.com/*.

6. Click **All Services**.

7. Search for **Intune** and select it.

8. Under Manage, click **Device Enrollment**. Note that the MDM authority now shows Office 365.

Change the MDM authority

There are two scenarios where an administrator can change their MDM authority. These include the following.

- **Intune Hybrid**   In this scenario an administrator can change the MDM authority from standalone Intune to ConfigMgr, or from ConfigMgr to standalone Intune. Both of these actions are completed in the ConfigMgr management console.

- **Office 365**   In this scenario an administrator can change the MDM authority from Office 365 to standalone Intune. This action is completed in the Azure portal.

INTUNE HYBRID

For this example, we are going to walk through changing the MDM authority from ConfigMgr to standalone Intune. This walk through assumes that your environment already has ConfigMgr set as the MDM authority and an active Intune subscription is configured in the ConfigMgr management console.

> **NOTE   CONFIGMGR VERSION**
>
> In this example we will be using ConfigMgr 1806. Earlier versions of ConfigMgr may not have these options available.

1. Click Start, search for **Configuration Manager Console** and select it.
2. Click the **Administration Workspace**.
3. Under Overview, expand **Cloud Services**.
4. Click **Microsoft Intune Subscriptions**.
5. Select the **Microsoft Intune** subscription. From the ribbon, click **Delete**.
6. On the Remove Microsoft Intune Subscription Wizard, review the available options (see Figure 1-13). Note that you have the option to remove the Intune subscription or change the MDM authority. Select the radio button next to **Change MDM Authority to Microsoft Intune** and click **Next**.

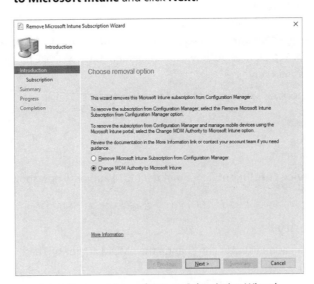

FIGURE 1-13 Remove Microsoft Intune Subscription Wizard

7. Review the warning presented before changing the MDM authority, as shown in Figure 1-14. This change will shift management from the ConfigMgr console to the Intune portal, and existing applications or policies will need to be recreated in Intune. Click **Yes**.

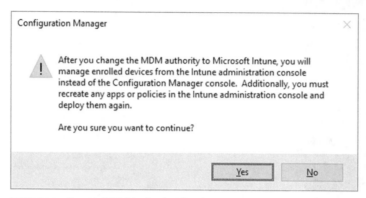

FIGURE 1-14 Change MDM Authority Warning

8. On the Subscription page, enter your credentials to sign-in to Microsoft Intune and click **Next**.

9. On the Summary page, review the requested changes and click **Next**.

10. On the Completion page, click **Close**.

11. To verify your MDM authority has changed, sign-in to the Microsoft Azure portal at *https://portal.azure.com/*.

12. Click **All Services**.

13. Search for **Intune** and select it.

14. Under Manage, click **Device Enrollment**. Note that the MDM authority now shows Intune.

OFFICE 365

For this example, we are going to walkthrough changing the MDM authority from Office 365 to standalone Intune. This walkthrough assumes that your environment already has MDM for Office 365 set as the MDM authority and that you have an active Intune subscription.

1. Sign-in to the Microsoft Azure portal at *https://portal.azure.com/*.

2. Click **All Services**.

3. Search for **Intune** and select it.

4. Under manage, click **Device Enrollment**. With Office 365 set as the MDM authority, you will automatically be taken to the Add MDM Authority blade, as shown in Figure 1-15.

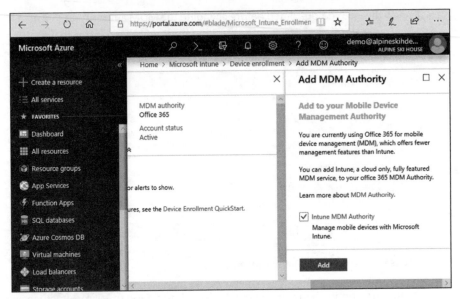

FIGURE 1-15 Add MDM Authority blade

5. Check the box for **Intune MDM Authority** and click **Add**.

6. Review the Azure portal notifications to confirm the MDM Authority was successfully changed to Intune (see Figure 1-16).

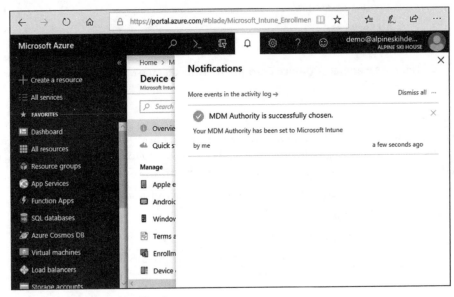

FIGURE 1-16 Azure Portal Notifications

Set device enrollment limit for users

This section covers the controls given to administrators to limit the number and type of devices a user can enroll. Why would you need to setup device enrollment restrictions for MDM? Limiting the number of devices assigned to a user can help with license constraints and organization. Restricting devices that are running an older operating system is a requirement for many organizations due to security and compliance. Blocking personally-owned devices may be a scenario you need to consider if your organization is not ready to support Bring Your Own Device (BYOD). These are a few of the examples that we'll be reviewing.

Plan for device enrollment restrictions

We have covered three MDM solutions in this chapter, and each of them has some basic ability to restrict device enrollment. Hybrid Intune and MDM for Office 365, however, cannot leverage the same enrollment restrictions available in standalone Intune. There are additional capabilities available beyond limiting the number of devices a user can enroll. For this section we will focus on the controls in the standalone Intune solution. Table 1-3 describes each of the restriction types and what their capabilities are.

TABLE 1-3 Device Enrollment Restrictions

Restrictions	Restriction Type	Description
Maximum number of enrolled devices	Limit restriction	Restrict the number of devices a user can enroll, ranging from 1 to 15.
Allow or block based on device platforms	Type restriction	Restrict device enrollment by device platform, including Android, Android work profile, iOS, Mac OS, and Windows (MDM).
Allow or block based on platform operating system	Type restriction	Restrict device enrollment by operating system, providing a minimum and maximum version number.
Allow or block personally owned devices	Type restriction	Restrict device enrollment by corporate-owned, requiring additional steps to define a device as corporate-owned.

> **NOTE PERSONALLY OWNED DEVICES**
>
> The ability to allow and block personally owned devices is dependent on other factors in your MDM configuration. For Windows (MDM), if the device was previously enrolled through a bulk provisioning package, ConfigMgr Co-Management or Windows Autopilot, it will be allowed to enroll.

Set device enrollment restrictions

With a high-level understanding of the possible enrollment restrictions, let's examine the interface and explore the controls. Device enrollment restrictions are available in the Azure portal under the Microsoft Intune service.

DEVICE LIMIT RESTRICTION

In this walk-through, we will implement a restriction to limit the number of devices a user can enroll with.

1. The first enrollment restriction covered focuses on limiting the number of devices a user can enroll. Sign-in to the Microsoft Azure portal at https://portal.azure.com/.

2. Click **All Services**.

3. Search for **Intune** and select it.

4. Under Manage, click **Device Enrollment**.

5. On the Device Enrollment blade, under Manage, click **Enrollment Restrictions**.

6. On the Device Enrollment – Enrollment Restrictions blade, review the items under Device Type Restrictions and Device Limit Restrictions. Refer to Figure 1-17 for an example. Take note that there is a default enrollment restriction for each restriction. Both can be modified, but not deleted.

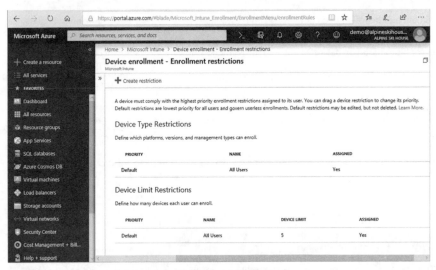

FIGURE 1-17 Device enrollment – Enrollment Restrictions

7. Click **Create Restriction**.

8. On the Create Restriction blade, fill in the following:

   A. **Name**   Custom device limit

   B. **Restriction Type**   Device Limit Restriction

   C. **Specify The Maximum Number Of Devices A User Can Enroll**   3

9. Click **Create**.

10. Review the Azure portal notifications to confirm that the new enrollment restriction was created successfully.

   At this stage you will have a new custom device restriction created and available on the Device Enrollment – Enrollment Restrictions blade. Here we worked with limit restrictions. Assigning a limit prevents users from enrolling more than the defined value. The default restriction allows users to enroll up to five devices. Attempting to enroll more than five will result in a notification. Now let's take a look at Device Type Restrictions.

DEVICE TYPE RESTRICTIONS

The second enrollment restriction we will work with is based on limiting enrollment by the type of device.

1. Sign-in to the Microsoft Azure portal at *https://portal.azure.com/*.

2. Click **All Services**.

3. Search for **Intune** and select it.

4. Under Manage, click **Device Enrollment**.

5. On the Device Enrollment blade, under Manage, click **Enrollment Restrictions**.

6. On the Device Enrollment – Enrollment Restrictions blade, click **Create Restriction**.

7. On the Create restriction blade, fill in the following:

   A. **Name**   Custom type limit

   B. **Restriction Type**   Device Type Restriction

8. Click **Select Platforms**.

9. On the Select Platforms blade, select the following options, as shown in Figure 1-18:

   A. **Android**   Block

   B. **Android Work Profile**   Block

   C. **iOS**   Allow

   D. **macOS**   Block

   E. **Windows (MDM)**   Allow

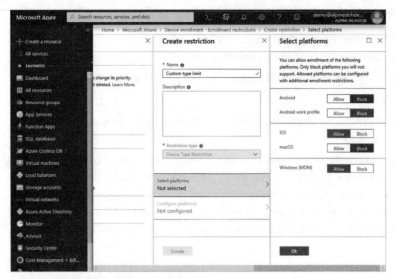

FIGURE 1-18 Create Restriction – Select Platforms

10. Click **OK**.

11. On the Create Restrictions blade, click **Configure Platforms**.

12. On the Configure Platforms blade, fill in the following, as shown in Figure 1-19:

   A. iOS Min Version   12.0

   B. iOS Personally Owned   Block

   C. Windows (MDM) Min Version   10.0.17134.345

   D. Windows (MDM) Personally Owned   Block

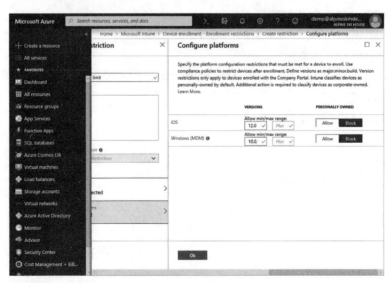

FIGURE 1-19 Create Restriction – Configure Platforms

13. Click **OK**.

14. Click **Create**.

15. Review the Azure portal notifications to confirm that the new enrollment restriction was created successfully.

With these steps complete, you should now have a custom device type restriction available on the Device Enrollment – Enrollment Restrictions blade. In this example we worked with platform restrictions. Platform restrictions provide a granular set of controls for approving specific device types and operating system versions. With an enrollment plan that supports BYOD, controlling the minimum and maximum operating system version can prevent known vulnerabilities or pre-release versions from entering your environment.

ASSIGNMENT

Let's examine the process for assigning enrollment restrictions. First, you need to understand the priority system. The priority value, shown on the Device Enrollment – Enrollment Restrictions blade, is for users that are members of multiple groups, but may have different enrollment restrictions assigned. You can change the priority value in the portal by dragging a device restriction up or down the list.

> **REAL WORLD**   **DEVICE RESTRICTION PRIORITIES**
>
> Ethan Rincon is a member of two Azure AD groups, IT and All Employees. The IT group has device enrollment restrictions that allow members to enroll all device types. This device restriction has a priority of 1. The All Employees group has device enrollment restrictions that only allow members to enroll Windows (MDM) devices. This device restriction has a priority of 2. In this situation Ethan will receive the IT device restrictions due to the higher priority.

Enrollment restrictions are assigned to Azure AD groups. The following walkthrough assumes you already have an Azure AD group created with the users you need to target.

1. Sign-in to the Microsoft Azure portal at *https://portal.azure.com/*.

2. Click **All Services**.

3. Search for **Intune** and select it.

4. Under Manage, click **Device Enrollment**.

5. On the Device Enrollment blade, under Manage, click **Enrollment Restrictions**.

6. On the Device Enrollment – Enrollment Restrictions blade, select the custom device limit restriction that was previously created.

7. On the Custom Device Limit blade, click **Assignments**.

8. On the Custom Device Limit – Assignments blade, click **Select Groups**.

9. Select an Azure AD group that you want to target and click **Select**, as shown in Figure 1-20.

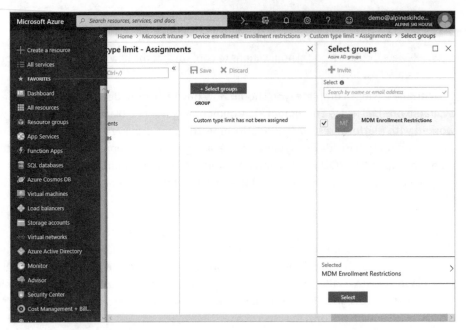

FIGURE 1-20 Enrollment Restriction Assignment

1. On the Custom Device Limit – Assignments blade, click **Save**.
2. Review the Azure portal notifications to confirm the device enrollment restriction was successfully assigned.

Once you have completed these steps you should have the device restrictions available in the portal and assigned to an Azure AD group of your choosing.

Skill 1.2: Manage device compliance

Device compliance is the practice of ensuring that the devices accessing your environment meet a distinct set of requirements, often defined by the IT and cybersecurity teams in your organization. For the purpose of this exam, device compliance is also referred to as a feature in Microsoft Intune. This feature is provided to aid administrators in defining their compliance requirements and using them to delegate access to data and services. As an administrator, it is your job to understand the use cases for device compliance and how to implement them.

The compliance policies that you define make up the connective tissue for several other actions in the platform. For example, the compliance status of a device can be leveraged as a determining factor for granting access to Exchange Online. This is accomplished using conditional access policies, another key feature covered in this chapter. Conditional access policies are a different type of policy, managed within Azure Active Directory (Azure AD), for allowing and denying access to data and services.

Plan for device compliance

This skill section covers planning considerations for device compliance. This includes topics such as prerequisites before implementation, compliance workflows, and possible use cases for your organization. Later in this chapter you will work with conditional access policies, and one of the dependencies for conditional access is the compliance status of the end user device. The MS-101 exam will present scenarios dealing with Intune enrollment, device compliance, and conditional access. As you prepare, take time to work with these technologies in the Azure portal and see what the dependencies are.

Understand the prerequisites for device compliance

Before you get started with creating device compliance policies, there are some technical prerequisites to plan for. Throughout this book you will see some trending prerequisites for each of the cloud technologies, particularly around the required subscriptions. Keep an eye on these for the exam and take some extra time to understand which features are included with the various subscription models.

These are the prerequisites for device compliance:

- **Subscriptions**   Device compliance is a technology with dependencies on Azure AD and Microsoft Intune. The device must be enrolled in Intune to receive a compliance policy, and the compliance flag is written to Azure AD for other features, such as conditional access. At a minimum you need a standalone Intune subscription and an Azure AD Premium P1 subscription. The higher tiered subscriptions, such as Azure AD premium P2, do not include additional capabilities focused on device compliance.

- **Platform support**   Device compliance policies support a wide range of platforms. For clarification, the term platform is referring to the operating system, not the physical hardware. Platform support is an important prerequisite if you are planning to manage devices that are not supported. At the time of this writing the following platforms are supported:

  - Android
  - Android Enterprise
  - iOS
  - macOS

- Windows Phone 8.1

- Windows 8.1

- Windows 10

- **Enrollment** Devices cannot report compliance until they are enrolled in Microsoft Intune.

> *MORE INFO* **CHOOSING A SUBSCRIPTION**
>
> For more information about the different editions of Azure AD and their corresponding subscription tier, visit: *https://azure.microsoft.com/en-us/pricing/details/active-directory/*. For more information about the subscriptions pertaining to Microsoft Intune, visit: *https://www.microsoft.com/en-us/cloud-platform/microsoft-intune-pricing*.

Understand the process flow for device compliance

Device compliance and conditional access are both policy-based technologies. You configure the policy to address your needs, and then assign that policy to the desired resources in Microsoft Intune. Devices will evaluate the policy and report back whether they meet the requirements or not. The compliance state is then written to the device object in Azure AD as a custom attribute. The state of that attribute will determine if the device is approved to access data and services. This is where conditional access enters the picture, which is covered in more detail later in this chapter.

Refer to Figure 1-21 for a diagram that illustrates the device compliance flow. In this example we are using the default configuration for device compliance. As an administrator, you have a few options to change this flow to meet your needs.

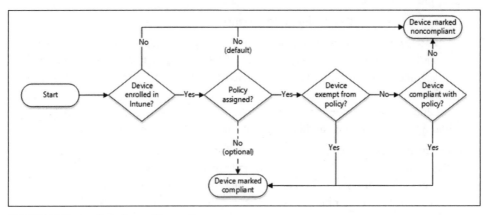

FIGURE 1-21 Device Compliance Process Flow

These next few items address controls that an administrator has available to alter the device compliance flow.

- **Intune enrollment** Devices that are not enrolled in Intune cannot receive device compliance policies. This rule also applies to devices that are Azure AD joined. This was covered earlier in the prerequisites section. In this context it can also be used to prevent compliance policies from applying to unmanaged devices.

- **Policy assignment** In the compliance policy settings for Microsoft Intune, you have the option to mark devices as compliant if they do not have a policy assigned. By default, all devices without an assigned policy are marked as noncompliant. But you do have the option to change this behavior, making all devices compliant by default. This is represented by the dashed line between the policy assigned and the device marked compliant in the illustration, also marked as optional.

- **Device exemption** Device exemption is another control you can configure. This is accomplished in the policy settings by defining which device platforms the compliance policy is scoped for. If your compliance policy includes all platforms except iOS, then iOS devices will be exempt from running that policy.

EXAM TIP

As you prepare for this exam, spend time looking at each of the device compliance options in the Intune portal. In this last section we reviewed the default behavior for devices that have no policy assigned. You may see questions that test your knowledge about the default behavior for device compliance policy, or where to change that behavior under certain circumstances.

Determine use cases for device compliance

In this section we are going to look at some potential use cases for device compliance. First, understand that compliance policies contain a series of rules that you define. These rules determine whether a device is compliant or not. Compliance policies can help to remediate certain conditions, but in most cases the device will be quarantined, and remediation will be left up to the user. For example, you have a device compliance policy that has a security rule that requires a password before unlocking a device. If a device is noncompliant with this policy, the user will be prompted to set a password on their noncompliant device.

Users with devices that are marked as noncompliant will receive notifications about the conflicting rules. As an administrator, you can also create a conditional access policy to block these devices until they are remediated. Refer to Table 1-4 for a series of compliance policies and corresponding use cases.

TABLE 1-4 Device Compliance Use Cases

Platform	Setting(S)	Example Use Case
Windows 10	Minimum OS version Valid operating system builds	Windows 10 devices that are not running the latest cumulative update are marked as noncompliant. Windows 10 devices running the latest release of 1709 are still valid while upgrades are rolling out.
macOS	Require system integrity protection	macOS devices that do not have system integrity protection enabled are marked as noncompliant.
Android	Rooted devices Encryption of data storage on device	Android devices that are rooted are marked as noncompliant. Android devices that do not have data storage encryption enabled are marked as noncompliant
iOS	Jailbroken devices Minimum OS version Restricted apps	iOS devices that are jailbroken are marked as noncompliant. iOS devices that are not running the latest major release of iOS are marked as noncompliant. iOS devices that have the Dropbox app installed are marked as noncompliant.

Design conditional access policies

In this skill section you will review the design aspects of conditional access policies. It is worth pointing out that a majority of this chapter is dedicated to conditional access: designing, creating, and managing policies. As you prepare for these skills plan to spend time working in the Azure portal and following along to review the interface and controls for conditional access.

This chapter began by covering what device compliance means from a cloud management perspective. Now you will see how device compliance is used to establish access requirements for data and services in your organization.

Design for the protection of data and services using conditional access policies

There are a variety of policy settings available for conditional access, and a mixture of configurations that you can implement. Let's first look at the Conditional Access Policies blade in the Azure portal. This will help set the stage for conditional access policies and introduce you to some key terms. Refer to Figure 1-22 for an example of the Policy Creation blade, as we drill down and take a closer look at each of the available options.

FIGURE 1-22 Conditional Access Policy Creation

- **Assignments** Assignments define the scope, criteria and conditions of the policy you are deploying. On the Policy Creation blade you are presented with three categories under assignments. These three categories include:

- **Users And Groups** They define who will receive the policy. You can either include or exclude users and groups. Although the creation screen will not prevent you from proceeding, all conditional access policies require a user and group assignment before it is applied. For includes you can select all users or specific users and groups. For example, if you have a group that only contains your marketing team you can select that as an option. For excludes you can select all guest users (defined by the userType attribute), specific directory roles such as "Application developer," or specific users and groups.

- **Cloud Apps** They define the services that users will access for productivity. You have the choice to include or exclude a pre-defined list of supported cloud apps. For includes you can select all cloud apps or specific apps, such as Microsoft Teams. For excludes you can select specific apps.

- **Conditions** They define when a policy is applied. Refer to Table 1-5 for a breakdown of each condition, the available options, and some example use cases.

TABLE 1-5 Conditional Access Options

Condition	Description	Options	Example Use Case
Sign-in risk	Azure AD determines a user's sign-in risk based on a configurable policy under Azure AD Identity Protection.	High, medium, low, or no risk	Enforce a MFA policy for users that are flagged with a medium sign-in risk.
Device platforms	Azure AD retrieves the operating system of joined device, but the information is not verified. This should be combined with a Microsoft Intune enrollment and device compliance policy.	Android, iOS, Windows Phone, Windows, macOS	Enforce an app restriction policy on iOS and Android devices only.
Locations	Locations are used to define trusted network locations. Trusted network locations are configured in Azure AD under Named Locations.	Trusted locations	Block access to Exchange online from the San Francisco office with an IP subnet of 10.20.11.0/22
Client apps (preview)	Set conditional restrictions based on specific client apps.	Browsers, mobile apps and desktop clients	Restrict access to mobile apps unless the device is marked as compliant.
Device state (preview)	Exclude corporate or trusted devices from conditional access restrictions	Hybrid Azure AD joined devices, devices marked as compliant	Enforce restrictions to Office 365 Exchange Online for noncompliant devices.

- **Access controls**   They define additional requirements for granting or denying access, along with session controls for limiting the experience within cloud apps. The following options are available from the access controls section:

- **Grant**   It enables you to block access based on the conditions that you defined under the assignments section. Alternatively, you can choose to grant access and enforce additional requirements. For example, you can require MFA or only grant access to devices that are marked as compliant through device compliance policies.

- **Session**   This control enables you to limit the experience within certain cloud apps. At the time of this writing, Exchange Online and SharePoint Online are the only cloud apps that support app enforced restrictions. Enabling this feature adds real-time monitoring and control capabilities to these apps.

Now that you have spent some time exploring the interface, let's look at how a conditional access policy is constructed. The policy is made up of two parts: the condition and the access control. You can also look at these in the following context: *when this happens* (condition), *then do this* (access control). For the exam you should be familiar with this formula and how it corresponds to conditional access restrictions. Refer to Table 1-6 for a few examples on how conditional access policies are assembled.

TABLE 1-6 Conditions and access controls

When This Happens (Condition)	Then Do This (Access Control)
Windows and macOS device owners are accessing SharePoint Online from an untrusted network. Additional security requirements are needed.	Grant access to SharePoint Online for Windows and macOS devices. Require multi-factor authentication and a compliant device when accessed from an untrusted network.
The sales team is accessing Exchange Online from their iOS and Android devices. These devices need to be compliant before access is granted.	Grant access to Exchange Online for the sales group. Require all sales team device owners to be enrolled in Intune and marked as compliant.
All users are accessing Microsoft Teams from trusted and untrusted networks. Users that are on an untrusted network need additional security requirements.	Grant access to Microsoft Teams for all users. Require multi-factor authentication when accessed from an untrusted network.
BYOD devices are accessing Exchange Online from their browser. Access needs to be restricted to approved apps.	Grant access to Exchange Online for all users. Restrict access to trusted client apps only.

The following list covers prerequisites that you need to be familiar with. Some of these are firm requirements and others are strategic questions to help prepare you for designing policies.

- **Subscriptions** The basic capabilities of conditional access are available with an Azure AD premium subscription. There are additional capabilities, however, that will not be available until you upgrade your subscription. These include the following:

  - **Azure AD Premium P1** The P1 subscription provides you with the basic capabilities of conditional access policies.

  - **Azure AD Premium P2** The P2 subscription enables identity protection, which is a requirement if you want to leverage sign-in risk. Sign-in risk is a capability that determines if a user sign-in is malicious and measures the risk level. This can be leveraged as part of your policy conditions.

  - **Microsoft Intune** Intune can be purchased standalone or through an EMS E3 or E5 subscription. Policy definitions that require a compliant device are dependent on the device being enrolled in Intune.

MORE INFO **SUBSCRIPTION DETAILS**

For more information about Azure AD subscriptions, visit: *https://azure.microsoft. com/pricing/details/active-directory/.* For more information about Microsoft Intune subscriptions, visit: *https://www.microsoft.com/cloud-platform/microsoft-intune-pricing.*

- **Permissions** Before you can start creating and managing conditional access policies, you will need the appropriate permissions assigned to your account. Conditional Access Administrator is a pre-defined role that that enables the necessary privileges.

- **Requirements to be delivered**   What requirements do you have for device compliance and conditional access? This is something you should start defining from the beginning. Determine if your goal is something straightforward, such as enforcing multi-factor authentication for users. Or something more advanced, such as restricting access to SharePoint Online from Windows devices when they are connected to an untrusted network.

- **Device management**   What kind of device management solution are you using today? The full capabilities of conditional access do have dependencies on Microsoft Intune, but if you are using ConfigMgr, you can enable co-management and start leveraging conditional access policies sooner.

- **Device platforms**   What types of devices and operating systems do you need to support? Conditional access policies support a variety of operating systems. At the time of this writing, the only current outliers are devices running Linux. Consider the devices in your environment and what type of restrictions you need to enforce.

- **Email requirements**   What are your access requirements around email? Email is often used as one of the first services for enforcing conditional access restrictions. If you have a goal to enable access restrictions for Exchange Online, then selecting the cloud app from the default list of assignments is straightforward, and something we will look at later in this chapter. If you have a goal to enable access restrictions for an on-premises Exchange server, you will need to plan for additional prerequisites, such as installing and configuring the on-premises Exchange connector.

> *NOTE* **PREVIEW FEATURES**
>
> New features are introduced on a monthly basis to the Azure portal. Some features are not fully production ready and will be introduced in a preview format, enabling you and other customers to try them and provide feedback to the developers. Elements in the portal that are in a preview state will be marked with "preview" following the name of the feature. For example, "Device state (preview)" is one of the features discussed in this skill section. At the time of this writing, there are features in a preview state and these may change over time. Keep these in mind and be sure to stay up to date on these features as you prepare for the exam.

Design device-based and app-based conditional access policies

First, understand that a conditional access policy can contain any mixture of options, including device-based and app-based restrictions. The distinction between device-based and app-based restrictions is relative to the controls that you select and how you structure your policies. That said, device-based and app-based policies can have different requirements and can operate independently of each other if you choose.

Let's look at a few examples:

- **Device-based**   This first policy focuses on device-based controls. In this example the policy requires multi-factor authentication on untrusted networks for iOS devices.

The policy is assigned to all users. In this example we have not defined any app-based restrictions, keeping the focus on the platform and network.

- **App-based**   This second policy focuses on app-based controls. In this example the policy requires approved client apps when accessing Exchange Online. This policy is assigned to all users. In this example we have not defined any device-based restrictions, keeping the focus on application controls.

- **Mixed**   This third policy includes a mixture of controls. In this example the policy requires all platforms to be enrolled in Intune and marked compliant before they can access Exchange Online from approved client apps. In this example we are specifying device-based restrictions and app-based restrictions to accomplish the desired result.

At this stage you should have a good understanding of the differences between device-based and app-based policies. Next, let's examine the individual controls related to each policy type. The following items are focused on device-based policy requirements:

- **Azure AD joined**   This requirement is available as both a condition and an access control item. When you are defining a condition, you have the option to exclude devices that are Azure AD joined. This is available through the device state blade and can be used in a scenario where you are locking down access, but want to ignore Azure AD joined devices. Alternatively, when you are defining the controls for granting access, you have the option to require Azure AD joined devices. This is available through the grant blade for access control and can be used as one of many required controls before enabling access to cloud apps.

- **Device compliance**   This requirement is available as both a condition and an access control item, similar to the Azure AD join requirement mentioned above. Devices must be enrolled in Microsoft Intune and be marked as compliant for this requirement to work. When you are defining a condition, you have the option to exclude devices that are marked as compliant. This is available through the device state blade and can be used in a scenario where you are locking down access but want to ignore enrolled devices that are compliant. Alternatively, when you are defining the controls for granting access, you have the option to require enrolled and compliant devices. This is available through the grant blade for access control and can be used as one of many required controls before enabling access to cloud apps.

- **Device enrollment**   This requirement is not directly defined through a conditional access policy but is a prerequisite for identifying device compliance.

- **Device platforms**   This requirement is available as a condition item. When you are defining a condition, you have the option to include or exclude the following operating systems: Android, iOS, Windows Phone, Windows, and macOS. This is available through the device platforms blade and can be used in a scenario where you are restricting access to a cloud app and want to exclude certain platforms.

Next, let's examine app-based requirements. We introduced session controls earlier in this skill section, which enable you to limit the experience within cloud apps. Two of the requirements we are going to cover are enabled using session controls. The following items are focused on app-based policy requirements.

- **Use app enforced restrictions** This requirement is available as an access control item. When you are defining access controls, you have the option to enable app enforced restrictions. This is defined on the session blade and could be used in a scenario where you need to provide limited access to Office 365 Exchange Online or SharePoint Online for noncompliant devices.

- **Use Conditional Access App Control** This requirement is available as an access control item. When you are defining access controls, you have the option to enable conditional access app control. This is defined on the session blade and could be used in a scenario where you need to monitor and control application access in real time. Access and session policies can then be configured through the Cloud App Security portal, enabling granular control over user access.

- **Available policies** Include access, activity, app discovery, app permission, cloud discovery anomaly detection, files, and session policies. Some of these are designed for monitoring and alerting, others have automated actions that can be enabled.

- **Require approved client app** This requirement is available as an access control item. When you are defining access controls, you have the option to enable the requirement for approved client apps. This is defined on the grant blade and can be used in a scenario where you need to ensure services are only accessed from approved client applications.

> **MORE INFO** **APPROVED CLIENT APPS**
>
> Enabling the requirement for approved client apps will prevent users from accessing services from native or third-party apps that Microsoft has not approved. For a list of approved client apps, visit: *https://docs.microsoft.com/azure/active-directory/conditional-access/technical-reference#approved-client-app-requirement.*

Create Azure AD Conditional Access policies

In this skill section we examine conditional access policies and how to create them. We leverage the design elements and controls that were reviewed in the previous skill section to assist with the creation process. At the time of this writing PowerShell support for conditional access policies is not available, so our walkthrough will be focused on the Azure portal. As with any policy, the controls you choose to enable will depend greatly on the needs of your organization and the goal you wish to achieve.

From an exam perspective, expect to see questions or scenarios that test your knowledge of the conditional access controls and what their capabilities are. We covered some of these fundamentals in the previous skill section, but now we will create the policies and assign them, so you can experience the end-to-end process. Over the next few sections we cover some of the more common conditional access use cases, which will provide you with the fundamentals you need. As always, try to follow along with the step-by-step instructions in your own lab.

Navigate and prepare for conditional access policies

Before creating conditional access policies, be aware that the restrictions you enforce can impact the productivity of your organization if assigned incorrectly. As a word of caution, always assign new policies to a dedicated test user or group and make it a priority to initially exclude admin accounts. Admin accounts can be re-introduced once you have tested the policy. This will prevent undesirable behavior, such as blocking Exchange Online for your senior management. Also, make sure you have the necessary subscription(s) active in your tenant.

To start off, let's take a look at the Conditional Access – Policies blade in the Azure portal. There are a number of controls here that are leveraged prior to policy creation. Depending on your objective, you may need to configure some of these options.

1. Sign-in to the Microsoft Azure portal at *https://portal.azure.com/.*

2. Click **All Services**.

3. Search for **Azure Active Directory** and select it.

4. Under Security, select **Conditional Access**. In Figure 1-23 you can see an example of the Conditional Access blade in the Azure portal.

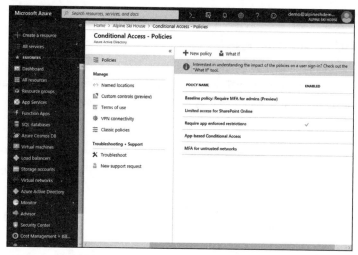

FIGURE 1-23 Conditional Access Policies blade

Let's look at the available options on the Conditional Access blade:

- **Policies**   The policies blade is where you will create and manage conditional access policies. In Figure 1-23 the Policies blade is selected. You can see on the right that we have a few policies already defined and one of them is enabled.

- **Named Locations**   The Named Locations blade enables administrators to configure network and region-based locations. Network locations are defined by an IP range. Regional locations are defined through a dropdown list of known countries and regions. Named locations that you define can later be used in your conditional access policies.

- **Custom Controls (preview)** The Custom Controls blade enables administrators to declare external services with additional authentication and validation steps. The administrator creates the control and provides the data input using the JSON format, interlinking conditional access and the third-party provider. At the time of this writing, the following providers offer integration with conditional access:

  Duo Security, Entrust Datacard, Ping Identity, RSA, and Trusona.

- **Terms Of Use** The Terms of Use blade enables administrators to upload a terms of use document, which can later be used by conditional access. Once uploaded, the terms of use are listed as another access control that you can require users to comply with before accessing data and services.

- **VPN Connectivity** The VPN Connectivity blade enables administrators to create and manage VPN certificates for Always On VPN. Once created, a conditional access policy can be configured to grant access to the VPN server cloud app.

- **Classic Policies** The class policies blade enables administrators to review and mange classic policies that were created using older versions of the Azure portal. This blade will list any existing classic policies and allow you to disable them as you migrate over to the new policy design.

Create conditional access policies

Now that you have some experience navigating the conditional access controls, let's examine an example scenario and configure a policy. This scenario includes a basic example of what controls you have as an administrator and how they apply in a real world scenario.

SCENARIO: REQUIRE MULTI-FACTOR AUTHENTICATION

As an example, let's say you have a requirement to enable multi-factor authentication and restrict access for cloud services to approved client apps only. The following conditions must be met:

- Applies to all users.
- Applies to iOS and Android platforms.
- Applies to Office 365 Exchange Online.
- Sign-in risk is medium or high.
- Location is untrusted networks.
- Devices are marked as compliant.

We are going to create a conditional access policy that meets these requirements. For each of these scenarios, consider any prerequisites that you may have to address before proceeding. For example, remember that sign-in risk does require an Azure AD premium P2 subscription and you will need to enable Azure AD Identity Protection for your tenant.

1. Sign-in to the Microsoft Azure portal at *https://portal.azure.com/*.

2. Click **All Services**.

3. Search for **Azure Active Directory** and select it.

4. Under Security, select **Conditional Access**.

5. On the Policies blade, click **New Policy**.

6. On the New blade, name the policy "ASH CA Policy."

7. Under Assignments, click **Users And Groups**.

8. On the Users and groups blade, on the Include tab, select the radio button next to **All Users** and click **Done**. Refer to Figure 1-24 for an example of this configuration.

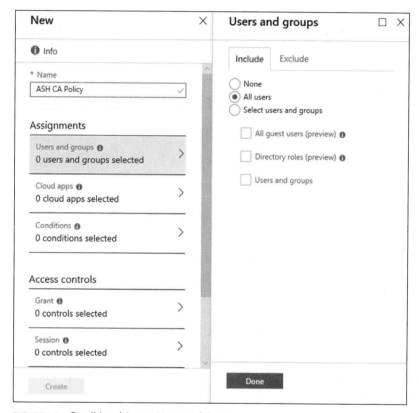

FIGURE 1-24 Conditional Access Users and Groups

9. Under Assignments, click **Cloud Apps**.

10. On the Cloud Apps blade, on the Include tab, select the radio button next to **Select Apps** and click **Select**.

11. On the Select blade, search for **Office 365 Exchange Online** and select it. Click **Select**. Refer to Figure 1-25 for an example of this configuration.

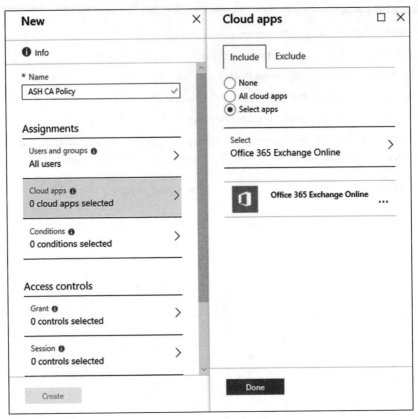

FIGURE 1-25 Conditional Access Cloud Apps

12. Click **Done**.

13. Under Assignments, click **Conditions**.

14. On the Conditions blade, click **Sign-In Risk**.

15. Under Configure, click **Yes** to configure this condition.

16. Check the boxes for **High** and **Medium** and click **Select**. Refer to Figure 1-26 for an example of this configuration.

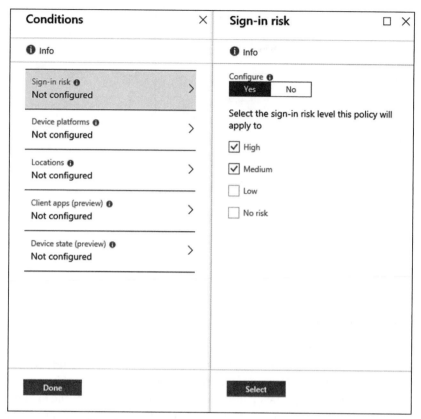

FIGURE 1-26 Conditional Access Sign-in Risk

17. On the Conditions blade, click **Device Platforms**.

18. Under Configure, click **Yes** to configure this condition.

19. On the Include tab, select the radio button next to **Select Device Platforms**.

20. Check the box next to **Android** and **iOS** and click **Done**. Refer to Figure 1-27 for an example of this configuration.

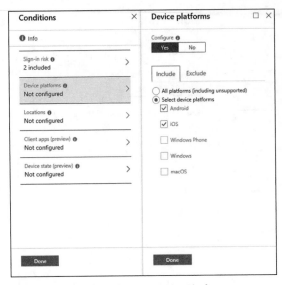

FIGURE 1-27 Conditional Access Device Platforms

21. On the Conditions blade, click **Locations**.

22. Under Configure, click **Yes** to configure this condition.

23. On the Exclude tab, select the radio button next to **All Trusted Locations** and click **Done**. Refer to Figure 1-28 for an example of this configuration. With this configuration we are including any location (default option on the include tab) and excluding all trusted networks. Once applied this policy will only affect users when connected from untrusted networks.

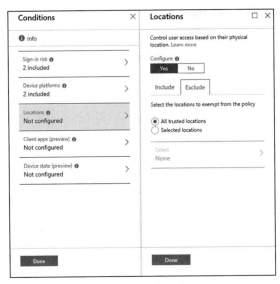

FIGURE 1-28 Conditional Access Locations

24. On the Conditions blade, click **Done**.

25. Under Access controls, click **Grant**.

26. On the Grant blade, select the radio button next to **Grant access**, check the box next to the following items and click **Done**. Refer to Figure 1-29 for an example of this configuration.

- Require Multi-Factor Authentication
- Require Device To Be Marked As Compliant
- Require Approved Client App

FIGURE 1-29 Conditional Access Grant

27. On the New blade, under Enable Policy, select **On**.

28. Click **Create**.

29. Review the Azure portal notifications to confirm that the conditional access policy was successfully created.

30. On the Policies blade, review the list of policies to confirm that the policy is present, and a check mark is present to indicate the policy is enabled.

After completing the above configuration, you should have a conditional access policy enabled that addresses both the device-based and app-based requirements outlined in this scenario. The goal for this scenario was to introduce you to the Conditional Access blades and build up your comfort level with navigating the various controls. Next, we will look at the What If tool to help assess which policies get applied to a user when certain criteria is defined.

Configure device compliance policy

This skill section covers the creation process for device compliance policies in Microsoft Intune. The examples cover common use cases for device compliance. Like conditional access policies, there are a variety of options and configurations for administrators to work with. This includes the ability to connect with third-party vendor solutions to further enhance the native capabilities. Also, as we navigate through the portal, remember that conditional access policies can leverage compliance status for restricting access to data and services.

Navigate and configure device compliance settings

When you access the Device Compliance blade for the first time, the first thing you might notice is the number of options available in comparison with the conditional access interface. The core functions are split into three groups: manage, monitor, and setup. Like we did with conditional access, let's take a look through these groups and identify the purpose for each.

1. Sign-in to the Microsoft Azure portal at *https://portal.azure.com/*.
2. Click **All Services**.
3. Search for **Intune** and select it.
4. Under Manage, select **Device Compliance**. In Figure 1-30 you can see an example of the Device Compliance blade in the Azure portal.

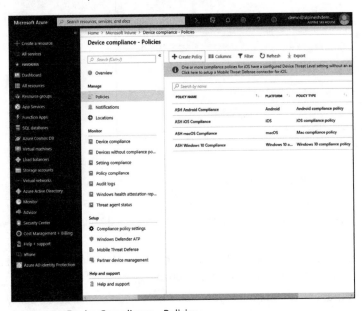

FIGURE 1-30 Device Compliance – Policies

Device compliance includes several built-in reports for administrators to review and export as needed. This includes an overview dashboard, providing a high-level look at overall compliance and areas of interest. Later in this section we will look at monitoring in more detail. For now, refer to Table 1-7 for a breakdown of each section.

TABLE 1-7 Device compliance blade

OPTION	CATEGORY	DESCRIPTION
Overview	Overview	This blade offers a compliance dashboard with summarization data for: ■ Device compliance status ■ Devices without compliance policy ■ Policy compliance ■ Setting compliance ■ Device protections status ■ Threat agent status
Policies	Manage	This blade is used for creating and managing device compliance policies.
Notifications	Manage	This blade is used for creating and managing notification templates that are used for compliance policies.
Locations	Manage	This blade is use for creating and managing locations for location-based compliance policy settings.
Device compliance	Monitor	This blade offers a report with all managed devices and their device compliance status.
Devices without compliance policy	Monitor	This blade offers a report with all managed devices that do not have a compliance policy assigned.
Setting compliance	Monitor	This blade offers a report with per-setting compliance information.
Policy compliance	Monitor	This blade offers a report that summarizes policy compliance by device count, including compliant, noncompliant and errors.
Audit logs	Monitor	This blade offers a report that shows recent administrative actions for compliances policies completed in the portal.
Windows health attestation report	Monitor	This blade offers a report that shows detailed information for health attestation, including the status for BitLocker, code integrity, secure boot, and more.
Threat agent status	Monitor	This blade offers multiple reports show detailed information for anti-virus enforcement, pending reboots, critical failures, and more.
Compliance policy settings	Setup	This blade is used for managing how the compliance service treats devices, such as compliance state when no policies are assigned.
Windows Defender ATP	Setup	This blade is used for integrating Windows Defender ATP with Microsoft Intune, enabling risk association for device compliance.
Mobile Threat Defense	Setup	This blade is used for creating and managing connection points with third-party vendors, enabling additional risk association visibility for device compliance.
Partner device management	Setup	This blade is used for creating and managing a connection with JAMF, a third-party MDM provider specializing in macOS and iOS devices.

When you first begin working with device compliance, there are some configurations that you should review. From the Conditional access blade, click **Compliance Policy Settings** under Setup. There are three controls on this blade that should be considered before you begin creating policies.

- **Mark Devices with No Compliance Policy Assigned As**   Compliant | Not Compliant
  - The default configuration for this setting is not compliant. In many cases this will be the desired setting because you want to have some understanding of the device state before granting it access to services. Consider a scenario where you assign a conditional access policy that requires devices to be compliant in order to access Exchange Online.
- **Enhanced Jailbreak Detection**   Enabled | Disabled
  - The default configuration for this setting is Disabled. Enabling this feature requires iOS devices to evaluate and report their jailbreak status more frequently in conjunction with leveraging location services. This will impact the battery life of the device while enabled.
- **Compliance Status Validity Period (Days)**   1 – 120
  - The default configuration for this setting is 30 days. This value determines the frequency in which devices must report back their device compliance status to Intune. If a device does not report compliance within the required timeframe they will be marked as noncompliant.

Create device compliance policies

Keep in mind that each compliance policy that you create is associated to a specific device platform, unlike conditional access policies, which enable you to select multiple platforms. Each platform has its own set of options. Some will be similar across platforms, but others will not. For example, macOS has a rule for requiring system integrity protection, which is exclusive to this platform. Based on this you should design your policies on a per-platform basis.

In the following example you are going to create a device compliance policy for Alpine Ski House. This goal is to cover common compliance rules and get you working with the technology.

SCENARIO: WINDOWS 10 DEVICE COMPLIANCE

For this example, you are the MDM administrator for Alpine Ski House. You have a requirement to create and assign a device compliance policy for the Windows 10 platform. This compliance policy will be focused on the security posture of the device and will be re-enforced using a conditional access policy for all cloud services. The following requirements must be met:

- BitLocker is required.
- Secure Boot is required.
- Minimum OS version is 10.0.17134.
- Encryption is required.

- Firewall is required.
- Antivirus is required.
- AntiSpyware is required.
- Windows Defender ATP machine risk is low.

Now that you have a list of requirements defined, follow these steps to create your device compliance policy:

1. Sign-in to the Microsoft Azure portal at *https://portal.azure.com/.*
2. Click **All Services**.
3. Search for **Intune** and select it.
4. Under Manage, select **Device Compliance**.
5. On the Device compliance blade, under Manage, click **Policies**.
6. On the Policies blade, click **Create Policy**.
7. On the Create Policy blade, name the policy "Windows 10 Security Compliance."
8. Under Platform, select **Windows 10 And Later**.
9. On the Windows 10 compliance policy blade, click **Device Health**.
10. On the Device Health blade, set the following options and click **OK**. Refer to Figure 1-31 for an example of this configuration.
    - Set **Require Bitlocker** to **Require**.
    - Set **Require Secure Boot To Be Enabled On The Device** to **Require**.

FIGURE 1-31 Device Compliance - Device Health

11. On the Windows 10 Compliance Policy blade, click **Device Properties**.
12. On the Device Properties blade, set the following option and click **OK**. Refer to Figure 1-32 for an example of this configuration.
    - Set **Minimum OS version** to **10.0.17134**.

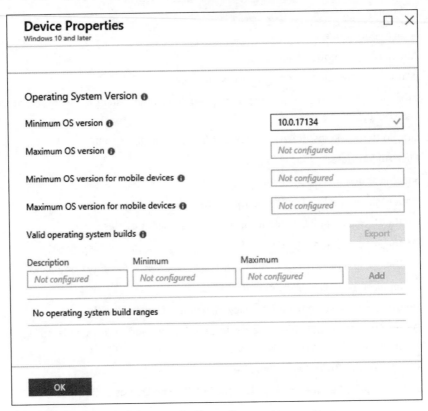

Device Properties
Windows 10 and later

Operating System Version ⓘ

Minimum OS version ⓘ   10.0.17134 ✓

Maximum OS version ⓘ   *Not configured*

Minimum OS version for mobile devices ⓘ   *Not configured*

Maximum OS version for mobile devices ⓘ   *Not configured*

Valid operating system builds ⓘ   Export

Description   Minimum   Maximum

Not configured   *Not configured*   *Not configured*   Add

No operating system build ranges

OK

FIGURE 1-32 Device Compliance – Device Properties

13. On the Windows 10 compliance policy blade, click **System Security**.

14. On the System Security blade, set the following options and click **OK**. Refer to Figure 1-33 for an example of this configuration.

   ■ Set **Encryption Of data Storage On Device** to **Require**.

   ■ Set **Firewall** to **Require**.

   ■ Set **Antivirus** to **Require**.

   ■ Set **AntiSpyware** to **Require**.

FIGURE 1-33 Device Compliance – System Security

15. On the Windows 10 compliance policy blade, click **Windows Defender ATP**.

16. On the Windows Defender ATP blade, set the following option and click **OK**. Refer to Figure 1-34 for an example of this configuration.

  ▪ Set **Require The Device To Be At Or Under The Machine Risk Score** to **Low**.

FIGURE 1-34 Device Compliance – Windows Defender ATP

17. On the Windows 10 Compliance Policy blade, click **OK**.

18. On the Create Policy blade, click **Create**.

19. Review the Azure portal notifications to confirm that the compliance policy was successfully created.

Once you complete these steps, you should have a compliance policy containing rules that pertain to Windows 10 device security. The next step is to assign this policy to your target audience and trigger an evaluation. For these steps it is assumed that you already have an existing AD group that contains Windows 10 devices.

1. On the Windows 10 Security Compliance blade, under Manage, click **Assignments**.

2. On the Assignments blade, click **Select Groups To Include**.

3. On the Select groups to include blade, select the group **Windows 10 Devices** and click **Select**.

4. On the Assignments blade, click **Save**.

5. Review the Azure portal notifications to confirm that the assignment was successfully saved.

6. On the Assignments blade, click **Evaluate** to force all group members to evaluate the compliance policy.

Manage conditional access policies

In this skill section we introduce two new tools in the Azure portal designed to help you manage their conditional access policies. The first tool is the What If tool. An administrator can define a user and specific criteria to determine which policies are getting assigned. The second tool is the Azure AD Sign-ins report. This report provides a record of user activity with the capability to drill down and view conditional access events. Over the next few sections these tools are examined in detail along with some examples of the interface.

Manage conditional access policies using the What If tool

As you begin designing the structure for your conditional access policies, you may find some policies start to overlap with others. For example, you might have a policy applied that enforces multi-factor authentication for all users. Then you introduce a new policy that does not enforce multi-factor authentication for a specific group of users with the condition that they are connected to a trusted network. The What If tool can help highlight exactly what policies are getting applied to each per-user. The What If tool is also a great solution for evaluating new policies before you enforce them across your organization, and should be considered as a first step in your rollout process.

The What If tool is available on the Conditional Access blade. Refer to the following steps to access the tool:

1. Sign-in to the Microsoft Azure portal at *https://portal.azure.com/*.

2. Click **All Services**.

3. Search for **Azure Active Directory** and select it.

4. Under Security, select **Conditional Access**.

5. On the Policies blade, click **What If** in the menu bar. In Figure 1-35 you can see an example of the What If tool in the Azure portal and what criteria is available.

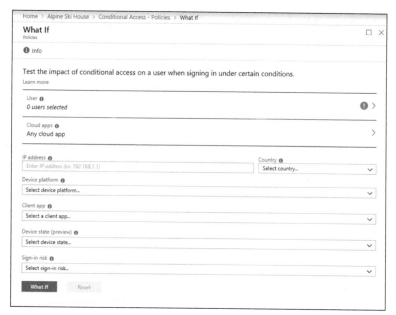

FIGURE 1-35 What If Options

The following list covers the available criteria on the What If blade. Each of these options should look familiar, as they directly correspond to the controls that were defined when creating the conditional access policy.

- **User**   This option enables you to select a single user account for analysis. You cannot select multiple users or groups. This is the only required option to run the What If tool.
- **Cloud Apps**   This option enables you to select one or multiple cloud apps. Any Cloud Apps is the default option. If you are troubleshooting a policy issue with a specific cloud app, you should select that app here.
- **IP Address**   This option enables you to enter an IP address for location-based queries. Typically, this is the IP address of the user's device. If you select this option, you must also specify a country.
- **Country**   This option enables you to select a specific country for location-based queries. Again, if you select a country you also must provide an IP address.
- **Device Platform**   This option enables you to select a specific device platform. This is helpful for troubleshooting policies that only apply to specific device platforms.
- **Client App**   This option enables you to select a specific client app. This is helpful for troubleshooting policies that apply to a combination of client app types.
- **Device State (preview)**   This option enables you to select Hybrid Azure AD join or device compliance. This is helpful for troubleshooting policies that have a device state requirement.
- **Sign-In Risk**   This option enables you to select a specific risk level. This is helpful for troubleshooting policies that have a sign-in risk level defined.

When you first start using the What If tool, you can begin by selecting any user in your tenant and clicking the What If button. This should provide you with some basic results regardless of whether the user has a conditional access policy assigned. In the following example the What If tool is used against a user account in our Alpine Ski House tenant. After running the tool you will be presented with the evaluation results at the bottom of the page. This includes two tabs. The first tab is for policies that will apply to the selected user account, and the second tab is for policies that will not apply.

In Figure 1-36 we have an example of the first tab. Take note of the Grant Controls column. This column will specify which access controls are being applied by the associated policy. You can use this information to determine where policies overlap, and drill down further by modifying the query criteria that we reviewed above. For example, set cloud apps to Exchange Online and rerun the tool to see if the same controls are being applied.

Evaluation result		
Policies that will apply	Policies that will not apply	
POLICY NAME	GRANT CONTROLS	SESSION CONTROLS
MFA for Sales and Marketing	Require multi-factor authentication	
Client Apps for All Users	Require multi-factor authentication AND Require approved client app	
Terms of Use for All Users	Alpine Ski House Terms of Use	

FIGURE 1-36 What If – Policies That Will Apply

Figure 1-37 shows an example of the second tab. Take note of the column: **Reasons Why This Policy Will Not Apply**, which is particularly helpful for identifying gaps in your policy design. For example, in this scenario we are reviewing the MFA policy for All Users, which should apply to iOS and Android devices. When running the tool, you selected iOS for the device platform, with the expectation that this policy would show applied. However, based on this evaluation, the tool has identified that this policy is not being applied due to the device platform, which is iOS in this case. With this information you now know that this policy needs to be reviewed to confirm that correct device platforms are selected.

Evaluation result	
Policies that will apply	Policies that will not apply
POLICY NAME	REASONS WHY THIS POLICY WILL NOT APPLY
Baseline policy: Require MFA for admins (Preview)	Policy not enabled
MFA for All Users	Device platform

FIGURE 1-37 What If – Policies That Will Not Apply

Manage conditional access policies using the Sign-ins report

Let's now examine the Azure AD Sign-ins report. This report is helpful for tracking and troubleshooting various events related to user activity with Azure AD. For conditional access, it provides a drill down view of each user event. Unlike the What If tool, these are actual events that have occurred in your environment, compared to a view that shows what will happen.

Refer to the following steps for accessing the Azure AD Sign-ins report. In this example we have some activity recorded in the report to help demonstrate what kind of data to expect.

1. Sign-in to the Microsoft Azure portal at *https://portal.azure.com/*.

2. Click **All Services**.

3. Search for **Azure Active Directory** and select it.

4. Under Monitoring, select **Sign-ins**. In Figure 1-38 you can see an example of the Sign-ins report that we will be working with in this example.

5. On the Sign-ins report, select an event that you would like to see more detail for. In this example, we have defined the following search criteria to help narrow down the results:

   - **User** Adam

   - **Application** Microsoft Office 365 Portal

   - **Status** Failure

   - **Date** Last 24 hours

> **NOTE SEARCH CRITERIA**
>
> As shown in Figure 1-38, all search criteria is case sensitive and supports the 'starts with' operator. For context, if you were to enter 'Office 365' for the application it would only return results that start with Office 365, such as Office 365 Exchange Online.

On the details pane there are five tabs. Each tab contains additional information about the selected event. Refer to the following list for a breakdown of each tab:

- **Basic Info** This tab contains basic details about the selected sign-in event. Some of this is visible in the main report but there are key items like Location, Sign-In Error Code, Failure Reason, and Client App.

- **Device Info** This tab contains details about the browser and device used during the sign-in event, including whether the device is enrolled in Intune and what the compliance status is.

- **MFA Info** This tab contains details that pertain to multi-factor authentication. This includes whether an MFA request was required, if the request was completed, the authentication method, and details about that method. For example, if the method was text message, the details would include the last two digits of the phone number.

- **Conditional Access** This tab contains details about the active conditional access policies, what the grant controls are, and the results of applying those policies during the sign-in event.

- **Troubleshooting And Support** This tab contains details related to failed events and includes information for submitting a support request. In the details pane select the **Conditional Access** tab (see Figure 1-38).

In the details pane select the **Conditional Access** tab. In our example you can see the conditional access events for Adam Brooks when he signed in to the Microsoft Office 365 Portal.

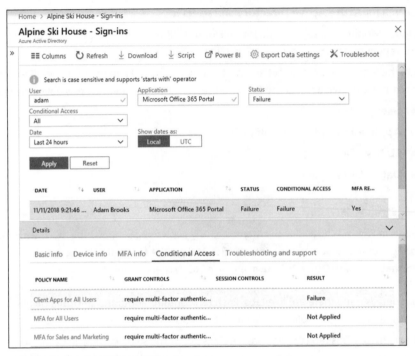

Home > Alpine Ski House - Sign-ins

Alpine Ski House - Sign-ins
Azure Active Directory

≡≡ Columns ↻ Refresh ↓ Download ↓ Script ▧ Power BI ⚙ Export Data Settings ✗ Troubleshoot

ⓘ Search is case sensitive and supports 'starts with' operator

User	Application	Status
adam ✓	Microsoft Office 365 Portal ✓	Failure ⌄

Conditional Access	
All ⌄	

Date	Show dates as:
Last 24 hours ⌄	Local / UTC

[Apply] [Reset]

DATE	USER	APPLICATION	STATUS	CONDITIONAL ACCESS	MFA RE...
11/11/2018 9:21:46 ...	Adam Brooks	Microsoft Office 365 Portal	Failure	Failure	Yes

Details ⌄

Basic info   Device info   MFA info   **Conditional Access**   Troubleshooting and support

POLICY NAME	GRANT CONTROLS	SESSION CONTROLS	RESULT
Client Apps for All Users	require multi-factor authentic...		Failure
MFA for All Users	require multi-factor authentic...		Not Applied
MFA for Sales and Marketing	require multi-factor authentic...		Not Applied

FIGURE 1-38 Azure AD Sign-ins Report

As you review the results for this conditional access event, you can see that there was a failure on the Client Apps for All Users policy. Clicking on the policy name will bring up the settings for that policy as a new blade, enabling you to make changes without having to navigate away from the Sign-ins report. In this example the policy is setup to require approved client apps when accessing all cloud apps. The failure was due to the user attempting to sign-in from an unsupported client app.

Skill 1.3: Plan for devices and apps

Most organizations assume responsibility for a range of devices and apps, which need to be maintained and supported in order to ensure that employees are productive, successful, and have a healthy work-life balance. There are common factors that organizations consider when planning for devices: the physical hardware and generation of that hardware, the operating system and version, and any peripherals such as display adapters or printers. For apps, planning considerations may include: line-of-business (LOB) applications, preferred publishers, licensing, and version control. As you plan for devices and apps, you must also consider how these planning considerations will be distributed, configured, and supported.

For the MS-101 exam, planning for devices and apps is focused on testing your knowledge of the Microsoft 365 ecosystem and how these technologies solve different problems. In this chapter we focus on device management and security. This includes a deep dive into device co-management, and a look at device profiles and security with Microsoft Intune. App deployment, management of apps, and app security will also be covered.

This section covers the following topics:

- Create and configure Microsoft Store for Business
- Plan app deployment
- Plan device co-management
- Plan device monitoring
- Plan for device profiles
- Plan for Mobile Application Management
- Plan mobile device security

Create and configure Microsoft Store for Business

The method in which applications are delivered to users and devices has evolved over the years. For traditional Win32 applications, some organizations may still have situations where their help desk staff is managing and installing these apps manually. Others may be leveraging features like ConfigMgr's application model, which offers a custom-tailored self-service method for employees to install traditional Win32 applications.

Another self-service app experience is available through the Microsoft Store. This service was first introduced in Windows 8 as a standalone application that was installed with the operating system. At that time, it was referred to as the Windows Store, and like many other app store platforms, consumers can navigate the store and install apps that Microsoft had approved for publication. The apps in the Microsoft Store are not packaged in the traditional Win32 format. Instead, they use the Universal Windows Platform (UWP) app type.

Enterprise and education customers have access to the Microsoft Store for Business (MSfB) or Microsoft Store for Education (MSfE). For this exam we will be focusing on the MSfB, but the two stores provide parallel offerings. Administrators have the option to configure a private store, enabling them to purchase apps in bulk, assign licenses, and deliver apps using self-service or direct assignment. This design has evolved with Windows 10 and will be the focus here.

Plan for Microsoft Store for Business prerequisites

The MSfB is designed for organizations that want to take a modern approach at managing their application portfolio. Managing and delivering apps using this solution provides IT administrators with several capabilities. Table 1-8 contains a list of core features included with the MSfB.

TABLE 1-8 Microsoft Store for Business Features

Feature	Description
Scaling flexibility	The MSfB is a cloud-based technology, providing a robust and reliable infrastructure for hosting and distributing apps across different geolocations and org sizes. Customers that already have Azure AD, Office 365, and Windows 10 deployed can enable an end-to-end app management solution using the MSfB. Customers that have an on-premises management solution can enable integration with the MSfB and begin modernizing their apps.
Purchasing and licensing	Administrators can procure apps and licensing in volume. Licenses can be assigned and reclaimed.
Private store	Administrators can enable a private store for their organization. This store can be customized with managed apps and collections, providing users with a tailored experience. The private store can be accessed from the Microsoft Store app on Windows 10 devices or from a web browser.
App distribution	Apps that are acquired through the MSfB can be distributed to users in multiple ways: ■ Apps can be assigned to users or groups and made available through the private store for download and installation. ■ Apps can be distributed using ConfigMgr, third-party management solutions, or during image deployment. ■ Apps can be distributed offline without connecting to the MSfB using the Deployment Image Servicing and Management (DISM) command-line tool or provisioning packages.
Line-of-business apps	Administrators can add LOB apps to the private store for management and distribution.
App updates	Apps that are purchased and managed online can receive automatic updates through the MSfB.

As you begin planning for MSfB there are a few prerequisites that you should be familiar with. First, you need to understand the difference between the two available licensing models: online-licensed apps and offline-licensed apps. Depending on the licensing model you choose can dictate which prerequisites you need to address.

- **Online-licensed apps**   Apps purchased using the online licensing model require users to connect to the Microsoft Store service in order to acquire the app and corresponding license. Licenses are maintained using the user's Azure AD identity. This is the default license model, and will be the primary option if your users have Azure AD accounts, and access to the Microsoft Store is enabled.

- **Offline-licensed apps**   Apps purchased using the offline licensing model do not require connectivity to the Microsoft Store. Instead, administrators can download their purchased apps and licenses for deployment within their internal network. Not all apps support offline licensing. It is up to the independent software vendor (ISV) to opt-in for this option in the development center by selecting *Disconnected (offline) licensing* during submission. Offline-licensed apps can be deployed at imaging time using a provisioning package or distributed to systems using a management solution such as ConfigMgr.

Next, we will cover the baseline prerequisites for setting up MSfB. These are items that you will need to plan for before you begin your implementation. Also, take note of the items that mention online and offline licensing requirements. These will differ slightly depending on which licensing model you choose.

- **Microsoft Store for Business account**   A global administrator needs to visit *https://businessstore.microsoft.com* and sign in to activate the private store.

- **Azure AD accounts for admins**   Administrators that will be tasked with acquiring apps, distributing apps, and manage licensing will also need an Azure AD account. These requirements are the same for both online and offline licensing.

- **Azure AD accounts for users**   An Azure AD account will be required for users that access the MSfB to download and install online-licensed apps. Users do not require an Azure AD account for offline-licensed apps.

- **Platform support**   Users that are accessing the MSfB will need to do so from a supported PC or mobile device. This includes Windows 10, version 1511, or later.

- **Browser support**   Administrators that are managing the MSfB will need to do so from a supported browser. MSfB is compatible with Internet Explorer 10 or later, current versions of Microsoft Edge, Chrome, or Firefox.

Setup the private store

The private store is designed to help organizations deliver a unified experience to their employees when browsing and installing apps. This feature enables administrators to customize their own private Microsoft Store and manage app purchasing and distribution. From a user experience perspective, this includes the ability to adjust app visibility in the store based on user or group membership, along with grouping and sorting apps to your liking.

In Figure 1-39 you can see an example of the Alpine Ski House private store. In this section we will walk through the process of setting up a private store for MSfB.

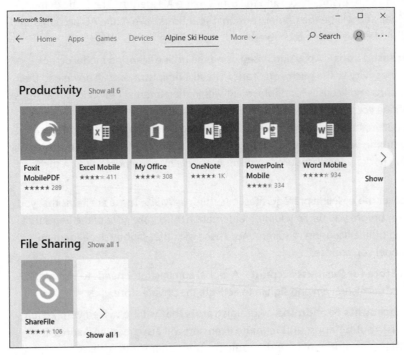

FIGURE 1-39 Private Store

In the following example you are an admin for Alpine Ski House. You have been tasked with creating a private store for your organization. Follow these steps to setup the private store:

1. Navigate to the **Microsoft Store For Business** at *https://businessstore.microsoft.com*.

2. Sign-in using an Azure AD Global Administrator account. Signing in without a global administrator account will only give you access to browse the standard Microsoft Store For Business.

3. In the menu bar at the top of the page, click the **Private Store** option. If this option is not visible, maximize your browser window or locate the collapse menu button in the upper left-hand corner. Click the menu button and select **Private Store** from the navigation menu, as shown in Figure 1-40.

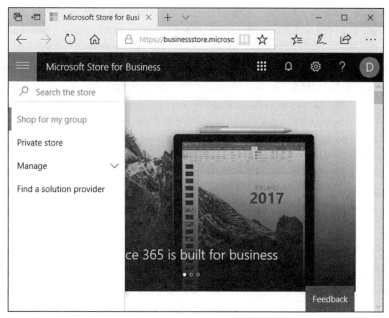

FIGURE 1-40 Microsoft Store for Business Portal

4. Review the Microsoft Store for Business and your data consent form. Check the box to consent and click Accept, as shown in Figure 1-41. Declining this consent form will automatically sign you out of the store.

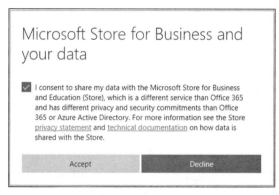

FIGURE 1-41 Microsoft Store for Business Consent

NOTE   FIRST TIME SIGN-IN

In this scenario we click the Private store in order to accept the consent form. The first time you sign-in to the MSfB as a global administrator, most actions will trigger the first-time consent form. For example, if you had clicked on Find A Solution Provider, it would have triggered the same form.

The private store has now been created and is associated with your Azure AD tenant. Once the private store is available you can access the Manage menu, which contains several administrative options that we will be reviewing in more detail in the next section.

At the time of this writing if you click the Private Store option after accepting the consent form you will see text that states: *Check with your admin. They need to set up your private store before you can use it.* This can be a bit confusing, because the store has already been created. It turns out that before you can access the private store and see apps, you need to accept a service agreement. You can do this by adding an app to your inventory. Continuing with our Alpine Ski House scenario, register a free copy of the OneNote app to trigger and accept the pending service agreement.

1. In the menu bar at the top of the page, type **OneNote** in the search field and select Enter. If the search field is not visible, maximize your browser window or locate the collapse menu button in the upper left-hand corner. Click the menu button and enter your search in the navigation menu.

2. From the search results, locate and click the free Microsoft OneNote app.

3. On the OneNote shop page, click **Get The App**.

4. Review the Microsoft Store For Business and Education Services Agreement. Check the box to accept the agreement and click **Accept**, as shown in Figure 1-42. This agreement is required to start using the private store.

FIGURE 1-42 Microsoft Store for Business Agreement.

5. On the Thanks for your order form, click Close. This confirms that the app has been purchased and added to your app inventory.

> **NOTE   GET NEW APPS**
>
> New apps that you add to your inventory can take up to 24 hours before they are visible in the private store. In the example above the OneNote app was visible in the private store within 5 minutes. This is a condition worth noting if you are troubleshooting why a recently added app has not appeared in the private store yet.

At the conclusion of this scenario the private store option on the menu bar will be replaced with the name of your organization (taken from your Azure tenant). When you click your organization name you should see the OneNote app listed in your app inventory. At this stage you can open the Microsoft Store on a compatible Windows 10 device, sign-in with your Azure AD credentials, and access your organization's private store.

> **REAL WORLD   ONLY SHOW THE PRIVATE STORE**
>
> The private store can provide organizations with an end-to-end app management solution. In some environments, once the private store is deployed, you may have a requirement to hide the default Microsoft Store. This can be achieved using Group Policy with the setting: Only Display The Private Store within the Microsoft Store. For more information on configuring this policy setting, visit:
> https://docs.microsoft.com/microsoft-store/manage-access-to-private-store#show-private-store-only-using-group-policy.

Configure Microsoft Store for Business

The management portal for MSfB contains several pages for app administration, licensing, and account management. Among these pages are a few controls to customize the private store. In this section we will introduce you to the portal, and walk through each of the available menu options.

Refer to Figure 1-43 for a preview of the MSfB management portal. In this screenshot we have the main navigation menu open and the Manage submenu is expanded. This submenu contains the administrative controls for managing your organization's MSfB experience. Let's take a closer look at the available options.

FIGURE 1-43 Microsoft Store For Business Management Portal

■ **Home** This page provides administrators an overview dashboard that contains summary information for various items such as license availability and recent purchases. The overview also includes drill down objects to other management options such as settings and permissions.

■ **Quotes** This page is used to view and interact with quotes that have been assigned to your organization for apps and other solutions. Expect this page to be blank unless you have a partner that has sent you a quote.

■ **Products & Services** This page is used to view your app inventory, benefits information and new LOB app. App inventory will include all registered apps for your organization, along with drill down details and customization options for each app. Benefits information is tied to your Microsoft agreement. LOB apps pertain to any newly registered LOB apps assigned to your organization.

■ **My Organization** This page is used to view account profile information, status information for your Microsoft agreements, connected tenants that you established with the Microsoft Products and Services Agreement (MSPA), and review requests that require admin approval.

■ **Devices** This page is used for managing your Windows AutoPilot deployments. AutoPilot is a technology that enables administrators to reduce traditional imaging needs by configuring automated system setup and configuration with Azure AD, Intune, Office 365, and MSfB.

- **Billing & Payments** This page is used to view invoices assigned to your organization and manage your account payment methods.
- **Order History** This page is used to view your order history and order details for software and subscriptions purchased by your organization.
- **Partners** This page is used to view the list of partners assigned to your organization. Partners are available to help organizations purchase and manage products and services. You can search for partner details by navigating to the Find A Solution Provider menu option.
- **Permissions** This page is used to view and manage the role-based access controls for your organization. This includes roles for admin, purchaser, basic purchaser, and device guard signer. Once your private store is active, it is important to review the default options and define the roles according to your business needs.
- **Settings** This page is used to view and manage the core settings for your organization's store experience. This includes shopping controls based on role-based access, distribution settings, and connectivity to your preferred MDM solution, device guard policies, and notification controls for invoices.
- **Support** This page is used for accessing support information about MSfB and opening support requests.

Now that you have a better understanding of the management portal, we will look at some customization controls for the private store. There are three primary locations that contain settings pertaining to the private store. The first location is the private store itself, which will be listed in the menu bar as the name of your organization. In this scenario the private store is called Alpine Ski House. Clicking on this link will present you with the store interface, as shown in Figure 1-44.

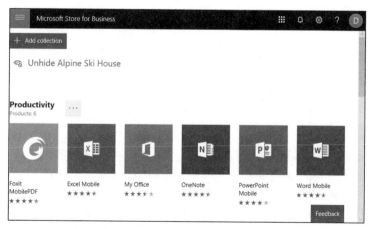

FIGURE 1-44 Microsoft Store for Business Private Store

This page enables administrators to customize the store interface for their employees. The changes you make here will be visible to employees when they access your organization's private store. Available options include the ability to create new collections by clicking on the **+ Add Collection** button. You can also remove collections and assign apps to collections by clicking on the more options icon (•••) next to the collection name.

In this example we are hiding the default collection, Alpine Ski House, which by default will contain all available apps. To replace this collection, we have created two new collections: Productivity (shown in the screen shot) and File Sharing (not shown). These new collections contain a custom list of apps based on our preference.

The second location for customizing the private store is under **Manage, Products & Services**, then **Apps & Software**. On this page you will see a list of apps from your inventory. Clicking on any one of these apps will take you to the product details page for that app. The lower half of this page has a tab for Private store availability, as shown in Figure 1-45.

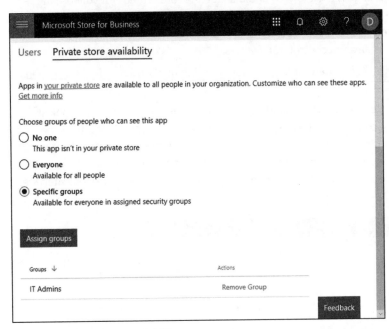

FIGURE 1-45 Private Store availability

The options on the Private store availability tab enable an administrator to control which users an app is visible to in the private store. In this example we have selected the radio button next to Specific groups, followed by an Azure AD security group that contains IT administrators. After saving these settings, the app will only be visible in the private store for users that are members of the IT Admins group.

Plan app deployment

In this section we will be working with app deployment in the cloud. App deployment with Microsoft 365 is centralized around cloud-based management. Traditional solutions for on-premises app deployment are still available, but working with apps in the cloud is the focus for this exam. The two major technologies that we will be focusing on are MSfB and Microsoft Intune. These technologies can operate independently, but are designed to be integrated for end-to-end coverage. For example, MSfB standalone can offer a suitable solution for Windows 10 devices, but if you need to distribute apps to iOS and Android then integrating Intune makes sense.

Plan for app deployment prerequisites

There are a few different ways to deploy apps in the Microsoft cloud. The prerequisites for these methods will depend on the requirements of the organization. For example, if your organization uses Office 365, but does not have an Intune subscription, you can still use the MSfB to help manage apps on Windows 10 devices. If your organization does have an Intune subscription, you can setup a MSfB account and integrate it with Intune to streamline the management and distribution of your apps across multiple platforms.

Based on the examples described above, many of the prerequisites for app deployment are going to be conditional. That said, you should be familiar with each of the available options and in what situations they apply.

- **Microsoft Store For Business Standalone**   If you choose to leverage the benefits of MSfB, your organization must have an active MSfB account.

- **Microsoft Store For Business + Intune**   If you plan to connect your MSfB account with Intune, you must activate Microsoft Intune. You can do this from the Intune portal, under **Manage**, **Settings**, **Distribute**, then **Management Tools**.

- **Microsoft Intune**   If you choose to leverage Intune for app management and distribution, your organization must have an active Intune subscription. This includes setting the MDM authority to Intune in the Azure portal.

- Device Enrollment   If you plan to require app installation on devices, those devices must be enrolled with Intune.

- **Supported Platforms**   MSfB supports Windows 10 devices. If you need to support other platforms, such as Android or iOS, you will need to consider an Intune subscription.

- **Supported App Types**   MSfB supports the conversion of multiple Windows app file formats into appx bundles for distribution. This conversion process requires an install sequence and capture of the app. Intune has a conversion process that converts the installer to a compatible intunewin bundle. The Intune solution is in preview at the time of this writing. Both scenarios should be planned for if you have a requirement to deploy Win32 apps.

Plan for app deployment types

In this section we are going to cover planning considerations for app deployment types. This topic refers to the various app deployment types that Microsoft Intune supports. In the management portal, administrators have access to a variety of app types that they can deploy to users and devices.

One of the first things to consider when planning your app management model is file formats. The file format of apps can vary based on publisher and platform. Variations by publisher is only true for Windows apps, where you have traditional file formats such as *.exe* and *.msi*, as well as newer formats such as .appx and *.msix*. This segmentation adds a lot of effort for IT admins that support a variety of apps. Variations by platform includes Android, iOS, and Windows. Modern and mobile apps are all platform-specific and need to be considered.

Next, you should know which app deployment types are available in Intune, and what options they provide. For this we will open the management portal and look at the client apps.

1. Sign-in to the Microsoft Azure portal at *https://portal.azure.com/*.
2. Click **All Services**.
3. Search for **Intune** and select it.
4. Under Manage, select **Client Apps**.
5. On the Client apps blade, under Manage, select Apps.
6. On the Client apps – Apps blade, click Add.
7. On the Add app blade, review the list of available app types. Refer to Table 1-9 for a breakdown of each app type and its capabilities.

TABLE 1-9 Client App types

Platform	App Type	Notes
Android, iOS, Windows Phone 8.1, Windows	Store app	All store apps require an app store URL that directs the app to the appropriate provider. With MSfB integration, Microsoft Store apps will automatically be synchronized with Intune every 24 hours.
Windows 10, macOS	Office 365 Suite	Office 365 apps can be bundled as a suite or created as standalone apps. Additional configuration options are available for architecture type, update channel, removal of previous MSI versions, automatic agreement acceptance, and shared computer activation.
Web link	Other	Web link enable you to create an app that launches a browser to a specific URL, such as your help desk portal.
Built-In app	Other	Built-In app enables you to quickly distribute curated managed apps, such as Office 365 or Adobe Reader for iOS and Android.
Line-of-business app	Other	Line-of-business app enables you to upload in-house apps. Accepted file formats include .msi, .msix, .msixbundle, .appx, and .appxbundle.
Windows app (Win32) - preview	Other	Win32 app enables you to upload a repackaged application using the .intunewin file format. At the time of this writing, this feature is in a preview state.

Create and deploy apps with Intune

In this section we are going to walk through the app creation process in Intune and cover how to deploy those apps to enrolled devices. The app deployment capabilities of Intune continue to evolve, with recent additions including Win32 app support. These are some notable milestones for the product, because Win32 app supports breaks the barrier from traditional on-premises app management requirements with new cloud capabilities.

MANAGE STORE APPS WITH INTUNE

Before you start working with apps in Intune, remember that you can synchronize Microsoft Store apps. Enabling this capability will simplify the management of Microsoft Store apps and provide us the ability to deploy them using Intune.

1. Navigate to the Microsoft Store for Business at *https://www.microsoft.com/business-store*.
2. Sign-in using an Azure AD account with admin access.
3. On the menu bar at the top of the page, click **Manage**.
4. On the Manage page, click **Settings** in the navigation list.
5. On the Settings page, select the **Distribute** tab.
6. On the Distribute tab, under Management tools, click **Activate** in the Action column for Microsoft Intune and Microsoft Intune Enrollment, as shown in Figure 1-46.

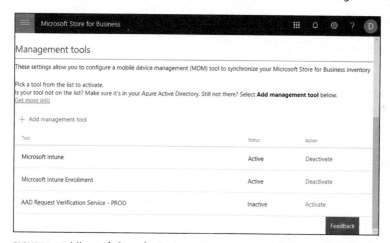

FIGURE 1-46 Microsoft Store for Business Management Tools

With Intune set as the active management tool for MSfB, you can verify the synchronization status in the Intune console.

1. Sign-in to the Microsoft Azure portal at *https://portal.azure.com/*.
2. Click **All Services**.
3. Search for **Intune** and select it.
4. Under Manage, select **Client Apps**.

5. On the Client apps blade, under Setup, select **Microsoft Store For Business**. This blade includes status and last sync information. You also have the option to change the language for apps in the console and force a sync.

After completing a sync, any Microsoft Store apps in your MSfB inventory will be visible in the Intune console. You can view and manage these apps by navigating to the Apps blade under Client Apps. In Figure 1-47 you can see an example of the synchronized Microsoft Store apps.

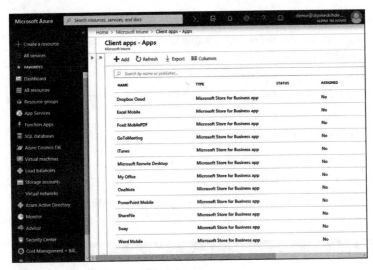

FIGURE 1-47 Microsoft Intune Client Apps

CREATING APPS IN INTUNE

We covered app deployment types earlier in this skill, which is one of the first options that you configure when creating apps in Intune. From there you can begin adding apps to your Intune library. In the following example we are going to add an Office 365 app to our Intune app library. This scenario will introduce you to the app creation process and get you comfortable with the portal.

1. Sign-in to the Microsoft Azure portal at *https://portal.azure.com/*.
2. Click **All Services**.
3. Search for **Intune** and select it.
4. Under Manage, select **Client Apps**.
5. On the Client apps blade, under Manage, select **Apps**.
6. On the Client Apps – Apps blade, click **Add** in the menu.
7. On the Add App blade, select **Windows 10** under the Office 365 Suite app type.
8. Click **Configure App Suite**. This blade will present you with each of the available products in the Office 365 suite.

9. On the Configure App Suite blade, select the following products, as shown in Figure 1-48, and click **OK**.

   ■ Excel, OneDrive Desktop, OneNote, Outlook, PowerPoint, Skype for Business, and Word.

FIGURE 1-48 Office 365 App Suite Configuration

10. On the Add app blade, click **App Suite Information**. This blade includes information pertaining to the app metadata, such as name and description. Because this is an Office 365 app some fields are prepopulated, such as the publisher and app icon.

11. On the App Suite Information blade, fill in the following values and click **OK**. Refer to Figure 1-49 for an example.

   ■ **Suite Name** This is a required field. Enter a name for the app. App names should be unique in order to prevent conflicts in the company portal.

   ■ **Suite Description** This is a required field. Enter a description for the app.

   ■ **Publisher** This field is pre-populated for Office 365 apps. For apps where the field is not populated, enter a publisher for the app.

   ■ **Category** This field is optional. There are nine categories to choose from and you can select as many as you want. Assigning a category will enable users to filter apps easier. Office 365 apps default to the productivity category.

   ■ **Display this As A Featured App In The Company Portal** This toggle sets whether the app is set on the main page of the company portal. Set the toggle to Yes. The company portal is used by employees to access and install apps. It can be accessed using the Microsoft Store app or by visiting *https://portal.manage.microsoft.com/*.

- **Information URL**   This field is optional. You can enter a web address that contains information about the app. Leave this field blank.

- **Privacy URL**   This field is optional. You can enter a web address that contains privacy information about the app. Leave this field blank.

- **Developer**   This field is optional. This field is prepopulated for Office 365 apps.

- **Owner**   This field is optional. This field is prepopulated for Office 365 apps.

- **Notes**   This field is optional. Leave this field blank.

- **Logo**   This field is optional. This field is prepopulated for Office 365 apps.

FIGURE 1-49 Office 365 App Suite Information

12. On the Add app blade, click **App Suite Settings**. This blade contains options for what version of the app will be installed and other actions such as activation.

13. On the App Suite Settings blade, fill in the following values and click OK. Refer to Figure 1-50 for an example.

- **Office Version**   64-bit.

- **Update Channel**   Monthly (Targeted).
- **Version To Install on End User Devices**   Latest.
- **Specific Version**   Latest version.
- **Remove Other Versions Of Office (MSI) From End User Devices**   Yes.
- **Automatically Accept The App End User License Agreement**. Yes.
- **Use Shared Computer Activation**. Yes.
- **Languages**. No changes.

FIGURE 1-50 Office 365 App Suite Settings

14. On the Add App blade, click **Add** to add the new Office 365 suite app to your Intune app library.

15. Review the Azure portal notifications to confirm that the app was created successfully.

   With these steps complete, you should have the new Office 365 Suite app listed on the Client Apps – Apps blade, alongside the MSfB apps that we saw earlier in this skill section.

ASSIGNING APPS IN INTUNE

Apps that are present in your Intune app library can be assigned to groups of users and devices for install or uninstall. When you create a new app assignment you are given three assignment types to choose from. These include:

- **Available for enrolled devices** This assignment type makes the app available to devices that are enrolled in Intune.
- **Required** This assignment type forces the app to install on the targeted group of users or devices.
- **Uninstall** This assignment type forces the app to be uninstalled from the targeted group of users or devices.

In the following example we will take our Office 365 suite app and assign it to the Alpine Ski House as a requirement for all devices.

1. Sign-in to the Microsoft Azure portal at *https://portal.azure.com/*.
2. Click **All Services**.
3. Search for **Intune** and select it.
4. Under Manage, select **Client Apps**.
5. On the Client apps blade, under Manage, select **Apps**.
6. On the Client Apps – Apps blade, locate the ASH Office 365 Suite app and select it.
7. On the ASH Office 365 Suite blade, under Manage, select **Assignments**.
8. On the Assignments blade, click the **aDD GROUP** button.
9. On the Add group blade, select **Required** for the Assignment type.
10. Click **Included Groups**.
11. On the Assign blade, fill in the following information and click **OK**:
    - **Make This App Required For All Users** No
    - **Make This App Required For All Devices** Yes
12. On the Add group blade, click **OK**.

EXAM TIP

Plan for questions on the exam that will test your knowledge of the assignment controls. Spend time creating groups, adding users and devices to those groups, and working with the include and exclude assignments. An example scenario might include two security groups and five computers with different membership between the groups. It will be your responsibility to solve question such as how to install app XYZ on two computers and uninstall app ABC from the other three computers.

Plan device co-management

In this skill we are going to dive into co-management. This delivers a new approach at transitioning device management workloads to the cloud. ConfigMgr is a traditional on-premises management solution with an extensive list of capabilities. Co-management is designed to bridge ConfigMgr and Intune, enabling administrators to choose which solution manages which workload. For example, ConfigMgr can continue managing compliance policies but endpoint protection is going to be managed by Intune.

In the past, ConfigMgr and Intune worked together in a hybrid format. This offered administrators a single pane of glass for managing a variety of platforms. However, it became apparent that enhancing a cloud solution like Intune moved at a much faster pace than customers supporting ConfigMgr. This introduced challenges. The hybrid format also didn't provide the tools needed to help customers move to a fully cloud managed solution at their own pace.

The co-management connector is a feature in ConfigMgr that you configure. From there administrators can selectively pilot and migrate specific workloads from their on-premises infrastructure to Intune.

Plan for co-management prerequisites

To prepare for co-management you need to be familiar with the prerequisites. This first list contains each of the core technical requirements that need to be addressed before you can establish a connection between ConfigMgr and Intune.

- **ConfigMgr Site Version**. Co-management is available in ConfigMgr 1710 or later.
- **Multiple ConfigMgr Sites**. Support for connecting multiple ConfigMgr environments to a single Intune tenant requires ConfigMgr 1806 or later.
- **Windows 10 Version. Devices that will be co-managed require Windows 10, version 1709 or later.**
- **Device Enrollment**. Devices that will be con-managed need to be enrolled in Intune and have a ConfigMgr client installed.
- **Intune Subscription. Co-management requires an active Intune subscription.**
- **MDM Authority**. The MDM authority for your Azure AD tenant must be set to Intune. MDM for Office 365 and hybrid ConfigMgr are not supported.

While co-management can help customers transition to Intune, it can also be used to support existing Intune customers that still need ConfigMgr for use cases such as operating system deployment. There are two supported scenarios that you should be familiar with when planning for co-management. Table 1-10 describes these scenarios and the corresponding prerequisites for each.

TABLE 1-10 Co-management Prerequisites

Scenario	Prerequisite	Description
Domain joined devices with ConfigMgr	Devices need to be hybrid Azure AD joined	This scenario supports customers that are transitioning their on-premises device management workloads to Intune.
Azure AD joined devices with Intune	Devices need to be Azure AD joined. ConfigMgr site needs to have a Cloud Management Gateway (CMG) deployed. The CMG enables Intune to deploy the ConfigMgr client to these devices.	This scenario supports customers with devices that are Azure AD joined and managed using Intune, but still require ConfigMgr for certain tasks. For example, customers using AutoPilot to deploy new devices.

Create the co-management connection

In this section we are going to walk through the process of creating the co-management connection in the ConfigMgr management console. For this example, we are running ConfigMgr version 1806.

1. Open the **Configuration Manager Console**.
2. Click the **Administration** workspace.
3. Under Overview, expand Cloud Services.
4. Click **Co-Management**.
5. In the ribbon, select **Configure Co-Management**.
6. On the Co-management Configuration Wizard, on the Subscription page, click **Sign In**, enter your Azure AD credentials, and click **Next**.

> *NOTE* **INTUNE PERMISSIONS**
>
> The account initiating the co-management connection does not need to be an administrator, but does require an Intune licensee assigned.

7. On the Enablement page, select **Pilot** from the Automatic enrollment in Intune drop-down and click **Next**. This will enable automatic enrollment to Intune for a limited set of devices in a pilot device collection.
8. On the Workloads page, move each of the sliders to the Pilot Intune column, as shown in Figure 1-51. This will shift the corresponding workloads to Intune for all devices in your pilot device collection.

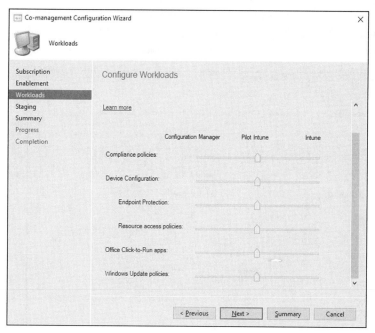

FIGURE 1-51 Co-management Workloads

9. On the Staging page, click **Browse**, select a device collection containing devices that are approved for co-management testing, and click **Next**. The devices in this pilot collection will automatically be enrolled in Intune and all workloads will be enabled for Intune management.

10. On the Summary page, review the configuration options and click **Next**.

11. On the Completion page, confirm the process was successful, and click **Close**.

After completing these steps, the co-management connector will be present in the ConfigMgr management console. If you need to modify the settings that you configured during setup, you can select the co-management connector in the console and click properties in the ribbon. From there you can make updates to your Intune enrollment settings, workloads, and pilot collection.

As a final step, you can validate that the targeted devices are communicating with Intune by locating them in the Intune console and viewing the device details. To locate a device, follow these steps:

1. Sign-in to the Microsoft Azure portal at *https://portal.azure.com/*.

2. Click **All Services**.

3. Search for **Intune** and select it.

4. On the Microsoft Intune blade, under Manage, select **Devices**.

5. On the Devices blade, under Manage, select **All Devices**.

6. On the Devices – All Devices blade, locate a device from your co-management collection and select it. This will bring up the details for that device. Refer to Figure 1-52 for an example of a co-managed device in the Intune console.

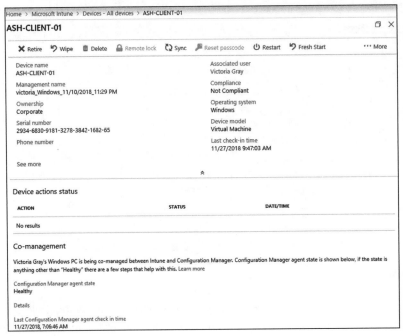

FIGURE 1-52 Microsoft Intune Co-managed Device

In this example ASH-CLIENT-01 has successfully enrolled in Intune and is being co-managed. We can see from Figure 1-52 that the compliance policies workload is being managed by Intune based on the **Compliance** field showing Not Compliant. The lower section shares specific details about the device's co-management status, including the health state of the ConfigMgr client, and the last time the device checked in.

> **NOTE** **NEW DEVICE MANAGEMENT PORTAL**
>
> Today administrators can continue managing Intune configurations through the Azure portal. As an alternative, you can access these same resources using the Microsoft 365 Device Management portal. To do so, visit: *https://devicemanagement.microsoft.com*.

Migrate your workloads to Intune

During the setup process for co-management we briefly showed the available workload options in the ConfigMgr console. The sliders on the Workloads page instruct devices where to receive the corresponding instructions. Refer to Table 1-11 for additional information about each of the workload options and their corresponding requirements.

TABLE 1-11 Co-management Workloads

Workload	ConfigMgr Version	Intune Controls
Compliance policies	1710	Device compliance policies are managed in Intune under Intune, Device compliance, then Policies. Intune device compliance can be used for monitoring and/or conditional access.
Device Configuration	1806	Device profiles are managed in Intune under Intune, Device configuration, Profiles. Intune device profiles apply rules, such as password requirements.
Endpoint Protection	1802	Endpoint protection profiles are managed in Intune under Intune, Device configuration, then Profiles. These profiles control the behavior of Windows Defender, including antivirus, antispam, firewall, and encryption.
Resource access policies	1710	Resource access policies are managed in Intune under Intune, Device configuration, then Profiles. These policies can control access to services such as email, wi-fi, VPN, and certificates.
Office Click-to-Run apps	1806	Office Click-to-Run apps are managed in Intune under Intune, Client Apps, then Apps. Administrators can create and assign Office Click-to-Run apps for deployment to users and devices.
Windows Update policies	1710	Windows Update policies are managed in Intune under Intune, Software updates, Windows 10 Update Rings. These policies control Windows Update behavior on managed devices.
Mobile apps (preview)	1806	Mobile apps are managed in Intune under Intune, Client Apps, then Apps. Administrators can create and assign mobile apps for deployment to mobile devices.

> **MORE INFO CO-MANAGEMENT WORKLOADS**
>
> For more information about co-management and the different workload options, visit: *https://docs.microsoft.com/sccm/core/clients/manage/co-management-overview*.

Plan device monitoring

In this skill section we are going to review the Device Health and Update Compliance solutions offered through Windows Analytics. These offerings enable organizations to monitor the health and compliance of the devices and apps in their environment. Both solutions are provided as part of the Operations Management Suite (OMS), a centralized repository that provides deeper insight and manageability controls for organizations.

Devices enrolled in Windows Analytics upload relative diagnostic data to Microsoft. That data is processed and analyzed in the Microsoft cloud and reported back to customers in a modern dashboard. Customers can navigate the dashboard, retrieve critical event information, and build custom queries. These solutions introduce a new landscape for monitoring devices in the enterprise.

UNDERSTAND YOUR OPTIONS FOR DEVICE MONITORING

Microsoft 365 provides a suite of solutions for monitoring the devices in your organization. At the time of this writing there are three solutions available: Upgrade Readiness, Update Compliance, and Device Health. In this skill section we are focusing on Device Health and Update Compliance as key sources for monitoring the pulse of devices and applications. In an upcoming chapter we will take a closer look at Upgrade Readiness, which provides customers with readiness details for Windows 10.

Refer to Table 1-12 for a summary of these solutions, include their core capabilities and the minimum required telemetry level for each (more to come on this).

TABLE 1-12 Windows Analytics Solutions

Solution	Telementry Level	Capabilities
Upgrade Readiness	Basic	Lifecycle management for Windows 10 compatibility and deployment readiness. Device and application inventory. Driver and application compatibility information for Windows 10. Application usage.
Update Compliance	Basic	Monitoring of Windows 10 quality and feature update compliance. Reports on update compliance and issues that require attention. Status information for Windows Defender signatures and threats. Status information for delivery optimization.
Device Health	Enhanced (limited)	Monitoring of Windows 10 device and application health. Crash report details related to applications and device drivers. Reports for login health and authentication method trends. Visibility into Windows Information Protection misconfigurations.

Plan for Windows Analytics prerequisites

Windows Analytics enables organizations to receive insights into their environment using Microsoft cloud services. Customers that choose to leverage Device Health and Update Compliance must opt-in and enable Windows telemetry on their devices. At the time of this writing, Microsoft does not offer a comparable on-premises solution for Device Health and Update Compliance.

The following list outlines the prerequisites required to configure Windows Analytics for use with Device Health and Update Compliance.

- **Azure Subscription** An Azure subscription is required to establish a connection with the log analytics workspace in OMS.
- **Commercial ID** After creating an OMS workspace, you are provided with a commercial ID for device enrollment. The commercial ID can be configured on devices using Intune, ConfigMgr, Group Policy, or an alternative management solution.
- **Windows 10** Device Health and Update compliance are compatible with Windows 10 devices (laptops and desktops only) running Professional, Education, and Enterprise editions.

- **Windows Telemetry**   Devices must have Windows telemetry enabled and set to certain diagnostic levels in order to support these monitoring solutions.

  - **Device Health**. Windows telemetry must be enabled and set to Enhanced. Devices running Windows 10, version 1709 or later, can optionally be configured to limit enhanced diagnostic data to the minimum required by Windows Analytics. This can be configured using a GPO.

  - **Update Compliance**. Windows telemetry must be enabled and set to Basic.

- **Data sharing**   There are several Microsoft cloud endpoints that your devices must be able to communicate with in order to upload diagnostic data. For a list of these endpoints, visit: *https://docs.microsoft.com /windows/deployment/update/windows-analytics-get-started#enable-data-sharing.*

> **MORE INFO   DIAGNOSTIC DATA LEVELS**
>
> Organizations that are interested in leveraging the capabilities of Windows Analytics are often concerned about the data they are required to upload. Take some time to study the four tiers of diagnostic data: Security, Basic, Enhanced (or Limited Enhanced), and Full.
>
> For more information about these diagnostic data levels and what data is sent to Microsoft, visit: *https://docs.microsoft.com/windows/privacy/configure-windows-diagnostic-data-in-your-organization#diagnostic-data-levels.*

Enable Windows Analytics

Now that you understand the prerequisites for Device Health and Update Compliance, we will walk through the process of enabling Windows Analytics on devices. This can be achieved in a variety of ways. In this example we will be using Group Policy to apply the configuration for Device Health. Each new release of Windows 10 includes a new set of Group Policy ADMX templates. For this walk through we will be using the Windows 10 1809 templates. Be sure to download the latest compatible templates for your environment.

In the following steps we will be configuring three policies to enable Windows telemetry for Device Health and Update Compliance. There are additional policies available that control other elements of Windows telemetry. While you are in the editor, take time to review the other options and what their capabilities are.

1. Open the **Group Policy Management Editor** on a server in your domain.

2. Create a new Group Policy Object (GPO) and name it Enable Windows Telemetry.

3. Right-click the new GPO and click **Edit**.

4. Under Computer Configuration, expand **Policies**.

5. Expand **Administrative Templates**.

6. Expand **Windows Components**.

7. Locate and click the folder for **Data Collection And Preview Builds**.

8. Locate and edit the policy: **Allow Telemetry**. This policy object enables Windows telemetry.

9. Select the radio button next to Enabled.

10. Select **2 – Enhanced** from the dropdown.

11. Click **OK**.

12. Locate and edit the policy: **Configure The Commercial ID**. This policy assigns the Commercial ID to devices. The Commercial ID uniquely identifies the devices in your organization so the corresponding data is available in log analytics.

13. Select the radio button next to **Enabled**.

14. Enter the Commercial ID value in the text field.

15. Click **OK**.

16. Locate and edit the policy: **Limit Enhanced Diagnostic Data To The Minimum Required By Windows Analytics**. This policy reduces the amount of data devices upload to the minimum required by Windows Analytics.

17. Select the radio button next to **Enabled**.

18. Select **Enable Windows Analytics Collection** from the dropdown.

19. Click **OK**.

20. Close the Enable Windows Telemetry policy.

This policy is now ready to be deployed to your compatible Windows 10 devices. Once deployed, expect to see data in the log analytics workspace within 24 hours for Internet-connected devices.

MORE INFO **DEPLOYMENT SCRIPT**

Microsoft provides customers with a deployment script that is designed to assist customers in establishing reliable data uploads. The provided documentation recommends running this script monthly in your environment to ensure that at least one full scan is completed and submitted. The script also provides log output for troubleshooting issues that you may not see otherwise, such as communication trouble with the cloud endpoints.

For more information about the deployment script, visit:
https://docs.microsoft.com/windows/deployment/update/windows-analytics-get-started#deploying-windows-analytics-at-scale.

Plan for device profiles

In this skill section we cover device configuration profiles in Microsoft Intune. In its simplest form, a device configuration profile enables administrators to assign a desired configuration change to a managed device. These profiles offer a variety of options across multiple platforms. Administrators can leverage them to automatically configure common tasks on managed devices such as corporate email accounts, VPN settings, and wireless configurations.

Determine which device profiles are available

For starters, this is one of those features that you need to get hands on with in the console. There are dozens of profile combinations available and if the out-of-box options don't fit your needs, each platform supports the capability to assign a custom profile. Custom profiles for Windows Phone 8.1, Windows 10, and Android use the Open Mobile Alliance Uniform Resource Identifier (OMA-URI) standard. macOS and iOS platforms use the Apple Configurator profile format.

Configuration service provider (CSP) is another term you should familiarize yourself with. A CSP functions similar to Group Policy. CSPs interface with the client operating system to read, set, modify, or delete configuration settings defined by an administrator. Many of the built-in device profile settings in Intune are established using CSPs, and custom settings can be added using OMA-URI strings.

Table 1-13 provides some example use cases where device configuration profiles can be leveraged. Depending on the needs of your organization, you can create scopes that are based on corporate-owned and personally-owned devices. This format can be used to help adopt the bring-your-own-device (BYOD) initiative.

TABLE 1-13 Device Profile Use Cases

Platform	Owner	Profile Type	Use Case
Android	Personal	Device restrictions	Create a device profile for enhanced security. The profile contains settings that require a password to unlock the device and encryption is enforced.
Android Enterprise	Corporate	Wi-Fi	Create a wireless profile for wireless connectivity. The profile contains settings for SSID, automatic connection, EAP type, certificates, and authentication methods.
macOS	Personal	Device restrictions	Create a device profile for enhanced security. The profile contains settings to block the following features: camera, file transfers using iTunes, AirDrop, all iCloud sync and backup capabilities.
Windows 8.1 and later	Corporate	VPN	Create a device profile for VPN connectivity. The profile contains the corporate VPN servers, VPN configuration file, and spit tunneling preferences.
Windows 10 and later	Corporate	Windows Advanced Threat Protection	Create a device profile for Windows ATP. The profile contains an ATP onboarding configuration package.

MORE INFO **CONFIGURATION SERVICE PROVIDER REFERENCE**

For more information about CSPs that are supported in Windows 10, visit: *https://docs.micro-soft.com/en-us/windows/client-management/mdm/configuration-service-provider-reference.*

Create device profiles

In this section we are going to walk through the process of creating a device profile for the iOS platform and assigning it to a group of managed devices. For this example, we are creating a configuration profile for the Alpine Ski House lodge. This location has several iPads available for customers to use. You need to configure a basic wireless profile that will enable the devices to access the guest wireless network. Once devices receive the profile, they will automatically connect to the wireless network when in range.

1. Sign-in to the Microsoft Azure portal at *https://portal.azure.com/*.
2. Click **All Services**.
3. Search for **Intune** and select it.
4. On the Microsoft Intune blade, under Manage, select **Device Configuration**.
5. On the Device configuration blade, under Manage, select **Profiles**.
6. On the Device configuration – Profiles blade, click **Create Profile**.
7. On the Create profile blade, fill in the following information:
   - **Name**   iOS Guest Wireless Profile
   - **Description**   iOS guest wireless profile for the Alpine Ski House lodge
   - **Platform**   iOS
   - **Profile type**   Wi-Fi
8. On the Wi-Fi blade, fill in the following information and click OK.
   - **Wi-Fi type**   Basic
   - **Network name**   AlpineSkiHouseLodge
   - **SSID**   ASH-Lodge
   - **Connect automatically**   Enable
   - **Hidden network**   Disable
   - **Security type**   WPA/WPA2-Personal
   - **Pre-shared key**   P@ssw0rd
   - **Proxy settings**   None
9. On the Create Profile blade click **Create** to finish the profile.
10. Review the Azure portal notifications to confirm that the profile was created successfully.
11. On the iOS Guest Wireless Profile blade, under Manage, select **Assignments**.
12. On the iOS Guest Wireless Profile – Assignments blade, on the Include tab, click **Select Groups To Include**.
13. On the Select groups to include blade, locate and select a security group containing the Alpine Ski House lodge iOS devices and click **Select**.
14. Click **Save**.

15. Review the Azure portal notifications to confirm that the assignment was created successfully.

After creating and assigning this wireless profile, you can monitor the progress of that profile assignment by navigating to the Device Configuration – Profiles blade and selecting it from the list. This will direct you to the Overview dashboard, which contains helpful information about the assignment status. This includes a chart that summarizes total success, errors, and conflicts—all helpful data points for troubleshooting and success tracking.

Plan for Mobile Application Management

In this skill section we cover planning considerations for application management on mobile devices. Application management refers to the protection of company data within an application. For example, say a user opens an email from their corporate account using Microsoft Outlook for Android. This email contains confidential information. Application management can be used to prevent the user from copying data from this email and pasting it into another application. For the exam you will need to be comfortable with creating and assigning these policies.

Plan for app protection prerequisites

The capability to manage the data within an application has evolved over the years. Microsoft's solution for this is called app protection policies. This is a feature available with Microsoft Intune. In the past, application management required the management of the device running the app. With app protection policies, the policy is assigned to the user. This alleviates the need for devices to be enrolled in an MDM. Instead the user signs into the app with their Azure AD account and the necessary policies get applied.

The following list covers the basic prerequisites for deploying app protection policies in an organization:

- **Azure AD subscription** A basic Azure AD subscription is required to establish Azure AD accounts.
- **Intune subscription** App protection policies are a capability of Microsoft Intune. You will need an Intune subscription in order to create and manage these policies. Users that have these policies assigned will require an Intune license.
- **Office 365 subscription** App protection policies assigned to Office 365 mobile apps will require users to have an Office 365 license assigned to their Azure AD account.
- **Azure AD account** Users must have an Azure AD account.
- **Supported platforms** App protection policies are supported for iOS, Android, and Windows 10.
- **Security groups** App protection policies are assigned to Azure AD security groups that contain user objects. You will need to create the desired groups in Azure AD or synchronize your existing on-premises groups using Azure AD Connect.
- **Supported apps** App protection policies are not available for all apps. The app must support the Intune SDK features that enable app management.

Configure app protection policies

In this section we proceed with creating an app protection policy and assigning it to a group of users. A common scenario that you may be presented with is app management for Office 365. These are often the core productivity apps for users, and company data is an important aspect to consider.

In the following example we are going to create an app protection policy for the Alpine Ski House sales team. These users travel often and use a mixture of corporate and personal mobile devices for accessing company resources. The app protection policy will control data for each of the core Office 365 mobile apps.

1. Sign-in to the Microsoft Azure portal at *https://portal.azure.com/*.

2. Click **All services**.

3. Search for **Intune** and select it.

4. Under Manage, select **Client Apps**.

5. On the Client Apps blade, under Manage, select **App Protection Policies**.

6. On the Client Apps – App Protection Policies blade, click **Create Policy**.

7. On the Create policy blade, fill in the following information:

   - **Name**   ASH APP for Android.

   - **Description**   APP for Office 365 apps on Android.

   - **Platform**   Android.

   - **Target To All App Types**   Yes.

8. On the Create policy blade, Click **Apps**.

9. On the Apps blade, select the following apps and click **Select**:

   - **Excel**

   - **OneNote**

   - **Outlook**

   - **PowerPoint**

   - **Word**

10. On the Create Policy blade, click **Settings**.

11. On the Settings blade, click **Data Protection**.

12. On the Data protection blade, select the following options and click **OK**. Refer to Figure 1-53 for an example of the configuration.

    - **Backup Org data To Android Backup Services**   Block

    - **Send Org Data To Other Apps**   Policy Managed Apps

    - **Receive Data From Other Apps**   Policy Managed Apps

    - **Save Copies Of Org Data**   Block

    - **Allow User To Save Copies To Selected Services**   Onedrive For Business

- **Restrict cut, copy, And Paste Between Other Apps** Policy Managed Apps
- **Screen Capture And Google Assistant** Disable
- **Encrypt Org Data** Require
- **Encrypt Org Data On Enrolled Devices** Require
- **Sync App With Native Contacts App** Disable
- **Printing Org Data** Disable
- **Share Web Content With Policy Managed Browsers** Require

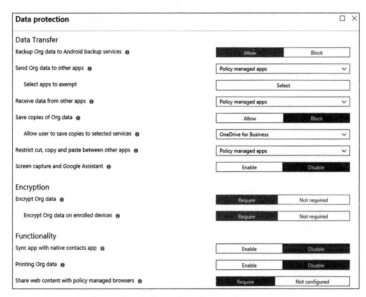

FIGURE 1-53 App Protection Policy – Data Protection

13. On the Settings blade, click **Access Requirements**.

14. On the Access requirements blade, select the following options and click **OK**. Refer to Figure 1-54 for an example of the configuration.

- **PIN For Access** Require
- **Pin Type** Numeric
- **Simple PIN** Block
- **Select Minimum PIN Length** 6
- **Fingerprint Instead Of PIN For Access (Android 6.0+)** Yes
- **Override Fingerprint With PIN After Timeout** Require
- **Timeout (Minutes Of Inactivity)** 30
- **App PIN When Device PIN Is Set** Enable
- **Work Or School Account Credentials For Access** Require
- **Recheck The Access Requirements After (Minutes Of Inactivity)** 30

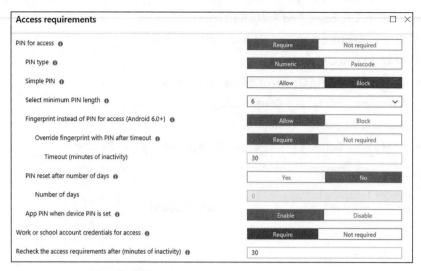

FIGURE 1-54 App Protection Policy – Data Protection

15. On the Settings blade, click **Conditional launch**.

16. On the Conditional Launch page, review the default options and click **OK**. Refer to Figure 1-55 for an example of the available options. Conditional launch enforces periodic checks to ensure that app protection policies are up-to-date and compliant. There are seven available settings:

   - **Max PIN Attempts**   If a user enters their PIN incorrectly more than the defined number of times, the user can be forced to reset their PIN, or the app data can be wiped.

   - **Offline Grace Period**   If the managed app does not check-in for a defined period, access to the app can be blocked or the app data can be wiped.

   - **Jailbroken/Rooted devices**   If the device has been jailbroken or rooted, access to the app can be blocked or the app data can be wiped.

   - **Min OS Version**   If the device OS does not meet the minimum version, the user can be warned, access to the app can be blocked, or the app data can be wiped.

   - **Min App Version**   If the app does not meet the minimum version, the user can be warned, access to the app can be blocked, or the app data can be wiped.

   - **Min Patch Version**   If the device OS does not meet the minimum patch version, the user can be warned, access to the app can be blocked, or the app data can be wiped.

   - **Device Manufacturer(s)**   If the device is not made by the specified manufacturer, access to the app can be blocked or the app data can be wiped.

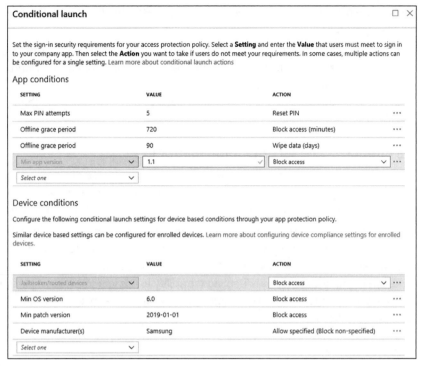

FIGURE 1-55 App Protection Policy – Data Protection

17. On the Settings blade, click **OK**.

18. On the Add a policy blade, click **Create**.

19. On the Client Apps – App Protection Policies blade, select the **ASH APP For Android** policy.

20. On the Intune App Protection blade, under Manage, click **Assignments**.

21. On the Intune App Protection – Assignments blade, on the Include tab, click **Select Groups To Include**.

22. Select the Alpine Ski House Sales group and click **Select**.

After completing this walk-through you should have a new app protection policy created and deployed. You can review the check-in information for users that access this app by navigating to the **ASH APP For Android** setting and selecting **Overview**. This blade provides insight into how many users are accessing the associated apps and the check-in count for each app in the policy.

Plan mobile device security

Planning for device security is something all organizations need to prioritize. Over the past few years Microsoft has invested considerable resources on improving the security posture of their products. This is seen in each of the solutions that we have discussed thus far, and makes up a large portion of this exam.

From a mobile device perspective, you have several tools at your disposal. Microsoft Intune and Azure AD give you access to device configuration profiles, device compliance, conditional access, and app protection policies. We cover each of these technologies individually in this book, but the focus for this section is to understand how they connect to improve the security of your mobile devices.

Design a mobile device security implementation

The cloud-based security offerings that are covered in this exam can operate independently of each other but are designed to work together. In combination they can form a layered defense structure that improves the security posture of your organization, your data, and your users.

Table 1-14 covers each of the core technologies used to manage and secure mobile devices. The defense layer column illustrates what components the corresponding technology is designed to manage. For example, device configuration profiles focus on the configuration of the device operating system, such as disabling the ability to use your device as a personal hotspot. The design considerations column highlights the capabilities of each technology and relative design suggestions.

TABLE 1-14 Mobile Device Security Layers

Technology	Product	Defense Layer	Design Considerations
Device configuration profiles	Microsoft Intune	Device	Device configuration profiles apply to enrolled and managed devices. Design configuration profiles to align with your device compliance requirements.
Device compliance policies	Microsoft Intune	Device, application	Device compliance policies apply to enrolled and managed devices. Design compliance policies to align with configuration profiles. Consider what conditional access restrictions will use device compliance.
Conditional access policies	Azure AD	Application	Conditional access policies apply to Azure AD joined and hybrid Azure AD joined devices. Design conditional access policies to incorporate device compliance requirements.
App protection policies	Microsoft Intune	Application	App protection policies apply to Azure AD accounts. Design app protection policies around managed and unmanaged devices.

Skill 1.4: Plan Windows 10 deployment

In 2015 Microsoft released Windows 10, an operating system that would completely shift the industry and the way in which enterprises managed and supported Windows. In the past you could expect a new version of Windows every 3-5 years, and the support lifecycle for those versions would overlap by a good margin. Organizations had very little pressure to quickly adopt the next major release. They could wait 12 months for major issues to be addressed, and then spend an additional 12-18 months testing and deploying the next release of Windows.

Windows 10 has evolved greatly since its original introduction. This version of the popular client operating system is delivered to customers as a service, meaning instead of waiting 3-5 years for new features or intermittent service packs, Microsoft deploys a major feature update every 6 months. These feature updates introduce new capabilities, security enhancements, bug fixes, and much more. In addition, the support lifecycle for Windows 10 releases are shorter than previous versions of Windows. This encourages organizations to stay current with Windows 10.

In this chapter we are going to cover Windows 10 in depth. This will include planning considerations around Windows as a Service (WaaS), a term you should become very familiar with. We will walk through the various deployment methods for Windows 10 and look at the pros and cons for each. We will cover upgrade readiness, a service that helps customers prepare for Windows 10 and maintain compatibility. Finally, we will look at the variety of security features introduced with Windows 10, which serves as one of the major benefits for adopting and staying current with Windows 10.

This section covers the following topics:

- Plan for Windows as a Service (WaaS)
- Plan the appropriate Windows 10 Enterprise deployment method
- Analyze upgrade readiness for Windows 10
- Evaluate and deploy additional Windows 10 Enterprise security features

---

Plan for Windows as a Service (WaaS)

IT organizations that have delivered and supported earlier versions of Windows will experience some significant changes once they adopt Windows 10. The upgrade to Windows 10 (moving from Windows 7 to Windows 10, for example) shares a lot of similarities with previous upgrades. Once your fleet of devices is running Windows 10, you need to establish guiding principles for supporting upcoming feature updates, such as hardware, driver, and application compatibility.

In this section we will introduce you to the core components and services relative to WaaS. This will include a closer look at servicing channels, which determine your feature update deployment cycle. We will also be covering Windows Insider for Business. This is a program based on Windows Insider that provides organizations a centralized approach for testing and providing feedback.

Identify the core components for WaaS

The term "as a Service" (aaS) has been largely adopted to represent a transformation in the way digital services are provided to customers. Some common examples of this model include Software as a Service (SaaS) and Infrastructure as a Service (IaaS). Both examples are built on cloud-based technologies. Customers now have the option to purchase Microsoft Office as a subscription (SaaS), providing frequent updates and new capabilities every month. Landing servers in your local data center may not be realistic when you can move those servers to the cloud (IaaS) and reduce on-premises support and maintenance.

With Windows 10, Microsoft introduced Windows as a Service (WaaS). The idea for WaaS is that customers no longer buy a new version of Windows every 3-5 years. Instead you purchase Windows 10 and receive frequent updates and features. Moving Windows to a semi-annual release schedule enabled Microsoft to make some foundational changes in how the operating system would be serviced moving forward. As part of that transformation, they introduced new components in Windows 10 to support the WaaS model.

Each of these terms is a key component of WaaS and relates to how you will manage Windows 10.

- **Feature updates** These updates deliver new functionality to the operating system. Feature updates are a core design change in Windows 10 and are the foundation to WaaS. Microsoft delivers these updates twice a year, one in the Fall and one in the Spring. From a deployment perspective, these updates are designed to be installed in-place, over the existing version of Windows 10. Users can expect to retain all their data and applications during the upgrade process. Microsoft has also introduced several tools to help administrators deliver these updates. We will be reviewing each of these tools in this skill.

- **Quality updates** These updates deliver security and reliability fixes to the operating system. Quality updates redefine the way administrators manage patching for Windows devices. Prior to Windows 10, Microsoft released a variety of individual updates on "patch Tuesday." In managed environments, administrators could then choose which updates to install. For example, some organizations might only install critical security updates each month or completely miss an important update from a prior month. This resulted in fragmented patch levels and reliability issues. Quality updates help address these issues. They are cumulative, meaning the patch content from the previous month is automatically rolled into the next month's update. They are also condensed, reducing the number of individual updates you need to deploy and manage. For example, instead of six individual security updates for August, you have a single quality update.

- **Servicing channels** Servicing channels represent the management controls available for determining which release of Windows 10 is deployed and when. Feature updates can be delivered using management solutions such as ConfigMgr, but they can also be delivered through Windows Update. Administrators must consider how they want to manage these updates and at what frequency they want them installed.

- **Deployment rings** Deployment rings represents a concept for rolling out Windows 10 feature updates in stages. A ring contains a collection of devices that you determine are ready for the upgrade. You might have a ring for pilot devices and a ring for production. These rings can also directly relate to different management solutions and deployment scenarios such as ConfigMgr with Windows 10 Servicing or Intune with Windows 10 Update Rings.
- **Windows Insider** The Windows Insider program was an original concept delivered in parallel with the first release of Windows 10. Customers were given the opportunity to join this program and test pre-release features. Participants had access to a feedback mechanism where they could share ideas and bugs. For enterprise customers, Windows Insider for Business was introduced to make enrollment easier.

Plan for servicing channels

We touched briefly on servicing channels in the last section. In this section we will cover servicing channels in detail. First, it is worth noting that the terminology for servicing channels has undergone changes since its original introduction. This was done to help align the update terminology between Windows 10 and Office 365. Earlier naming standards used branch identifiers. For example, Current Branch (CB), Current Branch for Business, and Long-Term Servicing Branch (LTSB). LTSB are still associated with some early editions of Windows Enterprise, but all other components are now referred to as servicing channels.

Servicing channels are broken down into three different types, each delivering a different service. As an administrator, it is your responsibility to identify and deploy the appropriate servicing channel based on the needs of your organization.

- **Insider Program** With Windows 10 Microsoft has encouraged customers to start their testing early. Windows Insider delivers a servicing channel that enables customers to enroll their devices and begin testing new features and capabilities before they are released to the general public. For business customers, this enables you to start compatibility testing earlier. Members of the Insider program also have a direct feedback link through the Feedback Hub application. The Insider program includes three deployment rings that you can configure.

    - **Fast Ring** Participants of the Fast Ring are the first to receive new features and changes. These enhancements are validated on a small population of devices before they become available to the Fast Ring. Customers should expect possible issues and blockers when enrolled in this ring.

    - **Slow Ring** Participants of the Slow Ring receive Insider builds after the Fast Ring. These builds include updates and fixes for issues identified by Fast Ring participants. There is still a risk that these builds could experience issues, but you can expect it to be more stable.

    - **Release Preview Ring** Participants of the Release Preview Ring will receive a release preview Insider build in advance of general availability. This enables organizations to start piloting the next release of Windows 10 with minimal risk, while still having access to provide feedback.

- **Semi-Annual Channel**   After a new feature update is released to the general public it enters the Semi-Annual Channel. At this point administrators can begin managing how these updates are delivered to their production devices. There are two deployment rings for this servicing channel.

  - **Semi-Annual Channel (Targeted)**   Newly released updates will enter this deployment ring first. Customers that choose this ring will receive the latest feature update, with the option to defer up to 365 days.

  - **Semi-Annual Channel**   After a period of time, usually about 4 months, feature updates are moved to the Semi-Annual Channel deployment ring. This provides organizations another option for postponing their rollout, in addition to the 365- day deferral rules.

- **Long-Term Servicing Channel**   Customers with specialized systems running Windows 10, such as medical equipment or heavy machinery, can leverage the Long-Term Servicing Channel to prevent the deployment of feature updates and receive extended support. Unlike Semi-Annual Channel, administrators must install the LTSB edition of Windows 10 Enterprise. There is no configuration option to quickly switch between Long-Term Servicing Channel and Semi-Annual Channel. Administrators will have to re-image devices if they need to make this change. Also, Long-Term Servicing Channel is not designed for systems that are used for productivity or content creation. Devices running Office should not be using Long-Term Servicing Channel.

Each servicing channel also has a different release cadence and support lifecycle. Refer to Table 1-15 for these details.

TABLE 1-15 Servicing Channel Support

Servicing Channel	New Releases	End of Support
Insider Program - Fast	Weekly	It varies based from release to release, but all Insider builds will eventually expire if you do not stay current.
Insider Program - Slow	Monthly	It varies based from release to release, but all Insider builds will eventually expire if you do not stay current.
Semi-Annual Channel	Every 6 months	Fall releases have 30 months of support. Spring releases have 18 months of support.
Long-Term Servicing Channel	Every 2-3 years	Up to 10 years of support.

Plan for Windows Insider for Business

Windows Insider delivers pre-release builds of Windows 10 to customers that enroll in the Insider program. Once enrolled, your device will start receiving Insider builds. As a participant you get to try new features and capabilities before they are released. The Insider build also includes a dedicated feedback channel for reporting issues or general feedback to the Windows development team. Through this program Microsoft is able to collect real-world data from a vast range of users and devices. That data helps address issues and improve Windows before an update is released to the general public. After joining the Insider program, you can enroll your existing Windows 10 device by navigating to the **Windows Insider Program** settings page, as shown in Figure 1-56. From there you click **Get Started** and enter your account credentials.

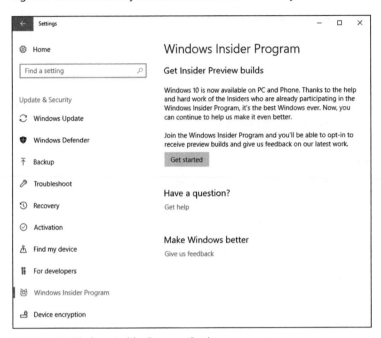

FIGURE 1-56 Windows Insider Program Settings

Windows Insider for Business is the same Insider program that we just reviewed, but with some extra controls to help organizations manage their enrolled users and devices. These controls include:

- **Domain registration** Customers that are synced with Azure Active Directory (Azure AD) can register their tenant with the Windows Insider Program. This enables employees to sign in with their Azure AD credentials.

- **Track feedback** The feedback submitted through the Feedback Hub is tagged with the corresponding user's Azure AD account. That feedback can then be tracked for internal analysis and data collection.

Registering your domain with the Windows Insider Program can be accomplished by following these steps:

1. Navigate to the Windows Insider registration page at *https://insider.windows.com/en-us/for-business-organization-admin/*.

2. Sign in with your Azure AD account and confirm you have access to complete the registration. Confirmation is shown at the top of the page under **Register Your Domain**

With The Windows Insider Program. Your account must meet the following require-ments. If these requirements are met, you will see a message prompting you to register your domain, as shown in Figure 1-57.

- Assigned the Global Administrator role in Azure AD.
- Existing participant of the Windows Insider Program.

> **You are signed in with an Azure Active Directory (AAD) account** that has been assigned a Global Administrator role on that Azure AD domain by your organization's IT administration.
>
> REGISTER YOUR DOMAIN WITH THE WINDOWS INSIDER PROGRAM FOR BUSINESS >

FIGURE 1-57 Windows Insider for Business Sign In

3. On the Manage Insider Preview Builds page, click the link: **Register Your Domain With The Windows Insider Program For Business**.

4. On the Register page, review the program agreement, check the box to accept the terms, and click **Register**.

5. Review the registration results to confirm your organization was successfully registered, as shown in Figure 1-58.

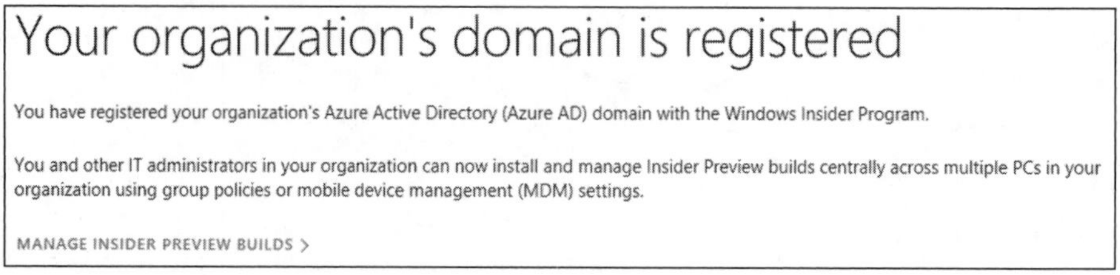

> # Your organization's domain is registered
>
> You have registered your organization's Azure Active Directory (Azure AD) domain with the Windows Insider Program.
>
> You and other IT administrators in your organization can now install and manage Insider Preview builds centrally across multiple PCs in your organization using group policies or mobile device management (MDM) settings.
>
> MANAGE INSIDER PREVIEW BUILDS >

FIGURE 1-58 Windows Insider for Business Registration

Plan the appropriate Windows 10 Enterprise deployment method

With Windows 10, deployment methods refer to both the initial deployment of the operating system and the deployment of future feature updates. Feature updates in Windows 10 are respon-sible for upgrading the operating system from one major release to the next. Both scenarios play an important role when you are supporting WaaS. Many of the techniques we review in this section can be used to manage new deployments of Windows 10 and support future feature updates.

Windows 10 supports many of the traditional deployment scenarios that you may already be familiar with. For example, deploying the latest version of Windows during an organization's next major hardware refresh has been a common scenario for earlier versions of the operating system. There are new methods available, however, such as the in-place upgrade, which can help simplify your migration if new hardware is not readily available.

For this section we will be looking at a variety of deployment methods available for Win-dows 10, along with the pros and cons for each. This will include capabilities available with modern servicing, such as Windows Update for Business. We will also be working with task sequences in ConfigMgr as part of the in-place upgrade. Finally, we will cover the traditional methods that are still supported with Windows 10.

Plan for deploying Windows 10 Enterprise

There are two main scenarios associated with Windows 10 deployment methods. The first scenario involves moving to Windows 10 from an early version of the operating system. For example, today your client devices have Windows 8.1 installed and you are planning a migration to Windows 10. The second scenario involves keeping Windows 10 current with the latest feature updates. For example, today your client devices have Windows 10, version 1803 installed. You are planning an upgrade to Windows 10, version 1809. There are deployment methods for each of these scenarios.

In some cases, a deployment method can be used for both deployments and upgrades, such as the in-place upgrade. Other methods are more specific, such as Windows Update for Business. The first thing you need to understand is what options are available and in what scenarios they apply.

- **Traditional methods**   This category covers several of the deployment methods used with earlier versions of the Windows operating system. Microsoft is continuing to support these methods and has released compatibility updates for tools such as the Microsoft Deployment Toolkit (MDT) and the Windows Assessment and Deployment Kit (Windows ADK), both of which support traditional imaging and upgrades.

  - **Bare metal**   This deployment method refers to scenarios where new hardware is procured, or existing hardware is repurposed. In both situations a Windows image is installed and configured according to the organization's IT standards. Bare metal deployments are seen at most organizations and are commonly leveraged in situations where you need to roll out a new version of the operating system or another major application, such as Microsoft Office. It can help consolidate efforts.

  - **Refresh**   This deployment method refers to scenarios where an existing device needs to be wiped and reloaded. In this situation the existing user state is backed up, the disk is wiped, the latest image is installed, and the user state is restored. Refresh deployments are often seen when a device becomes inoperable and needs to be wiped. This type of deployment can also be used in upgrade scenarios, such as moving from Windows 7 to Windows 10.

  - **Replace**   This deployment method is similar to the refresh method but includes new hardware as part of the process. For example, a user is running a 3-year old laptop with Windows 8.1 installed. You backup the user state on this device and restore it to a new laptop running Windows 10.

- **In-place upgrade**   This deployment method refers to scenarios where an existing version of Windows is installed, and you upgrade the device to a newer release of Windows 10. This method supports both upgrading to Windows 10 and staying current. For example, let's say you have a device running Windows 7 and you deploy an in-place upgrade for Windows 10, version 1809. Alternatively, you have a device running Windows 10, version 1803 and you deploy an in-place upgrade for Windows 10, version 1809. This process retains the applications, settings, and user data on the system. The old version of Windows is moved to a Windows.old folder for a configurable amount of time, which can then be referenced in the event that you need to roll back the operating system.

- **Modern servicing** This deployment method refers to scenarios where you need to keep current with new releases of Windows 10. Similar to the in-place upgrade, modern servicing can address situations where you are moving from one version of Windows 10 to the next. However, modern servicing technologies are specific to Windows 10, preventing them from being used with earlier versions of the operating system. Windows Update for Business, Windows Server Update Services (WSUS), and System Center Configuration Manager (ConfigMgr) are all tools that support modern servicing.

Now that we have covered the basic deployment methods for Windows 10, let's take a look at the different deployment formats. Windows 10 is available in two formats: Electronic Software Delivery (ESD), available through Windows Update or the Windows 10 Media Creation Tool, and Windows Imaging Format (WIM), available through traditional installation media (ISO). There are a number of solutions available for each deployment format, with pros and cons for each. Refer to Table 1-16 for a breakdown of these formats, followed by an introduction to each of the deployment solutions.

TABLE 1-16 Modern servicing techniques

Deployment Format	Delivery Solution	Pros	Cons
Electronic Software Delivery (ESD)	Windows Update for Business (WUfB) Windows Server Update Services (WSUS) System Center Configuration Manager (ConfigMgr)	Smallest package size. Fastest installation.	Limited control to handle pre and post upgrade tasks.
Windows Imaging Format (WIM)	System Center Configuration Manager (ConfigMgr) Microsoft Deployment Toolkit (MDT) Third-party management solutions	Full control over the upgrade experience end-to-end.	Highest administrative effort. Largest package size.

- **Windows Update for Business (WUfB)** WUfB is a series of new policies available to Windows 10 clients. These policies enable administrators to manage the servicing channel and deferral settings for Windows 10 feature updates and quality updates. This service delivers updates to clients through the public Windows Update network using the ESD deployment format. WUfB policies can be configured using a GPO or Intune MDM policy.

- **Windows Server Update Services (WSUS)** WSUS is an on-premises solution for organizations that need to fully manage the updates that they deploy to their clients. Administrators can synchronize with the Microsoft Update catalog and deploy approved updates for all supported versions of the Windows operating system. This includes feature updates and quality updates for Windows 10.

- **System Center Configuration Manager (ConfigMgr)**   ConfigMgr is an on-premises device management solution for organizations that need to fully manage the updates that they deploy to their clients. With ConfigMgr, administrators are given the option to use task sequences or Software Updates (WSUS). With task sequences you have additional control over the in-place upgrade scenario.

- **Microsoft Deployment Toolkit (MDT)**   MDT is a free deployment tool that enables administrators to support Windows 10 images and in-place upgrades. Similar to ConfigMgr, MDT uses task sequences for image creation and upgrades.

As you prepare to deploy Windows 10 using the in-place upgrade method, there are a number of items to consider. While there are several benefits to supporting this method, each of these items can impact the success of your implementation.

- **Compatibility**   Hardware, drivers, and applications all need to be reviewed for Windows 10 compatibility. Older hardware, including peripherals, may not support the latest release of Windows 10 or have supported drivers, in which case they would need to be replaced or updated. Applications that are incompatible can cause the upgrade to fail and need to be assessed as well. Later in this skill we will review Upgrade Readiness, a service provided by Microsoft to help identify compatibility issues.

- **Legacy BIOS to UEFI**   Windows 10 supports legacy BIOS and UEFI, both of which use different partition maps on the system drive. That said, there are security features, such as Secure Boot, that require UEFI. In this case you can complete an in-place upgrade on a device running legacy BIOS and then use the MBR2GPT tool to convert the partition map from Master Boot Record (MBR) to GUID Partition Table (GPT).

> **MORE INFO   RUNNING MBR2GPT**
>
> For more information about the MBR2GPT tool, including prerequisites and instructions, visit: *https://docs.microsoft.com/windows/deployment/mbr-to-gpt*.

- **Disk encryption**   The Windows 10 in-place upgrade supports BitLocker natively. If the system drive is encrypted with BitLocker, the upgrade will work without any additional administrative effort. If the drive is encrypted with a third-party solution, you will need to contact the vendor for instructions on how to address the encryption software during the upgrade.

- **Language packs**   The Windows 10 in-place upgrade will retain the system default user interface (UI) language. Any additional language packs that have been installed previously will need to be re-installed following the upgrade.

- **32-bit to 64-bit**   The Windows 10 in-place upgrade does not support upgrading devices from 32-bit versions of Windows to 64-bit. If this is a scenario you need to plan for, consider using the refresh or replace deployment methods.

- **Windows To Go** Windows To Go is a feature that enables customers to boot a Windows installation from a supported USB storage device. The Windows 10 in-place upgrade is not supported on Windows To Go devices running older versions of the operating system. Once on Windows 10, future Feature updates can be installed.

- **Existing images** If you have an existing operating system image for Windows 7 or Windows 8.1, installing that image, upgrading it to Windows 10, and recapturing it is not supported. A new operating system will need to be recreated for Windows 10 deployments. Alternatively, you can start utilizing offline servicing to avoid traditional reference image designs.

> **MORE INFO   WINDOWS 10 OFFLINE SERVICING**
>
> For more information about offline servicing for Windows 10, visit: *https://docs.microsoft. com/windows-hardware/manufacture/desktop/understanding-servicing-strategies.*

- **Dual-boot** The Windows 10 in-place upgrade supports devices running a single version of Windows. Devices configured in a dual-boot or multi-boot configuration are not supported.

Design an in-place upgrade for Windows 10

In this section we take a closer look at the in-place upgrade deployment method. This is a common starting point for organizations that are planning their migration to Windows 10. In the following example we work with a task sequence in ConfigMgr, version 1810. In this version of ConfigMgr a task sequence template is provided to support in-place upgrade scenarios.

To begin, you first need to download a copy of the Windows 10 installation media. This can be retrieved by downloading the latest Windows 10 ISO from the Microsoft volume license service center (VLSC). To access the VLSC, visit: *https://www.microsoft.com/Licensing/servicecenter/default.aspx.* Once downloaded, you will need to extract the files from that ISO in preparation for creating the operating system upgrade package required by ConfigMgr. Refer to Figure 1-59 for an example of the extracted files needed.

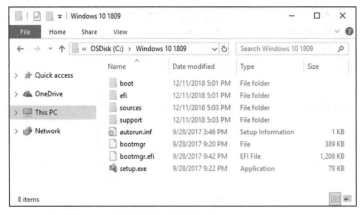

FIGURE 1-59 Windows 10 Installation Media

ConfigMgr requires the Windows 10 installation media in order to complete the in-place upgrade. The installation media is referenced in the task sequence as an operating system upgrade package. When this step runs, ConfigMgr is executing setup.exe with a series of command-line options that instruct setup how to complete the upgrade. Setup.exe can be executed independently of ConfigMgr and it is worth reviewing the variety of supported options.

> **MORE INFO**   **WINDOWS SETUP COMMAND-LINE OPTIONS**
>
> For more information about the supported Windows Setup command-line options, including examples on how to use these options, visit: *https://docs.microsoft.com/windows-hardware/manufacture/desktop/windows-setup-command-line-options*.

In Figure 1-60 you can see an example of the in-place upgrade task sequence template provided with ConfigMgr, version 1810. Each of the groups in this task sequence template are provided to assist you with creating a working upgrade deployment. You can add, remove, or modify any of these steps to meet your requirements. Each group contains a basic description to provide additional guidance.

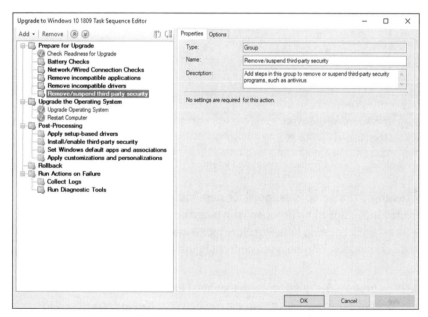

FIGURE 1-60 In-place Upgrade Task Sequence

- **Prepare for Upgrade**   This group is designed for steps that will run in the current operating system. These steps should be focused at pre-upgrade operations, such as checking for 20 GB of free disk space (a requirement for Setup) or ensuring that the computer is connected to a wired connection (if you do not support upgrades over wireless).

- **Upgrade the Operating System**   This group is designed for steps that trigger the in-place upgrade. The Upgrade Operating System and Restart Computer steps are included as part of the template. The Upgrade Operating System step includes a number of options, as shown in Figure 1-61. In this screen shot we have selected the checkbox: Perform Windows Setup Compatibility Scan Without Starting Upgrade. This setting runs setup using the /Comapt option. Windows setup will scan the device for possible incompatibilities. If any are found, a return code is generated with a series of logs that will need further analysis.

FIGURE 1-61 Task Sequence – Upgrade Operating System

- **Post-Processing** This group is designed for steps that need to run after the upgrade has completed successfully. This group will run based on the task sequence variable _SMSTSSetupRollback equaling false. Possible steps might include installing applications, resuming disk encryption, or running custom configuration changes for your organization.

- **Rollback** This group is designed for steps that need to run after an upgrade has failed and triggered a rollback. This group will run based on the task sequence variable _SMSTSSetupRollback equaling true. Possible steps might include sending an email notification to the device owner that the upgrade was unsuccessful, or automatically creating an incident in your service desk system.

- **Run Actions on Failure** Similar to the Rollback group, this group is designed for steps that need to run after an upgrade has failed. This group will run based on the task sequence variable _SMSTSOSUpgradeActionReturnCode not equaling 0. Possible steps might include running a log collector or diagnostic tool, such as SetupDiag.

> **MORE INFO   SETUPDIAG**
>
> SetupDiag is a diagnostic tool designed to analyze Windows setup failures and provide summarized results on what caused the failure. For more information about SetupDiag, visit: *https://docs.microsoft.com/windows/deployment/upgrade/setupdiag*.

Once you have configured this task sequence to meet your needs, you can use the deployment ring strategy discussed earlier in this chapter. In ConfigMgr this can be done using a series of device collections (groups of devices) followed by a phase deployment (a multi-phase deployment based on success criteria). For the exam you will want to be familiar with the in-place upgrade task sequence and what its capabilities are versus other deployment methods.

Design a servicing plan for Windows 10

In this section we are going to take a look at the modern servicing deployment method. This method delivers new feature updates to existing devices that already have Windows 10 installed. With modern servicing, feature updates are installed similar to a traditional Windows Update. In the following examples we are going to review three techniques for enabling modern servicing.

MODERN SERVICING WITH MICROSOFT INTUNE

The first solution we will look at is the Windows 10 update rings in Microsoft Intune. This solution requires the target devices to be enrolled in Intune. Once enrolled, devices that have this policy assigned will be configured to use Windows Update for Business. Follow these steps to create an update ring policy in Microsoft Intune.

1. Sign-in to the Microsoft Azure portal at *https://portal.azure.com/*.
2. Click **All Services**.
3. Search for **Intune** and select it.
4. Under Manage, click **Software Updates**.
5. On the Software updates blade, under Manage, click **Windows 10 Update Rings**.
6. On the Software updates – Windows 10 Update blade, click **Create**. Refer to Figure 1-62 for an example of the update settings available through this policy.

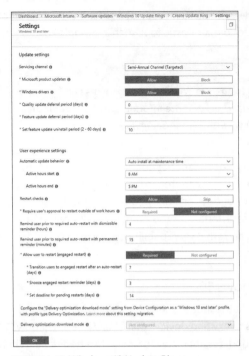

Dashboard > Microsoft Intune > Software updates - Windows 10 Update Rings > Create Update Ring > Settings

FIGURE 1-62 Windows 10 Update Rings

The Windows Update policy is split into two sections: Update settings and User experience settings. There are two controls under Update settings that are used to manage the deployment of feature updates. These include the following:

- **Servicing channel** The servicing channel dropdown includes each of the servicing channels that we reviewed in skill 4.1. Use this option to setup deployment rings for Windows Insider for Business, or configure this option to configure deployments of public releases once they reach semi-annual channel.

- **Feature update deferral period (days)** The feature update deferral period enables you to defer an update up to 365 days. This option is designed to give you an additional grace period to accommodate your deployment workflow.

After configuring and assigning this policy you have the option to pause the assignment for up to 35 days, in the event where you may need to halt all upgrades to troubleshoot an issue. The option to pause the assignment of a feature update can be done from the **Software updates – Windows 10 Update Rings** blade by selecting the policy and clicking **Pause** on the Overview page. If you are ready to resume the assignment you can do so from the same blade, otherwise the assignment will automatically resume after 35 days.

MODERN SERVICING WITH GROUP POLICY

The next solution we are going to review involves configuring WUfB using the Group Policy. The Group Policy settings are identical to Intune, so this will be a brief example. The major difference with Group Policy is how the various settings are split into individual policies. For example, the settings for user experience are broken down between multiple policies. In the following example we will configure a new GPO for WUfB. In this example we are using the latest ADMX templates provided with Windows 10, version 1809.

1. Open the **Group Policy Management Editor**.
2. Create a new Group Policy Object (GPO) and name it "WUfB".
3. Right-click the new GPO and click **Edit**.
4. Under Computer Configuration, expand **Policies**.
5. Expand **Administrative Templates**.
6. Expand **Windows Components**.
7. Expand **Windows Update**.
8. Expand **Windows Update for Business**.
9. Locate and edit the policy: **Select when Preview Builds and Feature Updates are received**.
10. Select the radio button next to **Enabled** and configure the following options. Refer to Figure 1-63 for an example of this policy configuration.

   A. Set the Windows readiness level to **Semi-Annual Channel**.

   B. Leave the deferral setting at **0**.

   C. Leave the pause value **blank**.

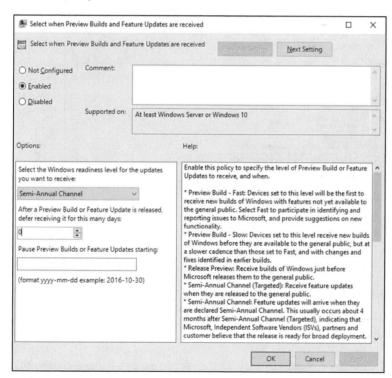

FIGURE 1-63 GPO for Feature Updates

MODERN SERVICING WITH CONFIGMGR

The last solution we will review is the Window 10 Servicing feature in ConfigMgr. This deployment method is ideal for environments that have chosen the ESD update format but still want to manage the update deployments through ConfigMgr.

Windows 10 servicing utilizes ConfigMgr's Software Update mechanics. The Software Update feature in ConfigMgr uses WSUS for synchronizing updates from the Microsoft Update catalog. Those updates can then be managed and deployed by ConfigMgr. The Windows 10 Servicing feature leverages these capabilities. The creation wizard will walk you through creating a servicing plan, setting up deployment rings, and creating the deployment. In this example we are creating a servicing plan in ConfigMgr, version 1810.

1. Click Start, search for **Configuration Manager Console** and select it.

2. In the Configuration Manager Console, click the **Software Library workspace**.

3. Under Overview, expand **Windows 10 Servicing**.

4. Under Windows 10 Servicing, select **Servicing Plans**.

5. In the ribbon, click **Create Servicing Plan**.

In Figure 1-64 you can see an example of a Windows 10 servicing plan created in ConfigMgr. The summary page outlines the configuration options for each of the various controls.

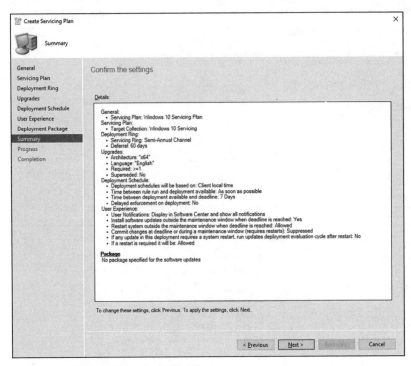

FIGURE 1-64 Windows 10 Servicing Wizard

- **General** The General page of the wizard is used to assign a name and description for the servicing plan.

- **Servicing Plan**   The Servicing Plan page of the wizard is used to select the device collection that will receive the deployment generated by this servicing plan.

- **Deployment Ring**   The Deployment Ring page of the wizard is used to select a servicing channel and delay deployment up to 120 days. Note that on this page your only options for servicing channels are Semi-Annual Channel (Targeted) and Semi-Annual Channel. You do not have options for Windows Insider builds.

- **Upgrades**   The Upgrades page of the wizard is used to define the criteria for the updates you are deploying with this servicing plan. For example, if you are creating a servicing plan for just 64-bit devices, you can configure the architecture attribute to only retrieve 64-bit updates.

- **Deployment Schedule**   The Deployment Schedule page of the wizard is used to define when the update will become available and when it will be enforced.

- **User Experience**   The User Experience page of the wizard is used to configure what notifications are displayed to the user and how reboot behavior will be handled. If you are using maintenance windows in ConfigMgr, you can configure whether they are acknowledged for this deployment.

- **Package**   The Package page of the wizard is used to assign a deployment package or to configure the servicing plan to use the Microsoft cloud, reducing the need to download and replicate content internally.

Analyze upgrade readiness for Windows 10

Earlier in this chapter we covered some of the requirements that you need to consider prior to deploying Windows 10. Most customers preparing to deploy a new operating system are going to do extensive testing and validation of their hardware, drivers, and applications before they start large scale deployments. This process can be time-consuming, even more so when that operating system is undergoing major changes every six months.

Upgrade readiness is a service provided by Microsoft to help customers identify compatibility concerns in support of WaaS. Customers that choose to enroll in this service can get metrics and visual indicators on which components need the most attention and which devices are ready to upgrade. This is made possible using Windows telemetry and the Microsoft cloud.

Plan for upgrade readiness

To prepare for upgrade readiness you need to be familiar with the requirements for Windows Analytics. In Skill 1.3 we introduced you to the various device monitoring services available with Windows Analytics. This included upgrade readiness, device health, and update compliance. Because all three of these solutions are delivered through Windows Analytics and are data-driven based on telemetry, the implementation is similar for each.

To begin, we will cover the fundamentals of upgrade readiness and items that you should be familiar with.

- **Telemetry** The upgrade readiness service requires that you set the Windows telemetry level to basic (minimum) for any devices that you enroll in the service.

- **Operating system support** Upgrade readiness supports devices running Windows 7 SP1, Windows 8.1, or Windows 10. For Windows 7 SP1 you must install KB2952664. For Windows 8.1 you must install KB2976978.

- **Target operating system** Upgrade readiness can provide you with compatibility information for one operating system version at a time. For example, in Figure 1-65 you can see the dropdown menu for **Target Version To Be Evaluated**. This option is configured as part of the solution settings in Azure. The operating system version you select will be used for data analysis. When a new Windows 10 feature update is released, you will need to update this field to the new build number. Change the target version can take up to 24 hours to apply.

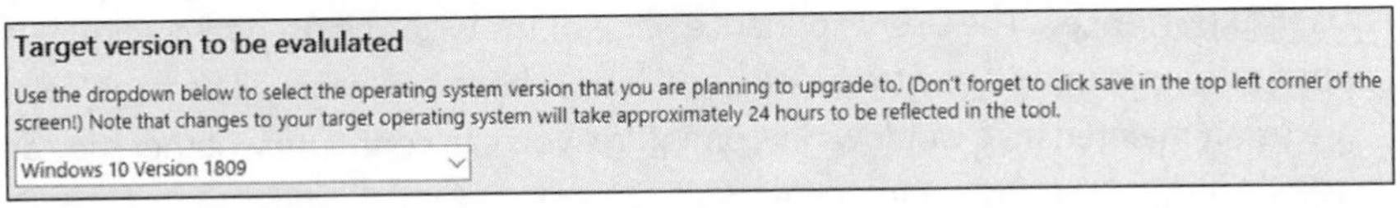

Target version to be evalulated

Use the dropdown below to select the operating system version that you are planning to upgrade to. (Don't forget to click save in the top left corner of the screen!) Note that changes to your target operating system will take approximately 24 hours to be reflected in the tool.

Windows 10 Version 1809   ⌄

FIGURE 1-65 Upgrade Readiness Solution Settings

- **Data availability** Once a device is configured to upload telemetry and associate it with a commercial ID, that data can take up to 72 hours before it is visible in upgrade readiness. After that you can expect to see updates every 24 hours. For example, if a device has an incompatible application and you update that application, the change will be reflected within 24 hours.

- **Cost** The upgrade readiness service has no cost. The free offering provides 7 days of historical data and up to 500 MB of storage. If your organization decides it needs to retain 90 days of historical data, you will need to procure Azure storage to accommodate this requirement.

Navigate upgrade readiness

Once you have your devices uploading telemetry to Microsoft with your organization's commercial ID, the results will be shown in the Log Analytics service in the Azure portal. From there you can begin navigating through the different blades and assessing your organization's upgrade readiness compatibility.

This next walk-through will introduce you to the upgrade readiness solution in the Azure portal. For this demonstration we have already created a Log Analytics workspace for Alpine Ski House, named ASH-Analytics. The devices in this organization are also configured for upgrade readiness. We will be looking at the Alpine Ski House environment to determine if they are ready to adopt Windows 10, version 1809. To access the upgrade readiness solution, follow these steps.

1. Sign-in to the Microsoft Azure portal at *https://portal.azure.com/*.

2. Click **All Services**.

3. Search for **Log Analytics** and select it.

4. On the Log Analytics blade, select the workspace containing your upgrade readiness solution. In this example we are selecting the workspace named **ASH-Analytics**.

5. On the ASH-Analytics blade, under General, select **Solutions**.

6. On the ASH-Analytics – Solutions blade, select the solution starting with **CompatibilityAssessment**. In this example the solution is named **CompatibilityAssessment(ASH-Analytics)**.

7. On the CompatibilityAssessment(ASH-Analytics) blade, click the **Upgrade Readiness** tile. This will present you with the upgrade readiness workflow page, consisting of multiple blades with data related to Windows 10 compatibility.

The upgrade readiness solution is designed as a workflow, with multiple steps that walk you through the end-to-end process for upgrading to Windows 10. The first information you are presented with is the Upgrade Overview blade, as shown in Figure 1-66. This blade provides an upgrade summary based on the targeted operating system version that you configured. In this example you can see at the bottom of the blade that Windows 10 Version 1809 is the target operating system. Total computers represent the total number of devices that have submitted telemetry to Windows Analytics. Completed upgrades represent the total number of devices that have successfully upgraded to Windows 10, version 1809.

FIGURE 1-66 Upgrade Readiness - Upgrade Overview

The next blade you are presented with relative to upgrade readiness is **STEP 1: Identify Important Apps**, as shown in Figure 1-67. This blade is designed to highlight applications in your environment that may need attention prior to deploying Windows 10. The first number on this blade, Total Applications, summarizes the total number of applications identified in your organization. The second number, Applications In Need Of Review, identifies applications that Microsoft does not have compatibility information for and recommends that you review. You can click either of these values to drill down into the various data categories.

Applications are automatically grouped based on importance. For example, applications that are installed on less than 2% of devices are grouped together. You also have the option to assign or modify the importance level with a selection of built-in options. This is accomplished by clicking on the Assign importance link at the bottom of the blade. Defining the importance level will assist in organizing your application portfolio, along with defining which applications are upgrade ready. These include the following.

- **Not reviewed**   This is the default importance level for applications that are installed on more than 2% of devices. To clearly understand which apps are important, you can modify this default value to something with additional meaning.

- **Mission critical**   This is an optional importance level, signifying a mission critical dependency on the application.

- **Business critical**   This is an optional importance level, signifying a business-critical dependency on the application.

- **Important**   This is an optional importance level, signifying the application is important to the organization.

- **Best effort**   This is an optional importance level, signifying the application is not important and compatibility will be approached as a best effort.

- **Ignore**   This is an optional importance level, signifying the application is not important and can be safely ignored from future compatibility reports. Selecting this option will mark the application as upgrade ready, removing it as a blocker.

- **Review in progress**   This is an optional importance level, signifying the application is currently under review and the importance level has not yet been identified.

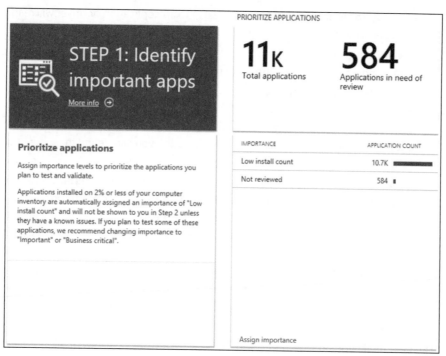

FIGURE 1-67 Upgrade Readiness - Identify Important Apps

The next blade you are presented with is **STEP 2: Resolve Issues**. This step in the workflow includes a series of blades for addressing issues that are considered to be upgrade blockers. Refer to the following list for more information about each of the blades in step 2.

- **Review Applications With Known Issues** This blade highlights applications with known issues. Applications that Microsoft has a fix for will be marked accordingly, reducing the number of applications that you need to review. As you review these apps you have the option to adjust the upgrade readiness value, approving or blocking applications from the upgrade. These values include:
  - **Not Reviewed** This is the default value for applications that are installed on more than 2% of devices and all drivers.
  - **Review In Progress** Assigning this value to an application or driver will prevent them from being approved until they can be marked ready to upgrade. This should be used for any applications or drivers that you still need to validate.

- **Ready To Upgrade** Assigning this value to an application or driver will mark it as upgrade ready.

- **Won't Upgrade** Assigning this value to an application or driver will mark all corresponding devices as not upgrade ready.

- **Review Known Driver Issues** This blade highlights drivers with known issues. Drivers that Microsoft has information on will be marked accordingly. For example, if a newer version of the driver is available through Windows Update, those drivers will be grouped together. Similar to the previous application blades, you can define the same upgrade readiness values to approve or deny drivers.

- **Review Low-Risk Apps And Drivers** This blade highlights applications and drivers that need review but are determined to be low risk based on various conditions. For example, if Microsoft has identified an application as highly adopted (installed on more than 100,000 devices) that application will be marked as low risk.

- **Prioritize App And Driver Testing** This blade highlights applications and drivers that are currently blocking the upgrade for your target operating system on more than 80% of devices. Reviewing and prioritizing these items can yield a high return for upgrade readiness.

The next blade you are presented with is **STEP 3: Deploy**, as shown in Figure 1-68. This step in the workflow consolidates all information that has been collected and categorizes devices based on upgrade readiness. There are three upgrade decisions included on this blade.

- **Review In Progress** Devices in this category have at least one application or driver installed that has been marked with review in progress. These markings are applied in step 1 and step 2 of the workflow.

- **Won't Upgrade** Devices in this category have at least one application or driver installed that has been marked with won't upgrade. Alternatively, these devices do not meet a system requirement to complete the upgrade, such as free disk space.

- **Ready To Upgrade** Devices in this category have all applications and drivers marked with Ready to Upgrade. When you are ready to deploy the upgrade to these devices, export the list of computers and target them with your preferred management solution.

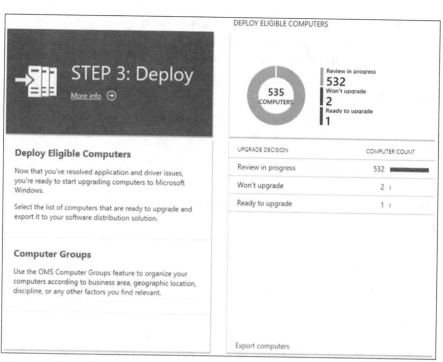

FIGURE 1-68 Upgrade Readiness - Deploy

The next blade you are presented with is **STEP 4: Monitor**. This step in the workflow includes a series of blades for monitoring the progress of your upgrade deployments. Refer to the following list for more information about each of the blades in step 4.

- **Update Progress (last 30 days)**   This blade highlights the deployment status for all of your devices. There are five deployment categories that group devices.

  - **Not Started**   This category contains devices that have not started the upgrade. This includes devices that are upgrade ready and those that are not.

  - **Upgrade completed**   This category contains devices that have successfully completed the upgrade to your target operating system.

  - **Failed**   This category contains devices that attempted to upgrade to your target operating system but were unsuccessful.

  - **In Progress**   This category contains devices that have started the upgrade to your target operating system and have not yet reported back their results.

  - **Progress stalled**   This category contains devices that have started the upgrade and stalled.

- **Driver issues**   This blade highlights drivers that are reporting issues following a successful upgrade. This information includes the problem code reported in device manager for the affected device(s).

- **User feedback** This blade highlights user feedback submitted through the Feedback Hub app. Users that have submitted feedback using their Azure AD account will be consolidated and displayed here for review.

> **MORE INFO** **UPGRADE READINESS**
>
> For more information about enabling upgrade readiness to support Windows 10, visit: *https://docs.microsoft.com/windows/deployment/upgrade/use-upgrade-readiness-to-manage-windows-upgrades*.

Evaluate and deploy additional Windows 10 Enterprise security features

For this section we will be exploring the core security features available with Windows 10, including which ones integrate with Microsoft 365, and what options you have available for evaluating these features in your environment. Windows 10 is a cloud-connected operating system, engineered to protect against modern day security threats. There are several security features in Windows 10, some of which can be connected to Microsoft 365 for centralized management and reporting. These features provide coverage across three main areas: identity and access management, information protection, and threat protection.

Determine what security features are available with Windows 10

Migrating to Windows 10 introduces a new collection of security features and enhancements that earlier versions of the operating system do not have access to. For the exam you will need to be familiar with these features and their capabilities. Moving to a semi-annual release cycle has enabled Microsoft to address major security vulnerabilities in a much shorter timeframe. This also means that these features are frequently evolving over time with new releases of Windows 10.

The security capabilities in Windows 10 are grouped into three categories. These include:

- **Identity and access management** Security features in this category are focused at enhancing security identities. This includes capabilities such as two-factor authentication and biometric credentials.

- **Information protection** Security features in this category are focused at protecting the data in your organization. This includes capabilities such as drive encryption, data leakage protection, and information protection.

- **Threat protection** Security features in this category are focused at protecting against vulnerabilities and threats. This includes capabilities such as antivirus, antimalware, and behavioral monitoring.

Table 1-17 includes a breakdown of each core Windows 10 security component, their protection category, the required Windows edition, and their capabilities description. In this table you will see references to S Mode. Alongside the variety of security features built-in to Windows 10, S Mode adjusts the behavior of the operating system. When activated, new security requirements are enforced, such as only allowing apps from the Microsoft Store and limiting browser usage to Microsoft Edge.

> **MORE INFO   WINDOWS 10 S IN MODE**
>
> For more information about Windows 10 in S mode, visit:
> *https://support.microsoft.com/help/4020089/windows-10-in-s-mode-faq.*

TABLE 1-17 Windows 10 Security Components

Technology	Protection Category	Windows Edition	Description
Windows Hello for Business	Identity and access management	S mode, Enterprise	Password replacement, enabling strong two-factor authentication for PCs and mobile devices. Leverages biometric credentials and supports Active Directory and Azure AD accounts.
Windows Defender Credential Guard	Identity and access management	S mode Enterprise, Enterprise	Virtualization-based security that protects secrets stored on the device, including NTLM password hashes, Kerberos credentials, and credential manager domain credentials.
BitLocker	Information protection	S mode, Pro, Enterprise	Drive encryption solution that is strongest when combined with a hardware-based Trusted Platform Module (TPM). Supports the escrowing of recovery keys in Azure AD.
Windows Information Protection	Information protection	S mode, Pro, Enterprise	Data leakage prevention (DLP) solution that can apply additional protection to company files, preventing data leakage.
Windows Defender Application Guard	Threat protection	S mode Enterprise, Enterprise	Enhanced security for Microsoft Edge that isolates untrusted sites to a Hyper-V enabled container, protecting the host operating system from potential threats.
Windows Defender Application Control	Threat protection	Enterprise	Policy-based protection that prevents access to non-approved applications.
Windows Defender Exploit Guard	Threat protection	S mode, Pro, Enterprise	Collection of host intrusion prevention tools focused at reducing fileless attacks. Features include exploit protection, attack surface reduction rules, network protection, and controlled folder access.
Windows Defender Antivirus	Threat protection	S mode, Pro, Enterprise	Antivirus and antimalware definition-based solution that is integrated with Windows 10.
Windows Defender Advanced Threat Protection (Windows Defender ATP)	Threat protection	Enterprise	Cloud-connected integration with the built-in security features in Windows 10. Provides behavioral-based analysis using machine learning and cloud-based analytics. Includes monitoring and alerts based on threat intelligence data generated by Microsoft and collected by other partners.

From an evaluation perspective, the majority of these features are built-in to the operating system. As long as you have a compatible edition of Windows 10, you can enable these features for testing without any additional licensing. To keep current with the list of available features, including requirements and deployment documentation, visit: *https://docs.microsoft.com/windows/security/.*

Thought experiment

In this thought experiment, demonstrate your skills and knowledge of the topics covered in this chapter. You can find the answer to this thought experiment in the next section.

Alpine Ski House is a global organization, spanning 200 locations and supporting 25,000 mobile devices. Some offices have slow WAN links, but all locations have fast Internet connections. The organization is using ConfigMgr for device management and deployment. All employees are registered in Azure AD and have an Office 365 license assigned. Last year they started introducing Windows 10 through a traditional bare metal deployment. 2,500 devices are running Windows 10, version 1803 and the remaining fleet is running Windows 8.1. Your manager has tasked you with creating a deployment plan for fully adopting Windows 10 over the next 6 months and keeping current with new releases. As the technical lead for enterprise device management, you have started testing the in-place upgrade using ConfigMgr, going from Windows 8.1 to Windows 10. Some devices upgraded successfully, and others failed. As part of your deployment design you need to address the following questions, while minimizing on-premises infrastructure:

1. The in-place upgrade from Windows 8.1 to Windows 10 has identified some compatibility issues. What solution should you implement to track compatibility for your fleet and what steps do you need to take to implement this solution?

2. Windows 10 Enterprise 64-bit is the target operating system for your fleet. Through a recent discovery you found 5% of your Windows 8.1 devices are 32-bit. What solution will you use to upgrade these devices?

3. What servicing channels should you adopt to keep current with the latest releases of Windows 10 and what steps do you need to take to implement them?

4. The 2,500 devices running Windows 10 need to be upgraded to version 1809. What solution should you implement to upgrade these devices?

5. Your CIO is asking you to begin migrating MDM workloads to Intune. What MDM solution addresses this requirement.

Thought experiment answers

This section contains the solution to the thought experiment. Each answer explains why the answer choice is correct.

1. To address compatibility issues with Windows 10 you should implement upgrade readiness. To accomplish this, you will need to create the Log Analytics workspace in Azure. After creating the workspace, you should create and deploy a GPO with Windows telemetry enabled and set to basic, along with your commercial ID. The Windows 8.1 computers will also need KB2976978 installed before they can upload data.

2. The Windows 8.1 computers will need to be upgraded using a refresh or replace deployment method. The user state can be captured with ConfigMgr and restored after the device has been re-imaged using a Windows 10 64-bit installation.

3. To support the latest release of Windows 10, you should adopt Semi-Annual Channel (Targeted) and plan for the Windows Insider channel to prepare for new versions of the operating system. You should use a GPO to configure the servicing channel.

4. You should use Windows Update for Business to manage the upgrade from Windows 10, version 1803 to Windows 10, version 1809.

5. The best solution is to use Microsoft Intune with co-management enabled in ConfigMgr. This solution will deliver a cloud-based MDM with support for iOS, Android, and Windows 10. This will also enable the organization to transition workloads for Windows 10 from ConfigMgr to Microsoft Intune. The existing devices enrolled in MDM for Office 365 can also be assigned EMS licenses and can be converted to Intune.

Chapter summary

- There are three MDM solutions that you can deploy with Microsoft 365. Standalone Intune, Intune with Co-management, and MDM for Office 365.

- Cloud-based MDM solutions can reduce on-premises server infrastructure, but network bandwidth needs to be sized appropriately.

- Policy conflicts should be reviewed and addressed as part of your planning phase for implementing Intune. Tools like MMAT can be used to help identify conflicts.

- Group Policy and ConfigMgr offer policies for configuring Hybrid Azure AD join and automatic MDM enrollment.

- Co-management provides a bridge for supporting Microsoft Intune. Administrators can select which workloads are managed by ConfigMgr and Intune.

- Setting an MDM authority is a requirement for managing devices with Intune.

- The MDM authority can be changed when moving between MDM solutions.

- There are pre-defined device enrollment restrictions with Microsoft Intune.

- You should be familiar with the enrollment restrictions interface in Microsoft Intune, including where to create restrictions.

- You should be familiar with the priority system used by enrollment restrictions and how to assign them to devices.

- You should be familiar with the subscription requirements for Microsoft Intune and Azure AD, along with the supported platforms for compliance policies.

- You should be familiar with the fundamentals of a compliance policy, how they are assigned to devices, and how a device is marked for compliance.

- You should have some understanding on what rules a device compliance policy can check for and use cases that align with those rules.

- You should be familiar with the conditional access formula and how it corresponds to the policies you create.

- You should be familiar with the conditional access controls available in the Azure portal, how these controls relate to each other, and how to design policies using these controls.

- You should be familiar with device-based and app-based policies, including how they are defined and what role they play in policy design.

- You should be familiar with navigating the Conditional Access blade, including items like named locations and terms of use.

- You should be familiar with how to create, assign, and enforce a conditional access policy to users and groups.

- You should be familiar with navigating the device compliance blade, with a focus on the available compliance configurations settings and relative use cases for changing the default values.

- You should be familiar with how to create, assign and evaluate device compliance policies. Keep in mind that compliance policies are created on a per-platform basis and are used by conditional access policies when referencing compliance status.

- You should be familiar with using the What If tool to evaluate new policies and troubleshoot policy assignments. Use this tool to help validate policies during your pilot phase, before assigning the policy to a larger audience.

- You should be familiar with the Azure AD Sign-ins report. This includes navigating the report, entering search criteria, and interpreting the details provided.

- You need to be familiar with the terminology used to describe WaaS. This includes terms such as feature updates, quality updates, and deployment rings.

- You need to be familiar with servicing channels and how they operate. This includes the available channels and configuration options.

- You need to be familiar with WIfB and its importance in supporting the WaaS model.

- You need to be familiar with the different deployment methods and what their capabilities are. This includes traditional deployments, in-place upgrades, and modern servicing.

- You need to be familiar with the Windows 10 in-place upgrade. This includes planning considerations, requirements, and solutions for deployment.

- You need to be familiar with modern servicing. This includes understanding the differences between servicing and in-place upgrades, the limitations, and the various solutions that can enable modern servicing.

- You need to be familiar with what upgrade readiness can provide and how it is implemented.

- You need to be familiar with the upgrade readiness workflow. This includes the different blades and they information they provide.

- You need to be familiar with each of the security features included with Windows 10. This includes an understanding of their capabilities and possible use cases.

- You should be familiar with MSfB, how to navigate the management portal, add apps, and connect it with Intune for centralized management.

- You should be familiar with app deployment prerequisites. This includes conditional requirements depending on the needs of an organization.

- You should be familiar with creating and assigning apps in Intune. This includes navigating the client app blades in the Intune console.

- You should be familiar with the requirements for implementing co-management. This includes versions of ConfigMgr and Windows 10, with an emphasis on certain versions.

- You should be familiar with how to setup co-management in the ConfigMgr management console. This includes navigating the setup wizard, account requirements for establishing the connection, and available workload options.

- You should be familiar with each of the workload options for co-management. This includes the basic capabilities and what version of ConfigMgr supports the different features.

- You should have a basic understanding of Device Health and Upgrade Readiness, including their requirements and capabilities.

- You should be familiar with how to enroll devices with Windows Analytics.

- You should be familiar with the capabilities of device profiles and the use cases they address. This includes platform support and profile types.

- You should be familiar with the device configuration blade in Intune, including how to navigate the portal for creating and assigning device profiles.

- You should be familiar with the requirements for app protection policies, with an emphasis on the required subscriptions and supported platforms.

- You should be familiar with navigating through the app protection policy blades, along with the extensive number of controls available for managing and securing app data.

- You should be familiar with the prerequisites and setup process required to activate the MSfB for an organization.

- You should be familiar with navigating the MSfB management portal. This includes searching for new apps in the Microsoft Store and adding them to an organization's app inventory.

- App collections and app visibility in the private store are managed through the MSfB portal, from the private store page.

CHAPTER 2

Implement Microsoft 365 security and threat management

In a traditional environment, applications and services are hosted and managed from an organization's on-premises data center. Intellectual property, employee data, and other sensitive information are contained within the confines of that organization. In the modern workplace, applications and services are hosted in cloud environments, such as Office 365, reducing overhead for IT and providing greater flexibility to the end user. This transition requires IT administrators to address new challenges around information protection and application security.

In this chapter we cover cloud-based security services for Microsoft 365. This includes a deep dive into Cloud App Security, Advanced Threat Analytics, and Windows Defender Advanced Threat Protection. With these services we walk through the various reports and alerts provided in each solution.

Skills covered in this chapter:

- Implement Cloud App Security
- Implement threat management
- Implement Windows Defender Advanced Threat Protection
- Manage security reports and alerts

Skill 2.1: Implement Cloud App Security

Cloud App Security is a Microsoft cloud solution that helps organizations address the challenges associated with information protection and application security. This solution interfaces with your cloud applications, providing enhanced visibility and control such as monitoring activity, enforcing policies, identifying possible risks, and addressing threats. There are two flavors of Cloud App Security: Microsoft Cloud App Security and Office 365 Cloud App Security. For the exam we are covering Microsoft Cloud App Security, which covers cross-SaaS support, as opposed to just the Office 365 stack.

In this skill section we work with Cloud App Security and administration. We begin by reviewing the prerequisites for enabling Cloud Discovery and the configuration settings that are necessary for the exam. Next, we walk through creating policies and connecting cloud apps to your subscription for monitoring and alerts. Finally, we cover configuring alerts in the portal and how to upload traffic logs for snapshot reporting.

> **This section covers how to:**
> - Plan for Cloud App Security
> - Configure Cloud App Security policies
> - Configure Connected apps
> - Design Cloud App Security Solution
> - Manage Cloud App Security alerts
> - Upload Cloud App Security traffic logs

Plan for Cloud App Security

Let's begin by focusing on identifying the prerequisites for the Cloud App Security solution. After addressing the prerequisites, we will have access to the portal and can begin reviewing the various configuration settings. The list of hard prerequisites is minimal. You will need to address the following requirements before accessing the Cloud App Security portal.

- **Licensing** A Cloud App Security license is required to use the product. Azure Active Directory Cloud App Security is included with Azure AD Premium P1, but has a limited set of features. The full Microsoft Cloud App Security solution is included with an EMS E5 subscription.

- **Security role** To administer Cloud App Security, you need to be a Global Administrator, Compliance Administrator, or Security Reader in Azure AD.

- **Web portal** Accessing the Cloud App Security portal is supported on the latest version of: Internet Explorer 11, Microsoft Edge, Google Chrome, Mozilla Firefox, and Apple Safari.

- **Networking** Accessing the Cloud App Security portal may require an update to your firewall's whitelist. For an updated list of IP addresses and DNS names, refer to the following link: *https://docs.microsoft.com/cloud-app-security/network-requirements*.

Beyond the list of prerequisites that Microsoft highlights, you should also plan to map out your organization's goals and objectives for this implementation. Consider setting up a trial account to evaluate the solution's capabilities and compatibility with your environment. This can help identify issues and areas where you can request support or provide feedback to Microsoft.

Configure Cloud App Security

Like many of the portals we cover throughout this book, the Cloud App Security portal has a series of configuration settings to meet different needs. For the best learning experience, consider setting up a trial account and navigating through the portal. The more you work with this solution, the more comfortable you will get with navigating these options.

Many of these settings are pre-configured with a standard default option. In Table 2-1 we cover each of the available settings, their functionality, and the default values.

TABLE 2-1 Cloud App Security Settings

Setting	Category	Description	Default Values
Organization details	System	Contains settings for configuring your organization's details, including name, environment, and managed domains.	The default values are pulled from your tenant details.
Mail settings	System	Contains settings for configuring the email settings for alerts, including custom email properties, and templates.	Mail settings is configured to use the Default settings.
Export settings	System	Contains the option to export your portal's configuration, including policy rules, user groups, and IP ranges.	N/A
Score metrics	Cloud Discovery	Contains settings for configuring the weight of each app property, customizing the score assigned to discovered apps.	All metrics are set to Medium (x2) with Exclude N/As enabled.
Snapshot reports	Cloud Discovery	Contains the option to upload traffic logs from your environment for analysis of app activity.	N/A
Continuous reports	Cloud Discovery	Contains the option to create custom continuous reports, filterable by user group, IP address tags, and IP address ranges.	N/A
Automatic log upload	Cloud Discovery	Contains options for creating and managing data sources and log collectors for automatic upload.	N/A
App tags	Cloud Discovery	Contains the option to create and manage tags for discovered apps, used for filtering apps in the portal.	The default tags include Sanctioned and Unsanctioned.
Exclude entities	Cloud Discovery	Contains options for creating and managing user and IP range exclusions. Entries on this page are excluded from all future Cloud Discovery.	N/A
User enrichment	Cloud Discovery	Contains the option to enable user enrichment. This feature replaces usernames found in traffic logs with the corresponding Azure AD username.	User enrichment is disabled by default.
Anonymization	Cloud Discovery	Contains options for enabling data anonymization for Cloud Discovery. This feature replaces username and device name information with encrypted values.	Anonymization is disabled by default.
Delete Data	Cloud Discovery	Contains the option to delete all Cloud Discovery data for the active tenant.	N/A

TABLE 2-1 Continued

Setting	Category	Description	Default Values
Admin quarantine	Information Protection	Contains the option to configure an admin quarantine location for files that violate your information protection policies.	The admin quarantine folder is not selected by default.
Azure Information Protection	Information Protection	Contains options for enabling Azure Information Protection to scan new files.	Azure Information Protection is not enabled by default.
Azure security	Information Protection	Contains the option to enable or disable monitoring of activities generated by the connected subscription.	Azure security is enabled by default.
Files	Information Protection	Contains the option to enable or disable monitoring of files in your software as a service (SaaS) apps.	File monitoring is enabled by default.
Default behavior	Conditional Access App Control	Contains the option to allow or block access to cloud apps when Cloud App Security is unavailable.	Allow access is enabled by default.
User monitoring	Conditional Access App Control	Contains the option to notify users that their activity is being monitored when accessing apps that have a policy assigned.	Notify users is enabled by default.
Device identification	Conditional Access App Control	Contains options for configuring device identification that can be leveraged for assigning access and session policies.	N/A
Provide feedback	Conditional Access App Control	Contains the option for enabling feedback collection for a list of defined users.	No usernames are provided by default.

There are a few important configuration settings you need to be familiar with as you begin working with Cloud App Security. The first area is covered on the Organization details page. Follow these steps to configure your organization details:

1. Sign-in to the Cloud App Security portal at *https://portal.cloudappsecurity.com*.

2. From the menu bar, click on the settings cog and select **Settings**.

3. On the Organization details page, fill in the following information:

   A. **Organization Display Name** The name you provide in this field will be included in emails and web pages sent to employees.

   B. **Environment Name** The name you provide in this field is used to differentiate between different environments owned by the same organization.

   C. **Organization Logo** The image you provide in this field will be included in emails and web pages sent to employees. The image must be in PNG format with a maximum size of 150x150 pixels.

   D. **Managed Domains** The domains you provide in this field determine which users are internal and external. This information is used for reports, alerts, and file sharing access levels.

4. Click **Save**.

After configuring your organization details, navigate to the Mail settings page and confirm that the applied values work for your environment. These settings include the following:

- **Default Settings**   This is the default option and will apply the following configuration to emails:
  - **Display Name**   Microsoft Cloud App Security
  - **Email Address**   no-reply@cloudappsecurity.com
  - **Reply-To-Address**   no-reply@cloudappsecurity.com
- **Custom Settings**   Select this option if you want to customize the mail sender identity.
  - **From Display Name**   Enter a custom display name.
  - **From Email Address**   Enter your preferred sender email address.
  - **Reply-To Email Address**   Enter your preferred reply-to email address.
  - **Custom Settings Approval**   You must agree to the terms of service when using custom mail settings.
- **Email Design**   Upload a custom email template, formatted in HTML.
- **Send A Test Email**   Initiate a test email.

The remaining configuration settings serve different purposes depending on your needs. Activities such as uploading logs, tagging apps, and customizing score metrics play an important role as you begin importing data and connecting apps. We will cover additional settings throughout the chapter.

Configure Cloud App Security policies

Let's examine the available policy types and cover some example scenarios. There are seven types of policies available in the Client App Security portal. These policies enable administrators to define what behavior is acceptable and what is not. Policies can be created to accomplish multiple automated tasks, such as generating email alerts, blocking access to apps, or quarantining suspicious files. Policies are a core component of Cloud App Security and are an important feature that you need to be familiar with for the exam.

Configure access policies

Access policies are the first policy type we are going to work with. An access policy delivers real-time monitoring and control when users login to your cloud apps. For example, you can create an access policy that generates an alert when a user accesses Office 365 from a non-US location.

Before you begin creating access policies there are some additional prerequisites that you need to consider. These include the following:

- **Licensing**   Access policies have a dependency on Azure AD Conditional Access. You will need an Azure AD Premium P1 subscription to use access policies in Cloud App Security.
- **Conditional Access**   Applications that you want to control with an access policy will need to be referenced in a Conditional Access policy with the option **Use Conditional**

Access App Control enabled. The Conditional Access policy also needs to be assigned to a test user so you can complete an initial sign-in for the app to be discovered.

After addressing these prerequisites, you can start creating access policies in the portal. In the following walkthrough we are going to create an access policy that generates an alert when non-domain joined devices access Microsoft Exchange Online.

1. Sign-in to the Cloud App Security portal at: *https://portal.cloudappsecurity.com*.

2. In the navigation menu, mouseover **Control** and select **Policies**.

3. On the Policies page, click **Create Policy** and select **Access Policy**.

4. On the Create access policy page, fill in the following information:

   - **Policy Name**   Enter a name that clearly identifies the policy. In this example we named our policy Access Monitoring For Non-Domain Joined Devices.

   - **Policy Severity**   Select a severity level for your policy. The policy severity is shown in the portal and can be used to determine if an alert should be generated. In this example we set the severity level to **Medium**.

   - **Category**   Select a category that best describes the policy. This field is for administrative use and can be used as search criteria to isolate policy types. In this example we kept the category set to access control (default).

   - **Activities Matching All Of The Following**   Define your activity filter(s) by selecting the desired conditions that you want the policy to monitor. Refer to Figure 2-1 for an example of the settings we are using.

FIGURE 2-1 Access Policy - Matching Activities

   - **Actions**   Select an action you want to take when this policy is triggered. In this example we are selecting **Test**, which will monitor activity, but will not block the user from accessing the application.

   - **Alerts**   Select which alerts you want to occur when this policy is triggered. In this example we are selecting **Create An Alert For Each Matching Event With The Policy's Severity** and **Send Alert As Email**.

5. Click **Create**.

Confirm your new access policy has been created successfully by reviewing the list of policies on the Policy page of the Cloud App Security portal.

Configure activity policies

The next scenario covers working with activity policies. An activity policy leverages the APIs in your cloud applications to collect metadata and generate alerts and actions. For example, you can create an activity policy that monitors user login events. If a user fails to login successfully multiple times in a row, the policy will generate an alert and notify the user.

In the following walkthrough we will create an activity policy that accomplishes this behavior.

1. Sign-in to the Cloud App Security portal at: *https://portal.cloudappsecurity.com*.
2. From the navigation bar on the left, mouseover **Control** and select **Policies**.
3. On the Policies page, click **Create Policy** and select **Activity Policy**.
4. On the Create Activity Policy page, review the available policy templates by clicking on the dropdown under Policy template. Microsoft provides you with a few pre-built templates to help you get started. Select the template **Multiple Failed User Log On Attempts To An App**.
5. Click **Apply Template** when prompted.
6. Review the options defined under Create Filters for the policy. Refer to Figure 2-2 for an example of the selections defined in the template. In this section you can control whether the policy triggers on single events or repeated activity, along with the minimum number of repeats and the timeframe.

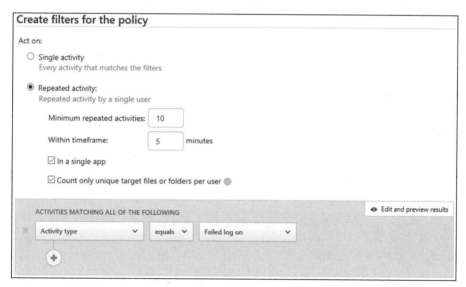

FIGURE 2-2 Activity Policy - Filters

7. Review the options defined under Alerts. Refer to Figure 2-3 for an example of the selections defined in the template. In this section you can control if an alert is generated, the maximum number of alerts for this policy per day, and what platform to deliver the alert

to. Note that Microsoft Flow is available as a preview feature at the time of this writing. Flow enables you to create additional automation when alerts occur.

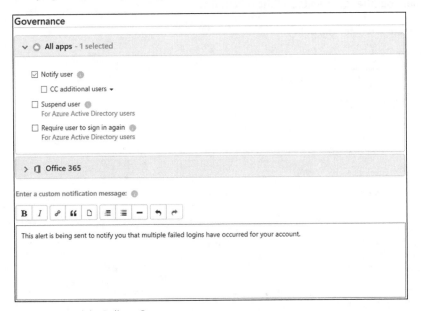

FIGURE 2-3 Activity Policy - Alerts

8. Expand the **All Apps** container under Governance. Review the available options. Check the box for **Notify User**. After checking this box, a new field will appear for you to enter a custom notification for this policy. Refer to Figure 2-4 for an example of the selected options. In this section you can control additional actions when an alert occurs, such as notifying the user, suspending the user, or requiring the user to sign in again.

FIGURE 2-4 Activity Policy - Governance

9. Click **Create**.

Confirm your new access policy has been created successfully by reviewing the list of policies on the Policy page of the Cloud App Security portal.

Configure app discovery policies

Next, we are going to work with app discovery policies. An app discovery policy enables you to receive alerts for events such as detecting new applications or identifying risky app behavior. For example, you can create an app discovery policy that generates an alert when a new app is detected across multiple users and has cloud storage capabilities.

In the following walkthrough we will create an app discovery policy that accomplishes this behavior.

1. Sign-in to the Cloud App Security portal at: *https://portal.cloudappsecurity.com*.
2. From the navigation bar on the left, mouseover **Control** and select **Policies**.
3. On the Policies page, click **Create Policy** and select **App Discovery Policy**.
4. On the Create App Discovery policy page, review the available policy templates by clicking on the dropdown under Policy template. Microsoft provides you with a few pre-built templates to help you get started. Select the template **New Cloud Storage App**.
5. Click **Apply Template** when prompted.
6. Review the following configuration options.

   A. **Apps Matching All Of The Following**   Define your app discovery filter(s) by selecting the desired conditions that you want the policy to monitor. Refer to Figure 2-5 for an example of the settings we are using.

FIGURE 2-5 App Discovery Policy - Matching Activities

   B. **Apply To**   Select which reports you want the policy to apply to. In this example it will apply to **All Continuous Reports**.

   C. **Trigger A Policy Match If All The Following Occur On The Same Day**   This setting differs slightly from the previous filter. These conditions must occur on the same day for the policy to trigger. Define your same day criteria by selecting the desired conditions that you want the policy to match on. Refer to Figure 2-6 for an example of the settings we are using.

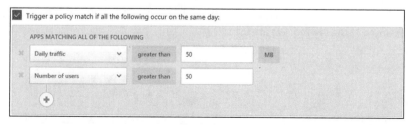

FIGURE 2-6 App Discovery Policy - Matching Activities

    D. Alerts   Select which alerts you want to occur when this policy is triggered. In this example we are selecting **Create An Alert For Each Matching Event With The Policy's Severity**.

    E. Governance   Select an app tag to apply to the app when this policy triggers. In this example we will leave all options unchecked (default template). If you would like to apply a custom tag you can create new ones by navigating to **Settings, and App Tags**.

7. Click **Create**.

Confirm your new app discovery policy has been created successfully by reviewing the list of policies on the Policy page of the Cloud App Security portal.

Configure Cloud Discovery anomaly detection policies

Next, we'll work Cloud Discovery anomaly detection policies. These policies are responsible for detecting unusual activity in application usage as part of the Cloud Discovery process. Cloud Discovery refers to the process of analyzing your network traffic logs. For this example, consider a policy that will generate an alert when suspicious activity is detected for cloud storage apps. Suspicious activity is determined using Microsoft's behavior analysis information. As an administrator, you can adjust the sensitivity of this feature.

In the following walkthrough we will create a Cloud Discovery anomaly detection policy that relates to this scenario.

1. Sign-in to the Cloud App Security portal at: *https://portal.cloudappsecurity.com*.

2. From the navigation bar on the left, mouseover **Control** and select **Policies**.

3. On the Policies page, click **Create Policy** and select **Cloud Discovery Anomaly Detection Policy**.

4. On the Create Cloud Discovery anomaly detection policy page, fill in the following information.

- **Policy Template**   Review the list of available templates. In this example we will not be using a template.

- **Policy Name**   Enter a name that clearly identifies the policy. In this example we named our policy Monitoring Unusual Activity For Cloud Storage Apps.

- **Description**   Enter a description for your policy.

- **Category**   The category value cannot be changed from Cloud Discovery.

- **Apps Matching All Of The Following**   Define your activity filter(s) by selecting the desired conditions that you want the policy to monitor. Refer to Figure 2-7 for an example of the settings we are using.

FIGURE 2-7 Cloud Discovery Anomaly Detection Policy - Matching Activities

- **Apply To** Select which reports you want the policy to apply to and whether you are targeting users, IP addresses or both. In this example we are Selecting **All Continuous Reports** and **Users And IP Addresses**.

- **Raise Alerts Only For Suspicious Activities Occurring After Date** Enter the current date (default value).

- **Alerts** Adjust the **Select Anomaly Detection Sensitivity** to **4**.

5. Click **Create**.

Confirm your new Cloud Discovery anomaly detection policy has been created successfully by reviewing the list of policies on the Policy page of the Cloud App Security portal.

Configure file policies

Next, we are going to work with file policies. File policies can be configured to scan for specific files or file types in your cloud apps. If detected, you can generate an alert or apply a governance action, such as quarantining the file. For example, you can create a file policy that monitors for Outlook data files (PST) with Microsoft OneDrive. If the policy detects a PST file being shared externally it will generate an alert and quarantine the file. To accomplish this behavior, you must enable two settings in the Cloud App Security portal.

- **File monitoring** Navigate to **Settings**, then **Files** and confirm that **Enable File Monitoring** is enabled.

- **Quarantine** Navigate to **Settings** then **Admin Quarantine** and select a folder location.

In the following walkthrough we will create a file policy that monitors PST file types and quarantines them if shared externally.

1. Sign-in to the Cloud App Security portal at: *https://portal.cloudappsecurity.com*.

2. From the navigation bar on the left, mouseover **Control** and select **Policies**.

3. On the Policies page, click **Create Policy** and select **File Policy**.

4. On the Create file policy page, fill in the following information.

   A. **Policy Template** Review the list of available templates. In this example we will not be using a template.

   B. **Policy Name** Enter a name that clearly identifies the policy. In this example we named our policy Monitoring Unauthorized Sharing Of PST Files.

   C. **Description** Enter a description for your policy.

   D. **Policy Severity** Set the severity level to **Medium**.

   E. **Category** Set the category to **DLP**.

   F. **Create A Filter For The Files This Policy Will Act On** Define your file filter(s) by selecting the desired conditions that you want the policy to monitor. For this example, create a filter where **Access Level Equals Public (Internet), Public, And External**. Create a second filter where **Extension Equals PST**. Refer to Figure 2-8 for an example of these settings.

Create a filter for the files this policy will act on

FILES MATCHING ALL OF THE FOLLOWING

Access level   ⌄   equals ⌄   Public (Internet), Exter... ⌄

Extension   ⌄   equals ⌄   pst

👁 Edit and preview results

FIGURE 2-8 File Policy – File Type Filter

G. **Apply To**   Set apply to **All Files** and **All File Owners**.

H. **Inspection Method**   Set to **None**.

I. **Alerts**   Check the box to **Create An Alert For Each Matching File** with a daily limit of **5**.

J. **Governance**   Expand the application **Microsoft OneDrive for Business** and check the box to **Put In Admin Quarantine**.

5. Click **Create**.

Confirm your new Cloud Discovery anomaly detection policy has been created successfully by reviewing the list of policies on the Policy page of the Cloud App Security portal.

Configure OAuth app policies

Let's take a look at OAuth app policies. Third-party cloud apps that utilize Open Authorization (OAuth) can introduce security risks on a per-user basis. If users accept the terms of the app, they may be granting access to their information without knowing the impact. OAuth app policies can trigger an alert if an unapproved cloud app requires a high level of permissions.

In the following walkthrough we will create an OAuth policy that accomplishes this behavior.

1. Sign-in to the Cloud App Security portal at: *https://portal.cloudappsecurity.com*.

2. From the navigation bar on the left, mouseover **Control** and select **Policies**.

3. On the Policies page, click **Create Policy** and select **OAuth App Policy**.

4. On the Create OAuth app policy page, fill in the following information:

A. **Policy Name**   Enter a name that clearly identifies the policy. In this example we named our policy Monitoring For Unapproved High Permission Apps.

B. **Description**   Enter a description.

C. **Policy Severity**   Set the severity to **Medium**.

D. **Category**   Set the category to **Threat Detection**.

E. **Create Filters For The Policy**   Define your OAuth filter(s) by selecting the desired conditions that you want the policy to monitor. For this example, create a filter where **Permission Level Equals High Severity**. Create a second filter where **App**

State Does Not Equal Approved. Refer to Figure 2-9 for an example of these settings.

FIGURE 2-9 OAuth Policy – App Filter

   F. **Alerts**   Check the box to **Create Alert** with a daily limit of **5**.

   G. **Governance**   Review the list of available apps and options. Leave these with their default options.

5. Click **Create**.

Confirm your new OAuth policy has been created successfully by reviewing the list of policies on the Policy page of the Cloud App Security portal.

Configure session policies

For our final scenario we will be working with session policies. Session policies have the same prerequisites as access policies. To review, these include the following:

- **Licensing**   Access policies have a dependency on Azure AD Conditional Access. You will need an Azure AD Premium P1 subscription to use access policies in Cloud App Security.

- **Conditional Access**   Applications that you want to control with an access policy will need to be referenced in a Conditional Access policy with the option **Use Conditional Access App Control** enabled. The Conditional Access policy also needs to be assigned to a test user so you can complete an initial sign-in for the app to be discovered.

With these prerequisites in place, a session policy will deliver session-level visibility to your cloud apps, enabling you to monitor the session or block specific activities within the session. For example, you can monitor for sessions accessing Exchange Online from untrusted devices. If a session is found, you can block the user from printing.

In the following walkthrough we will create a session policy that accomplishes this behavior.

1. Sign-in to the Cloud App Security portal at: *https://portal.cloudappsecurity.com*.

2. From the navigation bar on the left, mouseover **Control** and select **Policies**.

3. On the Policies page, click **Create Policy** and select **Session Policy**.

4. On the **Create Session** policy page, fill in the following information:

   A. **Policy name**   Enter a name that clearly identifies the policy. In this example we named our policy Block Print From Exchange On Untrusted Devices.

B. **Description**   Enter a description.

C. **Policy Severity**   Set to **Medium**.

D. **Category**   Set to **DLP**.

E. **Session Control Type**   Set to **Block Activities**.

F. **Activity Source**   Define your activity filter(s) by selecting the desired conditions that you want the policy to monitor. For this example, create a filter where **Device Tag Does Not Equal Compliant, Domain Joined**. Create a second filter where **App Equals Microsoft Exchange Online**. Create a third filter where **Activity Type Equals Print**. Refer to Figure 2-10 for an example of these settings.

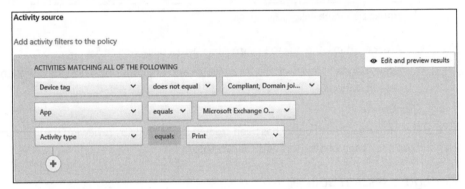

FIGURE 2-10 OAuth Policy – App Filter

G. **Actions**   Set to **Block**. Check the box to **Create An Alert For Each Matching Event With The Policy's Severity**.

5. Click **Create**.

Confirm your new session policy has been created successfully by reviewing the list of policies on the Policy page of the Cloud App Security portal.

 EXAM TIP

After completing this skill section, take time to explore each of the available policies in the portal. Plan for exam items that present you with a scenario and ask which type of policy you need to deliver the desired outcome. Most policies are unique in behavior. Access policies and session policies have some similarities. Be sure to understand the different capabilities between these two. An access policy can block access to an app. A session policy can monitor access, block access to specific activities, or block access entirely.

Configure Connected Apps

Cloud App Security supports multiple methods for consuming your data for analysis so that you can monitor and act on it. In this skill section we cover connected apps as one of these data sources. Cloud applications that offer an Application Programming Interface (API) can be connected to your Cloud App Security instance. This enables greater visibility into user activity and offers additional capabilities for governance.

Plan for Connected Apps

Before you get started with creating Connected Apps in the Cloud App Security portal, there are a few planning considerations that you should be familiar with.

- **Management Account**   As a best practice, plan to create a dedicated Cloud App Security management account for each cloud app that you connect using the API integration.

- **Networking**   Depending on the application, you may need to update your firewall's whitelist to allow connectivity. For an updated list of IP addresses and DNS names, refer to the following link: *https://docs.microsoft.com/cloud-app-security/network-requirements.*

- **Supported Apps**   At the time of this writing, the Cloud App Security portal supports nine Connected apps. These include the following:

  - **Amazon Web Services (AWS)**   There are no additional licensing requirements. For connectivity, create a new user account that has programmatic access in the AWS console.

  - **Box**   This app requires an enterprise license. The connecting account can either be a co-admin or full admin. However, the co-admin role will have limited visibility.

  - **Dropbox**   This app requires a business/enterprise license. The connecting account must be an admin.

  - **G Suite**   This app requires an enterprise or unlimited license. The connecting account must be a super admin.

  - **Exchange**   There are no additional licensing requirements. The connecting account must be a global admin.

  - **Office 365**   There are no additional licensing requirements. The connecting account must be a global admin.

  - **Okta**   This app requires an enterprise license. The connecting account must be an admin.

  - **Salesforce**   This app requires a Eureka license or higher. The connecting account must be an admin with the +RestAPI role.

  - **ServiceNow**   There are no additional licensing requirements. The connecting account must be an admin.

Configure Connected Apps

The process of creating a Connected App will depend largely on the app that you are working with. If you do not have an account available for the supported apps, trial accounts are an option in some cases. This can be useful for testing Connected Apps in a lab environment.

In this section we are going walkthrough the process of creating a Connected App. For this example, we will be working with a Dropbox business account for Alpine Ski House. We have an active business license and have created a dedicated admin user account for establishing the connection with Cloud App Security. To create the Connect App, follow these steps:

1. Sign-in to the Cloud App Security portal at *https://portal.cloudappsecurity.com*.

2. From the menu bar, click on the settings cog and select **App Connectors**.

3. On the Connected Apps page, take a moment to familiarize yourself with the interface. Refer to Figure 2-11 for an example of the Connected Apps page. Note that there are two tabs available. The App connectors tab shows all API connected apps. The Conditional Access App Control apps tab shows all apps connected through Azure AD Conditional Access. Refer back to this page when you need to manage app connectors or troubleshoot connectivity.

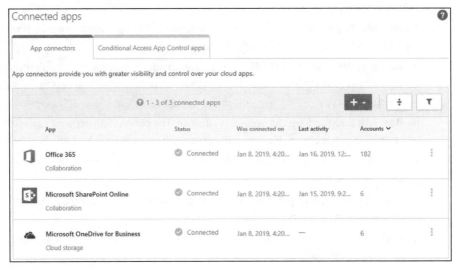

FIGURE 2-11 Connected Apps

4. On the Connected Apps page, click the plus button and select **Dropbox**.

5. On the Dropbox connection page, enter a name for the connected app instance and click **Connect Dropbox**. This name can be changed later from the Connected apps page.

6. On the Dropbox connection page, under Enter Details, enter the email address for the admin Dropbox account.

7. Under Save settings, click **Save Settings** and confirm the operation completes successfully.

8. Under Follow the link, click **Follow This Link**.

9. On the Dropbox sign-in page, enter the credentials for the Dropbox admin account and click **Allow**.

10. After completing the connection navigate back to the Connected Apps page and locate the new app. Click the app and select **Test Now** to verify the app is connected successfully. Refer to Figure 2-12 for an example of the connection test completing successfully.

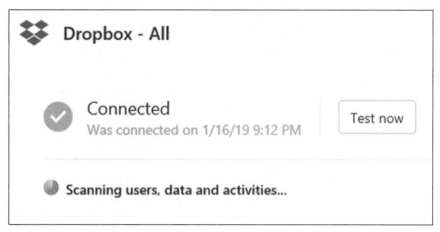

FIGURE 2-12 Connected Apps – Connection Test

After creating a new Connected App, you will see the app listed on supported policies with additional governance capabilities. If you come across a situation where you need to rename the Connected App instance or update the admin account information, navigate back to the Connected Apps page and click the more options button for the app in question.

> *NOTE* **REMOVING CONNECTED APPS**
>
> At the time of this writing there is no option to remove Connected apps from the Cloud App Security portal. If you identify an app that you need to remove, you will need to contact support and have them assist you with removing the app.

Design Cloud App Security solutions

Organizations that are moving their infrastructure, applications, services, and data to the cloud need a comprehensive security solution to protect against modern day security threats. Microsoft has positioned Cloud App Security as the solution for these needs. As you prepare to deploy Cloud App Security in your organization, you need to understand the requirements, capabilities, and connected technologies in order to design the best possible solution. In this skill we will review design consideration for Cloud App.

Design a Cloud App Security solution

There are several technologies that Cloud App Security uses or integrates with to deliver a full featured security solution. Table 2-2 outlines these technologies. Along with their requirements and the design considerations that you can use to build a solution appropriate to your organization's needs.

TABLE 2-2 Cloud App Security Designs

Technology	Requirements	Design Considerations
Connected apps	There are seven supported cloud apps available. Customers can request support for additional apps through the portal.	Review the list of supported connected apps and plan your solution accordingly. Connected apps give greater visibility and control to Cloud App Security, increasing your ability to manage threats.
Conditional Access App Control	Azure AD Premium P1 subscription.	Access and session policies require Conditional Access App Control. These policies enable you to restrict and monitor access to cloud apps based on defined criteria. Incorporating these in your design will enable you to automate actions that could prevent unwanted behavior.
Windows Defender ATP integration	Windows Defender ATP subscription Windows 10, version 1809 or later.	Integrating Cloud App Security with Windows Defender ATP enables extended visibility beyond your network and provides machine-based investigation. Consider designing a solution that leverages Windows Defender ATP and automatic log uploads for maximum coverage.
Microsoft Flow	Microsoft Flow subscription.	Integrating Cloud App Security with Microsoft Flow enables administrators to create custom automation and orchestration playbooks based on alerts. This integration can further automate remediation tasks for known threats.

As you design your Cloud App Security solution, identify the cloud apps that you need to prioritize monitoring for and establish a policy structure that meets your needs. For example, if you are using Dropbox Business for file sharing and backups consider first establishing an app connector for greater visibility into app usage. Next, consider creating the following policies.

- **Activity policy**   Create this policy to monitor for mass file downloads from a single user in a short period of time.
- **File policy**   Create this policy to monitor file sharing behavior in Dropbox with unauthorized domains.
- **Cloud Discovery Anomaly Detection policy**   Create this policy to monitor unusual behavior for all cloud apps.

This policy structure can be used as a starting point, with additional policies being created as you begin receiving alerts. For the exam expect to see multi-question scenarios that deliver an organization's design and outlines specific requirements. For these scenarios you will need to understand how the various technologies and policies interact.

Manage Cloud App Security alerts

Cloud App Security is a solution designed to keep you informed about your organization's usage of cloud apps. Unusual behavior or possible security risks will generate alerts in the portal. As you establish your policy design, you will find that managing these alerts is an important task and something that you will be working on regularly. Your goal should be to understand why the alert is being generated. Then you can determine if it is a true concern or a sign that one of your policies needs to be reworked. In this skill section we will be looking at the alerts page in the portal and how to interpret and manage this information.

Manage Cloud App Security alerts

To begin managing your alerts, you can access the alerts page by clicking **Alerts** in the left navigation bar. You can also refer to the alert icon in the navigation bar for an at-a-glance count of any pending alerts that need attention. The number will remain over the icon until the alerts are dismissed or resolved.

In Figure 2-13 you can see an example of the alerts page in the Cloud App Security portal. In this example there are six pending alerts that need attention. From this interface you can manage your alerts and investigate issues.

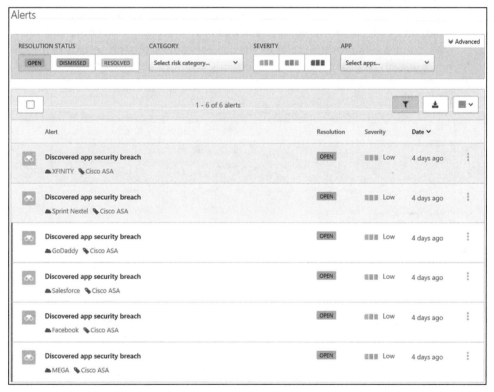

FIGURE 2-13 Cloud App Security – Alerts

The alerts page includes the following capabilities:

- **Filters** The filter bar at the top of the page includes multiple properties that you can use to narrow down the number of alerts you are viewing. These properties include: resolution status, category, severity, app, and user name. These controls are helpful when you start receiving alerts in high volume. For example, filtering on high severity alerts first is useful for addressing major issues quickly.

- **Bulk selection** On the Alerts table, the checkbox in the upper-left corner enables you to bulk select alerts for action. You can select all alerts, all alerts on the current page, or deselect alerts. This is helpful if you need to resolve or dismiss several alerts in one step.

- **Export** On the alerts table, the download icon in the upper-right corner enables you to export all alerts to a CSV file. This is helpful for offline review or sharing alerts with users that do not have access to the portal.

- **Dismiss/Resolve** Each alert has a more options button to the far right. This button gives you the option to dismiss or resolve an alert individually. Alerts that are of little value can be dismissed. Alerts that have been worked on and resolved can be marked as resolved. Both actions will prompt you with a comment window to provide input as to why you are dismissing or resolving the alert.

- **Alert details** Clicking on any of the alerts will provide a drilldown view with additional information about the discovered app. In Figure 2-14 you can see an example of the expanded view for a discovered cloud app that was marked with a security breach alert. The expanded view provides scores for the general status of the app, security of the app, industry-level compliance, and legal regulations.

FIGURE 2-14 Discovered Apps – Alert Details

MORE INFO   **MANAGING ALERTS BY TYPE**

For more information about the various types of alerts and recommendations for managing them, visit: *https://docs.microsoft.com/cloud-app-security/managing-alerts*.

Upload Cloud App Security (CAS) traffic logs

The network appliances in your organization generate traffic logs that Cloud App Security can import. These traffic logs contain important information about your network and the cloud applications running in your environment. These logs can reveal suspicious events, security risks, shadow IT incidents and much more. Once uploaded, this information can be analyzed and presented back to you in the portal for further investigation and action. In this skill we are going to review the different methods available for uploading traffic logs to the Cloud App Security portal.

Managing traffic logs

There are two methods available for uploading logs to your Cloud App Security instance. The first method accomplished through the snapshot reports feature. This feature is useful in situations where you need to review events that occurred on an isolated network where automatic uploads are not available, or at an earlier date in time.

The second method for uploading logs is through the automatic log upload feature. Automatic log upload enables you to configure a source server where Cloud App Security can connect and retrieve logs automatically. This feature is useful on networks where you need continuous monitoring and have approval from your cyber security partners to enable automatic uploads.

SNAPSHOT REPORTS

The snapshot reports feature is accessed by navigating to the **Settings** page and selecting **Snapshot Reports**. From this page you can see all previous uploads and access the report data associated with each upload. In Figure 2-15 you can see an example of a snapshot report generated by uploading a static traffic log taken from a firewall.

FIGURE 2-15 Cloud App Security – Snapshot Report

To upload a traffic log capture through the snapshot report interface, follow these steps:

1. Sign-in to the Cloud App Security portal at: *https://portal.cloudappsecurity.com*.

2. From the menu bar, click on the settings cog and select **Settings**.

3. On the Settings page, select **Snapshot Reports**.

4. On the Snapshot reports page, click **Create Snapshot Report**.

5. On the Create new Cloud Discovery snapshot report page, fill in the following information:

   A. **Report Name** Enter a name that clearly identifies the snapshot you are creating. In this example we named the snapshot report Cisco ASA Capture From November 2018.

   B. **Description** Enter a description for the snapshot report.

   C. **Data Source** Select the source appliance that you will be uploading your logs from. In this example we will be upload logs from a **Cisco ASA Firewall**. After selecting the data source, you may see some additional notifications appear, as shown in Figure 2-16. In this example the tool is providing a link to verify the logs are formatted correctly. There is also a note that the Cisco ASA data source only contains partial information, with links for more information and alternative formats.

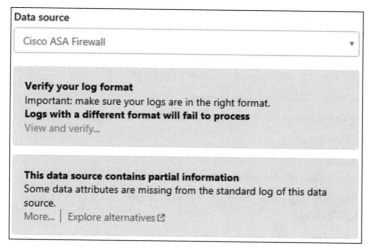

FIGURE 2-16 Snapshot Reports – Data Upload

    D. **Anonymize Private Information**   Leave this option unchecked or this example.

    E. **Choose Traffic Logs** Browse to the logs that you are going to upload and select them.

  6. Click **Create**.

Once uploaded, the logs will be processed and analyzed. Once complete you will receive a notification in the portal and the snapshot report will be available for viewing.

AUTOMATIC LOG UPLOAD

The automatic log upload feature is accessed by navigating to **Settings** and selecting **Automatic Log Upload**. On this page there are two tabs available. The Data sources tab is where you will manage your data sources, including the appliance that you are uploading logs from and the receiver, such as FTP or Syslog. The Log collectors tab is where you will manage your log collector connections. A log collector runs as a Docker container. The log collector runs on your network, collecting logs from your firewall and/or proxy, processing them, compressing them, and uploading them to the Cloud App Security portal.

> **MORE INFO** **DEPLOYING A LOG COLLECTOR**
>
> For more information about deploying a log collector in your environment, visit: *https://docs.microsoft.com/cloud-app-security/discovery-docker.*

To configure automatic log upload in the Cloud App Security portal we will begin by creating the data source. Follow these steps to create a new data source:

1. Sign-in to the Cloud App Security portal at: *https://portal.cloudappsecurity.com*.

2. From the menu bar, click on the settings cog and select **Settings**.

3. On the Settings page, select **Automatic Log Upload**.

4. On the Automatic log upload page, on the Data sources tab, click **Add Data Source**.

5. Fill in the following information:

    A. **Name**   Enter a name representing the data source and receiver type. In this example we will enter **CheckPointSmartView-SyslogTLS**.

    B. **Source**   Select the data source for your logs. In this example we will select **Check Point – SmartView Tracker**.

    C. **Receiver Type**   Select the receiver type for the log source. In this example we will select **Syslog – TLS**.

    D. **Anonymize Private Information**   We will leave this box unchecked for this example.

6. Click **Add**.

Our next step is to add the log collector. Follow these steps to add a new log collector:

1. On the Automatic log upload page, select the **Log Collectors** tab.

2. On the Log collectors tab, click **Add Log Collector**.

3. On the Create log collector page, fill in the following information:

    A. **Name**   Enter a name representing the log collector. In this example we will enter **ASH-LogCollector**.

    B. **Host IP Address Or FQDN**   Enter the IP address or FQDN for the host machine that will be running the log collector.

    C. **Data Source(s)**   Select the new data source that we created for our Check Point firewall.

4. Click **Update**.

After adding the log collector, follow the steps included on the creation page to deploy the log collector and configure it for automatic upload. Refer to Figure 2-17 for an example of the deployment instructions.

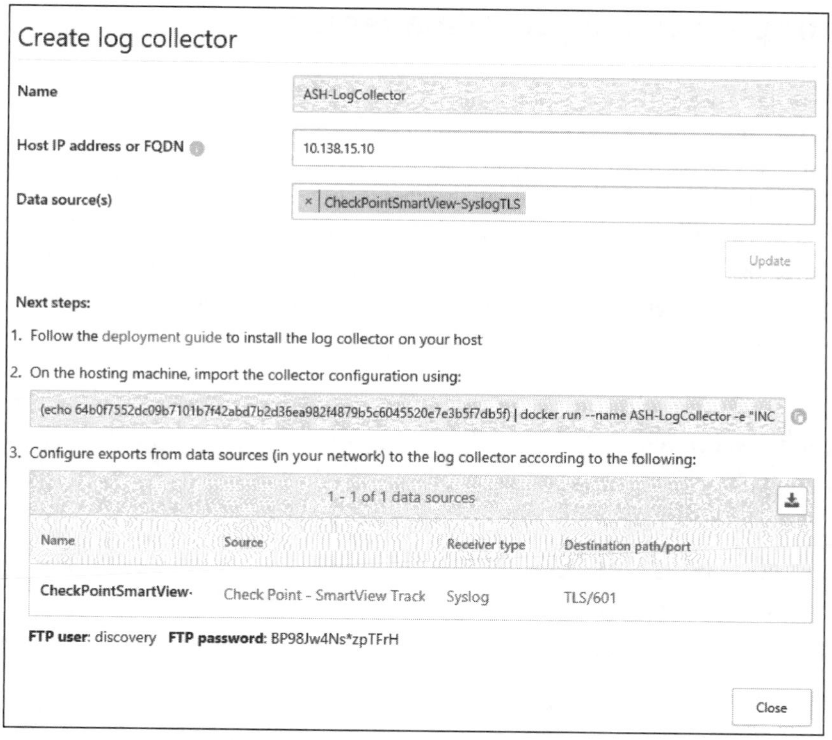

Create log collector

Name   ASH-LogCollector

Host IP address or FQDN ⓘ   10.138.15.10

Data source(s)   × | CheckPointSmartView-SyslogTLS

                                                                    Update

Next steps:

1. Follow the deployment guide to install the log collector on your host

2. On the hosting machine, import the collector configuration using:

   (echo 64b0f7552dc09b7101b7f42abd7b2d36ea982f4879b5c6045520e7e3b5f7db5f) | docker run --name ASH-LogCollector -e "INC ⓘ

3. Configure exports from data sources (in your network) to the log collector according to the following:

1 - 1 of 1 data sources				⤓
Name	Source	Receiver type	Destination path/port	
CheckPointSmartView-	Check Point - SmartView Track	Syslog	TLS/601	

FTP user: discovery   **FTP password:** BP98Jw4Ns*zpTFrH

                                                                    Close

FIGURE 2-17 Create Log Collector

Once your log collector is deployed, traffic logs will start being processed and uploaded automatically into your Cloud App Security instance. If you need to edit or delete a data source or log collector, navigate back to the Automatic log upload page and click the more options button for the corresponding item you need to update.

MORE INFO **WINDOWS DEFENDER ATP INTEGRATION**

Cloud App Security offers native integration with Windows Defender ATP. This integration enables analysis beyond your organization's network boundaries. This can operate independently as a Cloud Discovery source, or you can combine it with the other upload methods shared in this skill for better visibility of unmanaged devices on your network. Integration with Windows Defender ATP is supported on devices running Windows 10, version 1809 or later. For more information about this feature, visit: *https://docs.microsoft.com/cloud-app-security/wdatp-integration.*

Skill 2.2: Implement threat management

A threat is any activity that could cause problems for your information technology environment, whether on-premises or in the cloud. When you hear the term "threat," you might immediately think of a malicious person trying to gain unauthorized access to your device or your environment. That is a threat. But threats are also accidental, such as an accidental administrative action that brings down a critical service. And threats can also be environmental, such as a heavy rain or hurricane near you or your primary data center. Managing these threats is called threat management. In this chapter, we'll look at implementing threat management solutions including planning, designing, configuring, and monitoring.

> **This section covers how to:**
> - Plan a threat management solution
> - Design Azure Advanced Threat Protection (ATP) Policies
> - Design Microsoft 365 ATP Policies
> - Configure Azure ATP Policies
> - Configure Microsoft 365 ATP Policies
> - Monitor Advanced Threat Analytics (ATA) incidents

Plan a threat management solution

This skill section is a planning objective focused on threat management solutions. For this exam, the focus is on Azure Advanced Threat Protection (Azure ATP), and Advanced Threat Analytics (ATA). Office 365 ATP is focused on email security and is covered later in this chapter. You should understand Office 365 capabilities and limitations because the technology may be referenced on the exam. In this section, we will focus primarily on the planning aspects of ATP, along with some coverage of ATA.

When planning, focus on the bigger picture, such as what the architecture looks like, and which components are required. We will also examine what is nice to have, what the prerequisites are, and what the key considerations are (especially based on requirements presented in a scenario or an exam question).

Ascertain which technologies you need

The MS-101 exam focuses on two primary technologies to address threat management: ATP and ATA. Of the two, ATP is the primary focus, especially for this section of the exam. Even so, you need to be able to differentiate between the two and understand the capabilities of both. To begin, let's define, at a high-level, the two primary technologies:

- **Azure Advanced Threat Protection (ATP)** ATP is a cloud-based threat protection solution focused on users and user behavior. Its capabilities include the ability to monitor user activity, identify compromised users, and provide input on your identity configurations.

- **Advanced Threat Analytics (ATA)** ATA analyzes network traffic, learns how your organization's users work, and detects suspicious activities.

At a glance, ATP and ATA seem similar. That's because they are similar. ATA is an on-premises solution, however, while ATP is a cloud-based solution. Both solutions help protect your on-premises Active Directory Domain Services (AD DS) environment. Table 2-3 outlines some of the similarities and differences between the two solutions.

TABLE 2-3 ATP versus ATA

Solution	Products	Location of analysis and reporting	Protection zones
ATP	Azure Advanced Threat Protection Windows Defender Advanced Threat Protection (Windows Defender ATP) Office 365 Advanced Threat Protection (Office 365 ATP)	In the cloud (Microsoft Azure)	On-premises (Azure ATP, Windows Defender ATP), cloud (Office 365 ATP), hybrid (Windows Defender ATP)
ATA	Advanced Threat Analytics	On-premises (in your data center)	On-premises only

For the exam, you must be able to differentiate between the high-level offerings (ATP and ATA) and the products (Azure ATP, Windows Defender ATP, and Office 365 ATP). This chapter focuses on Azure ATP and Microsoft 365 ATP.

As part of your planning, you also need to think about integrations. Exam scenarios often present environments with existing implementations and known issues or challenges. In such scenarios, organizations often have goals. You must plan your threat protection strategy around integrating your solution with the existing implementations. In the list below, we outline key integration technologies and information.

- **Azure Security Center** Many organizations in the cloud have Azure Security Center or plan to deploy it as part of their move to the cloud. ATA integrates with Azure Security Center. This enables you to review all of your alerts in Azure Security Center.
- **Windows Defender ATP** You can integrate Azure ATP with Windows Defender ATP. This enhances the overall threat protection because you cover a wider variety of devices (ATP for your domain controllers, and Windows Defender ATP for your client devices).
- **VPN** Azure ATP and ATA can integrate with VPN solutions. RADIUS accounting events are forward to Azure ATP or ATA. For Azure ATP, you must open UDP port 1813 inbound to domain controllers if using Azure ATP sensors. If using standalone sensors, you must open UDP port 1813 inbound to the servers with the ATP standalone sensors. For ATA, you must open UDP port 1813 inbound to ATA Gateway servers or domain controllers with the ATA lightweight gateway.

- **SIEM / Syslog** Azure ATP can send notifications to a syslog server or your security information and event management (SIEM) solution.

EXAM TIP

You must download and install an agent to integrate ATA with Azure Security Center. During the integration steps, a download link will be provided. Additionally, you need a Log Analytics workspace to handle your on-premises computers in Azure Security Center.

Figure 2-18 shows the high-level architecture of Azure ATP.

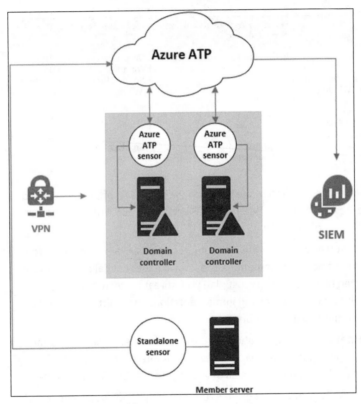

FIGURE 2-18 Azure ATP architecture

Figure 2-18 shows the high-level architecture of Azure ATP. Depending on the configuration you choose, and your on-premises environment, there are additional components not shown. The bulleted list describes the components from the diagram:

- **Azure ATP** Azure ATP, in the Azure cloud, is the service providing the threat protection features. It provides an Azure ATP portal where you can perform the administration of Azure ATP, including monitoring and managing your environment.

- **Azure ATP Sensor** The Azure ATP sensor is installed directly on a domain controller to monitor the network traffic. Optionally, you can use standalone sensors or a mix of both types of sensors.

- **Domain controller** Domain controllers are the source of information for Azure ATP. They either have sensors installed on them or there are sensors on member servers that gather the data remotely.

- **VPN** Azure ATP integrates with VPN solutions and gathers data about the VPN connections. At the time of this writing, there is support for Microsoft VPNs, F5 VPNs, Check Point VPNs, and Cisco VPNs.

- **SIEM** Azure ATP integrates with SIEM solutions and can send notifications to SIEM solutions. For the purposes of the exam, a SIEM solution is equivalent to a syslog server.

- **Standalone Sensor On Member Server** You can deploy a standalone sensor if you do not want to deploy a sensor on a domain controller. You install a standalone sensor on a member server.

> **MORE INFO   AZURE ATP SIEM LOG REFERENCE**
>
> You can look at the specific information Azure ATP sends to SIEM by reviewing the Azure ATP SIEM log reference at *https://docs.microsoft.com/azure-advanced-threat-protection/cef-format-sa*.

Figure 2-19 shows the high-level architecture of ATA.

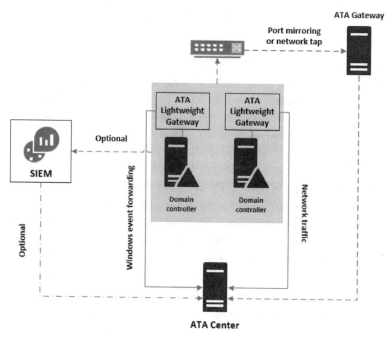

FIGURE 2-19 ATA architecture

Figure 2-19 shows the high-level architecture of Microsoft ATA. Depending on the configuration you choose, and your on-premises environment, there are additional components not shown. The bulleted list describes the components and technologies from the diagram:

- **ATA Gateway** The ATA Gateway is deployed to a server, but not to a domain controller. It requires port mirroring or a network tap to monitor domain controller traffic.

- **ATA Center** The ATA Center is a server that receives data from gateways, whether they are ATA gateways or lightweight gateways.

- **ATA Lightweight Gateway** The ATA Lightweight Gateway is a gateway that is installed directly on domain controllers. It enables direct monitoring of domain controller traffic without requiring port mirroring or a network tap.

- **Windows Event Forwarding** You can configure events to forward directly to ATA Center. Optionally, you can use a SIEM solution and forward event to the SIEM solution and have the SIEM solution forward the events to ATA Center.

While the exam section titled "Implement threat management" only has one dedicated topic for ATA (Monitor Advanced Threat Analytics (ATA) Incidents), ATA could be seen more on the exam because it falls under the "Implement threat management" umbrella. ATP is, by far, the most important topic for the exam.

> **MORE INFO** **WHAT'S NEW IN AZURE ATP?**
>
> Microsoft is routinely adding new features and functionality to Azure ATP. At the time of this writing, Azure ATP is on release 2.50. You can visit *https://docs.microsoft.com/azure-advanced-threat-protection/atp-whats-new* to review the latest release information.

Understand the prerequisites to move forward

Now that you have a good understanding of the available threat management technologies, let's examine what it takes to move forward with the solutions. From the exam perspective, you need to understand minimum requirements, understand the requirements if you want to deploy everything, and be aware of key limitations and restrictions.

ATP-RELATED PREREQUISITES

There are several components for Azure ATP. Each has its own prerequisites, as follows:

- **Azure ATP Portal Requirements** While the portal has minimum requirements, most are not going to be tested on the exam. For example, there are minimum browser version requirements, but these are unlikely to be tested. One thing to focus on is the network requirements. Know the FQDN of the Azure ATP portal (atp.azure.com) and understand that communicating with the portal goes over TCP port 443. This information might come into play during a troubleshooting scenario.

- **Azure ATP Standalone Sensor Requirements** All of the following minimums must be met:

- Minimum of Windows Server 2012 R2 for the member server where you plan to install the standalone sensor. The member server can be joined to the domain or joined to a workgroup. Server Core is supported on Windows Server 2016 and later.

- 5GB of free disk space.

- VMs must not use dynamic memory or memory ballooning.

- Outbound communication on TCP port 443 to *.atp.azure.com.

- Time synchronized to within 5 minutes of domain.

- At least two network adapters.

- Port mirroring.

- Communication to Azure ATP, domain controllers, DNS servers, connected components (SIEM, RADIUS), and other devices on the network. From a port perspective, we don't recommend memorizing all of the ports, but it is a good idea to know the key ports (LDAP on 389, LDAPS on 636, DNS on 53, Global Catalog, insecure, on 3268, Global Catalog, and secure on 3269).

- **Azure ATP Sensor Requirements** All of the following minimums must be met:

  - Minimum of Windows Server 2008 R2 SP1 (note that this is a difference compared with the standalone sensor which requires Windows Server 2012 R2 or later). Server Core is supported on Windows Server 2016 and later.

  - 5GB of free disk space.

  - Minimum of two cores and 6 GB of RAM.

  - VMs must not use dynamic memory or memory ballooning.

  - Time synchronized to within 5 minutes of domain.

  - Communication to Azure ATP, DNS servers, connected components (SIEM, RADIUS), and other devices on the network. Note that the Azure ATP sensor has less port requirements than the standalone sensors. Refer to Figure 6-3 for details on ports.

Beyond the published requirements, there are a couple of other requirements that might not be apparent if you browse through the documentation.

- Incompatibility with some packet capture technologies. If you have the WinPcap software installed on a domain controller (common in troubleshooting scenarios for capturing packets), the Azure ATP sensor install will fail. Removing the installation (sometimes manually) will fix the issue.

- Wireshark and other packet capture utilities often bundle WinPcap in the installation. If you have Wireshark or a similar packet capture utility installed on a domain controller, it will likely need to be removed before you install the Azure ATP sensor.

- Incompatibility with some NIC teaming. Be aware that NIC teaming might prevent the Azure ATP sensor from installing.

Figure 2-20 shows the port requirements for an Azure ATP implementation.

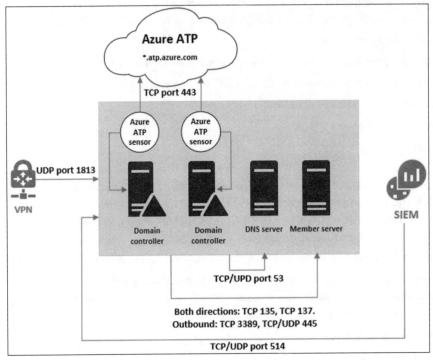

FIGURE 2-20 Azure ATP sensor port requirements

We don't recommend memorizing all of the ports for the various deployment options for the exam, but you should be familiar with the common communication requirements to the cloud and the differences between the port requirements for standalone sensors and Azure ATP sensors. This will help you solve troubleshooting items and plan the right deployment options in a given scenario.

For standalone sensor deployments, the port requirements are identical to Azure ATP sensor deployments, plus the following outbound communication to domain controllers (since your standalone sensors are on member servers):

- TCP and UDP port 389
- TCP port 636
- TCP port 3268
- TCP port 3269
- TCP and UDP port 88
- UDP port 123

Evaluate the pros and cons of different deployments

At this point, you understand the technologies at a high-level and you have a good understanding of the prerequisites. Now, let's look at the pros and cons of various design choices. This section contains key information to help you plan a threat management solution.

REVIEWING THE PROS AND CONS OF DEPLOYMENT OPTIONS FOR AGENTS

For Azure ATP, you can deploy Azure ATP sensors directly on domain controllers or you can deploy standalone sensors on member servers or standalone servers. For ATA, instead of sensors, there are gateways. You can deploy them on domain controllers (ATA Lightweight Gateway) or on standalone servers (ATA Gateway). For the purposes of this topic, the pros and cons of the deployment options are the same for Azure ATP and ATA.

The pros of deploying Azure ATP sensors or ATA Lightweight Gateways on domain controllers are:

- You don't need dedicated servers for the sensors.

- You don't need to worry about port mirroring.

- You don't need to open as many open ports for communication.

- You automatically receive events from the Windows Event Log service, instead of having to forward events when using a standalone sensor.

The cons of deploying Azure ATP sensors or ATA Lightweight Gateways on your domain controllers are:

- You must install and maintain extra software on your domain controllers. To maximize the stability and performance of your domain controllers, it is a good practice to minimize the installed software and services.

- You must enable communication directly from your domain controllers to the public cloud (in this case, Azure ATP). While the communication is encrypted, it is a good practice to severely limit (or eliminate) communication directly from domain controllers to the Internet.

- Attackers can more easily discover the presence of Azure ATP when using Azure ATP sensors on domain controllers.

The pros of deploying Azure ATP standalone sensors or ATA Gateways are:

- You don't need to install and maintain extra software on your domain controllers.

- You don't need to enable direct communication from your domain controllers to the Internet.

- For Azure ATP specifically, standalone sensors make it harder for attackers to discover the presence of Azure ATP.
- The cons of deploying Azure ATP standalone sensors or ATA Gateways are:
- You must deploy dedicated servers for the sensors or gateways.
- You must configure and maintain port mirroring.
- You must open more ports for communication.
- You must specifically configure Windows event forwarding to offer the same features and functionality you get automatically with Azure ATP sensors and ATA Lightweight Gateways.

EVALUATING AGENT DEPLOYMENT DISTRIBUTION OPTIONS

For ATP and ATA, you have three agent deployment options:

- Deploy all agent software directly on domain controllers.
- Deploy all agent software directly on dedicated servers, but not on domain controllers.
- Deploy some agent software directly on domain controllers and some agent software directly on dedicated servers.

From an Azure ATP perspective, each sensor type provides the same capacity and performance. However, for ATA, the ATA Gateway supports up to 50,000 packets per second, compared to only 10,000 packets per second for the ATA Lightweight Gateway. Thus, you can deploy less ATA Gateways while providing the same capacity and performance. One other factor for the agents is performance. Deploying agents onto domain controllers requires CPU and memory. For example, to get the maximum performance out of the ATA Lightweight Gateway, you need a minimum of 10 CPU cores and 24 GB of RAM. If you have physical domain controllers and are constrained with CPU or memory (or if you have constraints for your virtual DCs), you might want to opt for the out-of-band agents (those installed on dedicated servers). Our preference is to opt for one agent deployment option and use it throughout your environment. For example, choose to use dedicated servers for all agent software. When you combine both agent deployment types, you build complexity into your environment. It makes it harder to deploy and harder to maintain and support. If you can provide the same functionality with a simpler deployment, you should opt for that.

Design ATP policies

The MS-101 exam calls out two topics related to designing policies: designing Azure ATP policies and designing Microsoft 365 ATP policies. Azure ATP doesn't have policies in this sense, however, the exam blueprint was developed early on, before all the capabilities of Azure ATP were known. For this section, we'll focus strictly on Office 365 ATP, which is included with Microsoft 365 E5. Licensing can get a bit confusing, so pay close attention to the details. While it might seem like you would get Office 365 ATP with Enterprise Mobility + Security E5, you don't. Instead, you get Microsoft ATA and Azure ATP (and a bunch of other stuff, just not Office 365 ATP).

Microsoft 365 ATP provides threat protection for email by providing four components. Each component has its own policies or configuration.

Design anti-phishing policies

Anti-phishing policies are used to minimize or eliminate phishing attempts at your organization. Remember, phishing is the act of trying to fool recipients into clicking on a malicious link, open a malicious attachment, or provide sensitive information (spear phishing is the same thing but targeted at a specific person). While phishing can happen over email, telephone, or in person, we will focus on phishing over email since that is the focus of the exam.

Office 365 includes built-in anti-phishing technology (through the Office365 AntiPhish Default policy). However, you can expand on that by adding additional anti-phishing policies. The following list describes the capabilities of custom policies, presuming that you have Office 365, such as E3, but not:

- You can deploy policies to domains, specific recipients, or groups. Thus, you can deploy one policy for a department and a separate policy for another department.
- Instead of moving spoofed messages to the Junk Email folder, you can quarantine the messages.
- You can turn off anti-spoofing protection.

When you have Office 365 ATP, you have greater control over your anti-phishing policies and more features. Office 365 ATP comes with Office 365 E5 and Microsoft 365 E5. Don't get hung up on all the licensing options, but be aware of the high-level differences. Figure 2-21 shows the initial edit screen for a custom policy for an Office 365 E3 subscription. Notice how sparse it is.

Priority	0	
Status	On	
Last modified	October 24, 2018	
Policy setting	Policy name	ASH Anti-Phishing Custom Policy
	Description	
	Applied to	If the recipient domain is: alpineskihouse.com
Spoof	Enable antispoofing protection	On
	Action	Move message to the recipients' Junk Email folders

FIGURE 2-21 Anti-phishing options in Office 365 E3

Figure 2-22 shows the initial edit screen for a custom policy for an Office 365 E5 subscription. Note the additional features and greater control.

Priority	0	
Status	On	
Last modified	October 24, 2018	
Policy setting	Policy name	ASH Anti-Phishing Custom Policy
	Description	Extends anti-phishing capabilities from default.
	Applied to	If the recipient domain is:
		alpineskihouse.com
Impersonation	Users to protect	Off
	Protect all domains I own	Off
	Protect specific domains	Off
	Action > User impersonation	Don't apply any action
	Action > Domain impersonation	Don't apply any action
	Safety tips > User impersonation	Off
	Safety tips > Domain impersonation	Off
	Safety tips > Unusual characters	Off
	Mailbox intelligence	On
Spoof	Enable antispoofing protection	On
	Action	Move message to the recipients' Junk Email folders
Advanced settings	Advanced phishing thresholds	1 - Standard

FIGURE 2-22 Anti-phishing options in Office 365 E5

The following list describe the key capabilities you get with E5.

- **Greater control of who and what to protect**   You can add up to 60 users to protect from being impersonated.

- **Automatic domain protection**   You can configure a policy to automatically protect all of the domains you own.

- **You can control the actions during impersonation**   You can delete the message, deliver it and BCC somebody, or redirect the email to a different email address.

- **Mailbox intelligence**.   This feature analyzes user email to help identify phishing attempts.

- **Add trusted senders and domains**   You can add specific senders or trusted domains to a safe list so that message from the senders or domains won't be classified as imper-sonation.

- **You can adjust the aggressiveness of the anti-phishing engine**   Setting it to 1 is the default and represents a standard level of aggression. You can set it to 2, 3, or 4 where 4 is the most aggressive setting. As you increase the aggressiveness of the engine, the chances of having false positives increases (whereby a legitimate email is marked as a phishing attempt).

Outside of the anti-phishing policies, you can control anti-phishing in anti-spam policies too. In anti-spam policies, you have additional options for acting on email identified as phish-ing email. For example, you can redirect the phishing email to a shared mailbox that is moni-tored by your information security team.

Design anti-spam policies

When you think about spam, you think about unwanted email. Whether it is marketing-related email or unsolicited advertisements, spam is generally benign. With anti-spam policies, however, you can also control how potential malicious email is handled. For example, with control over some phishing email settings, you can block email from specific regions or countries, and you can block specific senders or domains.

When studying the anti-spam policies for the exam, you should keep something in mind: there are tons of settings and a myriad of ways to configure things. You won't possibly be able to memorize every setting or combination of settings. And you won't need to for the exam. For this section of the exam, focus on the design components. You need to know, at a high level, what your design options are, the pros and cons of various choices, and some of the most common settings.

Standard settings

By default, the standard anti-spam settings are turned on. This provides a basic level of protection and includes many of the most commonly used options. Table 2-4 shows the standard settings and default values.

TABLE 2-4   Standard Settings For Anti-Spam

Setting name	Description	Default Value
Spam action	What to do with messages classified as spam.	Move message to Junk Email folder
Mark bulk email as spam	Whether to mark bulk email as spam.	On
Bulk threshold	A numerical value is assigned to each message. The threshold determines when a message is classified as bulk.	7
Mark NDR backscatter as spam	Backscatter messages are email bounce messages sent to you when your email address is spoofed or forged.	Off
Safety Tips	Color-coded message that warns you about potentially malicious messages.	On
Bulk email	What to do with messages classified as bulk (for example, marketing or newsletters).	Move message to Junk Email folder
Phishing email	What to do with messages classified as phishing attempts.	Quarantine message

Want to adjust the standard settings? Then, you must switch to custom settings. When you use custom settings, you can modify the default spam filter policy and create your own policies. Custom settings are discussednext.

Custom settings

You have complete control of anti-spam when using custom settings. You can also have multiple policies (each having a specified priority). Using custom settings, however, also requires more administrative overhead (design time, setup time, testing time). Be sure to understand the different policies and what they are used for. Table 2-5 outlines these policies.

TABLE 2-5 Custom Settings and Multiple Policies for Anti-Spam

Setting name	Description
Default spam filter policy	This is the default policy, which you can adjust. The default spam filter policy, however, applies to all users and you cannot change that.
Connection filter policy	You can use the connection filter policy to add safe IP address to the IP Allow List, which will ensure messages are always accepted. You can also add IP addresses to the IP Block List to always block messages from those IP addresses. You can turn on the safe list that ensures that messages from senders on the safe list are not checked for spam.
Outbound spam filter policy	This is a built-in policy to scan outbound messages for spam. This policy is always on. You can't turn it off. The only updates you can make to the outbound spam filter are to send a copy of suspicious outbound emails to somebody (such as your information security team) and notify specific people if a sender is blocked due to sending outbound spam.
Spoof intelligence policy	This policy is always on. You can review senders that have spoofed your domain and decide if you want to block them or not.

When you use custom settings, you gain access to a wider array of anti-spam settings. The following custom setting sections are available:

- **Spam and bulk actions** This is the section where you decide which action to take. For example, with spam, you can move messages to the Junk Email folder, add an X-header, prepend a subject line with text (such as "<Possible spam>"), redirect messages to a specified email address, delete messages, or quarantine messages. You get the same options for high confidence spam, phishing emails, and bulk email. You set the spam threshold. The default is 7 and 1 represents the most aggressive while 9 is the least aggressive threshold. Finally, you can turn off safety tips.

- **Allow lists** Here, you can add specific senders or domains to ensure that email is always delivered from them.

- **Block lists** Here, you can mark all email from specific senders or domains as spam.

- **International spam** You can filter email messages based on the language used, or based on country or region.

- **Spam properties** Here, you can adjust the spam score based on email message attributes such as whether an email address has links to remote sites or uses an IP address in a URL. You can also flag email messages as spam if they meet certain criteria, such as having object tags in HTML. And you can also configure SPF, Sender ID filtering, and NDR backscatter.

- **Applied to** You can apply a policy to a user, a group, or a domain. You can also use exceptions for granular control.

There are some key points to keep in mind for the exam:

- You cannot configure the default spam policy to apply to specific groups, users, or domains. Instead, create a new policy that can be targeted at groups, users, or domains.
- You cannot target the connection filter policy to specific groups, users, or domains.
- The outbound spam filter cannot be turned off.
- You cannot disable the spoof intelligence policy.

Design anti-malware policies

With anti-malware, you start with one default policy. It can be modified, but it cannot be disabled, and it has some limitations. For example, you cannot target the policy at specific groups or users. If you want more control, you must create a new anti-malware policy. Like anti-spam, Office 365 ATP does not enhance anti-malware (in other words, there isn't an ATP anti-malware like there is an ATP anti-phishing solution).

Table 2-6 describes the available anti-spam policies.

TABLE 2-6 Description of Anti-Malware Settings

Setting name	Description	Default value
Malware detection response	Whether to notify recipients if their messages are quarantined	Notify with default notification text
Common attachment types filter	Whether to block attachment types that might be harmful to a computer	On
Notifications	Whether to notify a sender of the quarantined message	Off
Administrator notifications	Whether to notify an administrator about quarantined messages	Off
Custom notifications	Whether to customize the name, email address, subject, and message when notifications are used	Off

If you create a new anti-malware policy, you will be able to adjust the same settings. In other words, it has feature parity with the default policy. A custom policy can be targeted at specific domains, groups, or users. For the exam, this is important to remember.

In Figure 2-23 the scoping of a policy is targeted at members of Group1, with an exception for a user named Brian Svidergol.

FIGURE 2-23 Scoping an anti-malware policy

There are some key things to remember about anti-malware for the exam:

- Messages are scanned when sent or received, however, messages are not scanned when viewed.

- Custom policies take precedence over the default policy. The default policy always has the lowest precedence.

- You can have multiple custom policies and specify a policy that takes precedence over other custom policies.

- You can test anti-malware policies by creating a text file named EICAR.TXT. In the file, type the following string: **X5O!P%@AP[4\PZX54(P^)7CC)7}$EICAR-STANDARD-ANTIVIRUS-TEST-FILE!$H+H***. Then, attach the file to an email message and try to send it to another mailbox. Note that your desktop anti-virus program might intercept the file. To avoid that, you can put it in a folder excluded from anti-virus scanning to test anti-malware.

- You can run a message trace to find out if a message was detected as malware.

Design DomainKeys Identified Mail

DomainKeys Identified Mail (DKIM) provides a method for validating a domain name associated with an email message. With DKIM, you can greatly reduce the chances of your domain name being used maliciously, especially outside of your network (such as during spoofing). DKIM can help cut down on spam and malicious email, although this requires more widespread adoption. The high-level process involves the following steps:

1. Add required CNAME records for DKIM.

2. Add DKIM signature to your domain.

3. Send email.

4. The receiving organization receives an email message and the email server recognizes that it is signed by DKIM. A DNS query obtains the public key from the domain, which allows for the DKIM verification.

Table 2-7 shows the two CNAME record formats for the DNS records.

TABLE 2-7 DNS configuration items for DKIM

DNS item	Value
Hostname	selector1-<domainGUID>._domainkey.<initialDomain>
Points to address or value	selector1-<domainGUID>._domainkey.<initialDomain>
TTL	3600
Hostname	selector2._domainkey.<domain>
Points to address or value	selector2-<domainGUID>._domainkey.<initialDomain>
TTL	3600

You might be wondering how to obtain the domainGUID. You can check the MX record for the domain. Use the nslookup command, as follows:

```
Nslookup
set type = MX
alpineskihouse.com
```

The output will contain the mail exchanger:

```
alpineskihouse.com   MX preference = 0, mail exchanger =
alpineskihouse-com.mail.protection.outlook.com
```

The part of the mail exchanger before mail.protection.outlook.com is the domainGUID (in this example, alpineskihouse-com). Full discloser: alpineskihouse.com (on the Internet), doesn't have this MX record. If you want to try this on the Internet, use microsoft.com.

There are a few key points to note about DKIM for the exam:

- Your initial domain in Office 365, such as alpineskihouse.onmicrosoft.com, will have DKIM enabled by default.

- It is a good practice to use DKIM, Sender Policy Framework (SPF), and Domain-based Message Authentication, Reporting, and Conformance (DMARC) together to prevent spoofing of your domain. SPF and DMARC use DNS TXT records to help prevent spoofing. While the exam blueprint doesn't specifically call out SPF and DMARC, you should familiarize yourself with them.

- Office 365 supports inbound validation of DKIM messages. You can use a transport rule to process messages based on the results of the DKIM validation.

- There is a default Office 365 DKIM policy that applies to all domains. If you enable DKIM for your customer domain, then it takes precedence over the default DKIM policy.

MORE INFO   **HOW OFFICE 365 USES SPF TO PREVENT SPOOFING**

To understand more detail about how SPF works in Office 365, see *https://docs.microsoft. com/office365/securitycompliance/how-office-365-uses-spf-to-prevent-spoofing*.

Configure ATP Policies

Let's examine the configuration of ATP policies. This section covers day-to-day tasks associated with working with policies, especially when you initially create and configure them. You should use the design information from the previous section to help you configure policies to meet the design.

When preparing for the exam, try to gain some hands-on experience configuring ATP policies. Obtain a trial of Office 365 E5 or use Microsoft 365 E5 if you have access to it. Optionally, you can add on Advanced Threat Protection to other subscription types. The main point is, you need to get to the interface, explore PowerShell options, and configure these policies to cement your knowledge.

Configure anti-phishing policies

By default, you will not have an anti-phishing policy. Instead, you have built-in anti-phishing protection, which is built into the other policies such as the anti-spam default policy. If you want additional protection, you should create a new anti-phishing policy. To create a new policy, you need to be in the Azure ATP security groups (such as Azure ATP *<workspace name>* Administrators) or be an Azure AD global administrator or Azure AD security administrator. When you create a new anti-phishing policy, you give it a name, an optional description, and then specify who the policy applies to (domain, group, or user). Thereafter, you can increase the priority of the policy, if desired. So, where are the settings? After creation, you can edit the policy. That's where you'll find the settings. There aren't many configuration options. The following settings can be adjusted in the anti-phishing custom policy:

- **Description**   A description helps you identify the purpose of a policy.
- **Who the policy applies to**   You can apply a policy to a domain, a group, or directly to a user. You can have multiple conditions and can also include exceptions. For example, you can configure a policy to apply to all users except the executive team. Then you configure a separate policy to only apply to the executive team.
- **Whether anti-spoofing protection is enabled**   This can be enabled or disabled but should be enabled for anti-spoofing protection.
- **The action to apply when somebody spoofs your domain**. You can choose to move messages to the Junk Email folder (default option) or to quarantine the message.

While there aren't many settings with the default anti-phishing solution, ATP anti-phishing gives you access to impersonation settings and advanced settings, such as:

- **Define protected users**   You can define up to 60 protected users. For example, you might define the CEO of your organization. If an email comes from outside the company and attempts to impersonate the CEO, all users who have the ATP anti-phishing policy will be protected. Don't confuse protected users as the only users protected from the phishing attempt.
- **Show tip for impersonated users**   This is a safety tip that notifies users of impersonated users.

- **Show tip for impersonated domains**   This is a safety tip that notifies users of impersonated domains.

- **Show tip for unusual characters**   This is a safety tip that notifies users if a message contains unusual characters (such as symbols).

- **Mailbox intelligence**   This optional feature enhances impersonation results. This option is only available for mailboxes hosted in Office 365 (not for mailboxes hosted on-premises).

You receive an attack simulator toolset separately from ATP anti-phishing, as part of Office 365 Threat Intelligence. At least one of these tools is helpful to find out if your organization is susceptible to phishing attacks. Office 365 Threat Intelligence offers three tools to simulate attacks. These tools are meant to help you test your environment for susceptibility to attacks. Office 365 Threat Intelligence is available as part of Office 365 Enterprise E5. Beyond the three tools we cover here, there is also a threat tracker (which helps you track publicly known campaigns or specific malware and phishing policies you've earmarked), a threat explorer that enables you to browse malware and phishing activity for your organization, and a threat management review tool that is a high-level view of incidents, quarantine, and blocked users.

- **Spear Phishing**   This attack is designed to harvest credentials by tricking people into clicking links or otherwise divulging information. Often, phishing attacks have users click links that appear legitimate but are nefarious. There are two built-in templates. One is named "Prize Giveaway" that tells users how they won a prize. The other is named "Payroll Update" and tells users that their payroll information needs to be urgently updated. You can customize the templates or create a completely original email. You can configure an attack to target a single user or a group of users (up to 500). After the spear phishing campaign, you can review reports that show you:
  - Total users targeted
  - Successful attempts
  - Overall success rate
  - Fastest click
  - Average click
  - Click success rate
  - Fastest credentials
  - Average credentials
  - Credential success rate

- **Brute Force Password**   A brute force password attack is targeted against a single user. The attack tries passwords that are contained in a text that that you upload. The file format is one password for each line in the file. After a brute force password campaign, a report is generated showing the total number of successful attempts and the success rate.

- **Password Spray Attack**   A password spray attack also targets passwords. Instead of using a list of passwords, it uses a single password against a (typically) large group of users. After a password spray attack is run, a report is generated showing the number of users targeted, the successful attempts, and the overall success rate.

From an implement perspective for the exam, be aware of the following information:

- **Most of the anti-phishing policies are configured in the Security and Compliance portal at https://protection.office.com**   There are wizards that walk you through tasks, step-by-step. We've opted not to show step-by-step walkthroughs if they are very simple (Next, Next, Next) and don't add value to the book.

- **Be familiar with permissions**   You can be in the Organization Management role, Security Administrator role, or Security Reader role to view reports. Organization Management enables you to control permissions for others and configure everything. Security Administrator has less permissions than Organization Management, but more than Security Reader. Security Reader is a read-only view of the Office 365 Security & Compliance Center.

- **ATP anti-phishing is only available with Advanced Threat Protection**. Advanced Threat Protection is included with Office 365 Enterprise E5. You can buy it as an add-on with other Office 365 Enterprise subscriptions.

Configure anti-spam policies

The most important aspect of configuring anti-spam policies is knowing what the settings do. The configuration part is simple; mostly you configure a setting in a dropdown menu, click to enable features, and gives names and descriptions to policies.

Below are the steps to use custom settings in Office 365 anti-spam and create a basic anti-spam policy.

1. Sign in as an administrator to the Office 365 Security & Compliance portal at *https://protection.office.com*.

2. In the left pane, expand **Threat management**.

3. Under Threat management, click **Policy**.

4. In the right pane, click the **Custom** tab at the top and then use the **On** slider button to turn on custom settings.

5. Click the + **Create a policy** button.

6. In the New spam filter policy, type a name for the policy, and then type a description for the policy.

7. Expand the six configuration areas and configure your desired settings.

8. Click **Save** to finish creating the new policy.

9. After creating a policy, you can adjust the priority of the policy (if you have more than one policy.

Here are additional key exam points about configuring anti-spam in Office 365:

- **Anti-spam protection is enabled by default** By default, all users are protected. Many organizations will need to customize the anti-spam settings to reduce spam and improve the user experience.

- **Changes can take up to 1 hour to propagate** Office 365 is spread across multiple data centers. Changes that you make in the services can take up to one hour to propagate throughout the centers.

- **Anti-spam isn't enhanced in Office 365 ATP** Instead, anti-spam settings are the same. Only anti-phishing is enhanced. Additionally, you get ATP safe attachments and ATP safe links functionality with Office 365 ATP.

- **Use the Message Trace tool to find email messages** If you want to find out if an email was dropped due to being flagged as spam, you can use the Message Trace tool to figure that out.

MORE INFO **OFFICE 365 ANTI-SPAM POLICY SETTINGS**

To understand more detail about Office 365 anti-spam policy settings, see *https://docs.microsoft.com/office365/SecurityCompliance/configure-your-spam-filter-policies.*

Configure anti-malware policies

Office 365 anti-malware has a default policy. You can customize that. Or, optionally, you can create your own anti-malware policies. Many organizations use multiple policies based on departmental or organization needs. For example, you might create a custom policy for executives and ensure that the executives are not notified about malware detection. Instead, you could route notifications to the IT executive support team to handle.

Let's talk through the process of creating a new anti-malware policy and discuss these options.

1. Sign in as an administrator to the Office 365 Security & Compliance portal at *https://protection.office.com*.

2. In the left pane, expand **Threat Management**.

3. Under Threat Management, click **Policy**.

4. In the right pane, click **Anti-Malware**.

5. Click the + icon to create a new anti-malware policy.

6. Type a name for the new policy. For example, type "Executive anti-malware policy."

7. Type a description for the policy. For example, type "Disables notifications for executives and routes notifications to executive IT support team."

8. Choose a malware detection response setting. By default, it is set to not notify recipients if malware is quarantined. You can opt to notify recipients with the default text or notify with custom text.

9. Choose a common attachment types filter. By default, the feature is on and blocking dangerous file types (such as .exe and .vbs). You can turn it off, add more file types, or remove some file types.

10. Configure the sender notifications. By default, senders are not notified if an email is not delivered due to malware. You can opt to notify senders if they are internal, notify senders if they are external, or notify all senders.

11. Configure administrator notifications. By default, administrators are not notified. You can opt to notify an administrator (based on email address) when undelivered messages originate from an internal sender or an external sender.

12. Configure customized notifications. By default, customized notifications are not enabled. You can enable custom notification text including the from name, from address, subject, and message. The subject and message can be unique based on whether the sender is internal or external.

13. Configure who the policy applies to. You can specify users, groups, or domains. You can also add conditions and exceptions. For example, you can configure the policy to apply to alpineskihouse.com if the recipient is a member of Group1, but isn't named Brian.

14. Click **Save** to complete the creation of the anti-malware policy.

For the exam, also know the following information about Office 365 anti-malware.

- **Standalone customers - most email messages are scanned**   Whether sent or received, most messages are scanned. Messages sent from an internal recipient to another internal recipient are not scanned. Also, scanning does not occur upon email access.

- **Exchange Online customers (such as Office 365 Enterprise plans) - all email messages are scanned**.   This includes messages sent from one internal recipient to another internal recipient.

- **The message trace tool can help you find out what happened to an email message**   If you want to watch an email go through the Office 365 email service, use the message trace tool. It will also tell you if a message contains malware.

- **You can use PowerShell to manage anti-malware**   Be familiar with the Get-MalwareFilterPolicy cmdlet, the Set-MalwareFilterPolicy cmdlet, the New-MalwareFilterPolicy cmdlet, and the Remove-MalwareFilterPolicy cmdlet.

- **You can use the EICAR.TXT file to test anti-malware functionality**   As we discussed earlier with anti-spam, you can use EICAR.TXT to test the functionality of your anti-malware settings.

Monitor Advanced Threat Analytics incidents

This skill is specific to monitoring Advanced Threat Analytics (ATA) incidents. While much of this chapter is focused on ATP, this section does not cover ATP. ATA and ATP are, however, virtually identical so much of the information contained herein is applicable to ATP. We'll focus on monitoring incidents and some of the prerequisites. Before we begin, understand that "incidents" is a generic term referring to suspicious activities captured in ATA.

Understanding what ATA incidents are

To understand what ATA incidents are, it helps to look at the type of attacks ATA is looking for. Based on version 1.9 and higher, ATA looks for compromised credentials, lateral movement, privilege escalation, and reconnaissance. ATA doesn't detect external reconnaissance or compromised computers.

Here are the ways that ATA provides information.

- **Alerts** Microsoft ATA raises alerts for suspicious activities it detects. You can use the ATA Health Center to review alerts, close alerts, and suppress alerts.

- **Suspicious activities time line** The time line is the first thing you see when you go to the ATA console. It lists suspicious activities based on the date and time.

- **Notifications** ATA can use email to notify you about suspicious activities. Or, ATA can forward events to your SIEM solution (or syslog server). In turn, your SIEM solution or syslog server can notify you.

- **Reports** You can run reports to look at the health of your environment and the suspicious activities detected in a specified time. The built-in reports are:

    - **Summary report** This is an overview of what's happening in your environment, suspicious activities, and open health issues.

    - **Modification of sensitive groups** This report shows all the changes to sensitive groups.

    - **Password exposed in cleartext** This report shows you the accounts that have had passwords exposed in cleartext (plain text).

    - **Lateral movement path to sensitive accounts** This report lists the sensitive accounts (such as a member of the Domain Admins group) that are exposed via lateral movement paths. For example, if you have a utility server that is used by all the IT department and by members of the Domain Admins group, then this would be identified as a lateral movement path because anybody that has access to the utility server could potentially use that to try to gain access to higher privileged user accounts. Ideally, sensitive user accounts should only sign into hardened computers where standard users or lesser privileged IT users do not have access.

You should also understand some of the key detections ATA provides. We don't recommend memorizing every potential detection, but you should know about these detections: changes to sensitive groups, brute force attacks, pass-the-hash and pass-the-ticket, and remote execution attempts.

Maximizing the information ATA gathers and alerts on

ATA gathers information from domain controllers. But it can gather information from additional sources too. Consider expanding ATA with the following tasks:

- **Configure Windows event forwarding** If you install the ATA Lightweight Gateway directly on a domain controller, then you already get the necessary event information (presuming ATA version 1.8 or higher). For ATA gateways on dedicated ATA server (using port mirroring), you must configure event forwarding. See Table 2-8 for the list of events and what they are.

- **Configure VPN integration** ATA can obtain accounting information from various VPN solutions. This integration relies on RADIUS accounting events that are forwarded. Once VPN accounting information is coming in, ATA will be aware of the VPN connections, locations, and IP addresses—this information provides additional context for investigations.

- **Tag sensitive accounts** Without any additional configuration, some groups and user accounts are tagged as sensitive. For example, the Domain Admins group and members of that group are tagged as sensitive. This enhances detections, especially for group modification and lateral movement. You should identify additional sensitive accounts and tag them as sensitive to maximize detection capabilities for those accounts.

- Table 2-8 shows the events that ATA requires to enhance detection capabilities.

TABLE 2-8 Event IDs to enhance ATA capabilities

Event ID	Description
4776	DC authenticates a user by using NTLM.
4732	Group membership addition for Domain Local group.
4733	Group membership removal for Domain Local group.
4728	Group membership additional for global group.
4729	Group membership removal for global group.
4756	Group membership addition for universal group.
4757	Group membership removal for universal group.
7045	A new service was installed/added.

Reviewing health, reports, and notifications

Beyond receiving email notifications from ATA or your SIEM solution or syslog server, you need to understand how to review information on demand too. The good news is that ATA is simple to use. There are three sections in the ATA portal to review information:

- **Timeline** The timeline is a chronological breakdown of suspicious activities. It is a good place to view everything in chronological order.

- **Reports** The reports section provides you the ability to run reports on demand. You can choose the from and to date and download the report. Note that you cannot download reports for suspicious activities that have not been detected. For example, if passwords have never been exposed in cleartext, then you can't generate and download a report.

- **Health** The health section shows you all the health events. Health event might be related to your gateways (for example, if one stopped communicating), other configuration issues, or suspicious activities.

Skill 2.3: Implement Windows Defender Advanced Threat Protection

Windows Defender Advanced Threat Protection (Windows Defender ATP) is a post-breach analysis tool to help organizations assess how a breach occurred, when the breach occurred, and the behavior of the malware. It complements, but does not replace, Windows Defender, other advanced threat protection products, and anti-virus or anti-malware products. Think of Windows Defender ATP as another tool your organization can use to help keep the environment secure. While Windows Defender ATP protects your Windows 10 devices, it is a cloud solution, with all components in the cloud. This makes it appealing from an implementation perspective and from a performance perspective, because the solution can use the power of the public cloud.

This section covers how to:

- Plan Windows Defender ATP Solution
- Configure preferences
- Implement Windows Defender ATP Policies
- Enable and configure security features of Windows 10 Enterprise

---

Plan Windows Defender ATP solution

Planning for Windows Defender ATP involves looking at licensing, integration points, learning how Windows Defender ATP is architected, and the options for deploying it in your environment. Like other security solutions, integration brings out more features or data and you want to plan ahead of time to reduce issues with your implementation. Your goal should be to understand the suitability for a given solution, the prerequisites, an understanding of the capabilities, and being able to distinguish solutions from alternative solutions.

How to acquire Windows Defender ATP

Windows Defender ATP has specific licensing requirements that you need to be familiar with. From an operating system perspective, there are only two qualifying Windows 10 editions for Windows Defender ATP:

- **Windows 10 Enterprise E5**   It is available as an online service. Without the appropriate licensing, a Windows 10 Enterprise E5 operating system reverts to Windows 10 Pro. Note that Microsoft 365 E5 comes with Windows 10 Enterprise E5.

- **Windows 10 Education E5**   E5 can be purchased to add-on to an existing Windows 10 Education E3 or you can obtain it as a standalone offer. Note that Windows Defender ATP does not come with the "Student Use Benefit" (a feature of Windows 10 Education licensing whereby educational institutions can provide Windows 10 Education to students for free).

> **NOTE   SUPPORT FOR EARLIER CLIENTS**
>
> There is a preview feature that will be released into the mainstream Windows Defender ATP product, which enables integration with down-level Windows client operating systems. We cover this with more detail in the section titled "Plan for integrating Windows Defender ATP."

Beyond the operating systems licensing requirements, you also need to have Windows Defender ATP licensed. You can check the status of your licensing using the Office 365 admin center or the Microsoft Azure portal. If you aren't licensed at all (you don't have a subscription for Windows Defender ATP), then you get an error message when you try to go to the Windows Defender Security Center site (*https://securitycenter.windows.com*), as shown in Figure 2-24.

 No subscriptions found

Before you can start using Windows Defender Advanced Threat Protection, you need to subscribe to the service.
See Windows Defender ATP product site or contact your Microsoft account team for information.

Already subscribed to a trial or commercial license?
Windows Defender ATP license settlement can take up to 30 minutes. Please try to log in again later.

Need further assistance? Contact support

Click here to retry now

FIGURE 2-24 No Subscriptions Found error

To evaluate Windows Defender ATP, you can request a free trial. Visit *https://www.microsoft. com/WindowsForBusiness/windows-atp?ocid=docs-wdatp-main-abovefoldlink* for details. For Windows Defender ATP, a trial must be approved by Microsoft. This is a bit of a divergence from past trial offerings that are typically approved automatically for everybody. If you aren't approved for a Windows Defender ATP and are not able to gain hands on experience with the product before taking the exam, plan to spend extra time studying for it, including reading the release notes and official documentation.

Once licensed, whether via trial or through your enterprise agreement or similar, you can visit the Windows Defender Security Center at *https://securitycenter.windows.com/.* A setup wizard will guide you through the initial configuration, which includes choosing where to store your data, the industry your organization is in, and whether you want to enable the preview experience.

Plan for integrating Windows Defender ATP

Integrating Windows Defender ATP into your environment has many steps. You need to ensure that your clients run a supported operating system. And you need to ensure that your clients have internet connectivity and communication with Windows Defender ATP service URLs. The bulleted list below outlines the key connectivity points for clients.

- Clients must be able to communicate with the Windows Defender ATP service URLs over port 80 and port 443. The complete list of service URLs is shown in Table 2-9.

- The traffic is considered anonymous and is not tied to the client's users.

- If you use SSL inspection, exempt or whitelist the service URLs so that traffic isn't inspected.

- You can use the `netsh` command to set a static proxy, if applicable in your environment. For mobile devices, such as laptops, use a registry-based static proxy configuration to avoid connectivity issues.

- You can use Group Policy to configure a registry-based static proxy server. While you can also manually update the registry, it isn't efficient if you have more than a few computers. The Group Policy setting is Configure Connected User Experiences And Telemetry, which must be set to Enabled. Once enabled, you set the fully qualified domain name (FQDN) of the proxy and, optionally, a port. The registry path for the proxy server and port is HKLM\Software\Policies\Microsoft\Windows\DataCollection\TelemetryProxyServer (which would be set to the FQDN or the FQDN followed by a colon and the port number).

- You can test connectivity using the Windows Defender ATP Connectivity Analyzer tool, as a free download from Microsoft. Download it from: *https://go.microsoft.com/fwlink/p/?linkid=823683* and install it on a Windows Defender ATP client.

Table 2-9 shows the Windows Defender ATP service URLs.

TABLE 2-9 Windows Defender ATP service URLs

Location	service URL	NOTES
Common URLs applicable to all	*.blob.core.windows.net crl.microsoft.com ctldl.windowsupdate.com events.data.microsoft.com	
EU	eu.vortex-win.data.microsoft.com eu-v20.events.data.microsoft.com winatp-gw-neu.microsoft.com winatp-gw-weu.microsoft.com	The v20 URL is applicable if clients are running Windows 10, version 1803 or later.
UK	uk.vortex-win.data.microsoft.com uk-v20.events.data.microsoft.com winatp-gw-uks.microsoft.com winatp-gw-ukw.microsoft.com	The v20 URL is applicable if clients are running Windows 10, version 1803 or later.
US	us.vortex-win.data.microsoft.com us-v20.events.data.microsoft.com winatp-gw-cus.microsoft.com winatp-gw-eus.microsoft.com	The v20 URL is applicable if clients are running Windows 10, version 1803 or later.

When you plan for a Windows Defender ATP deployment, a key consideration is the integrations you want to have. Often, integrating security products together brings greater insight and data. We are not talking about integrating with other anti-virus products, because that is sometimes not supported, or results in a degraded implementation. Instead, we are talking about integrating with complementary products. The following integrations are available for Windows Defender ATP.

- **Microsoft Cloud App Security**   Cloud App Security is a Microsoft SaaS offering that helps organizations control cloud app usage. You can approve apps for use, deny apps for use, and gain an understanding of how cloud apps are used within the organization. At the time of this writing, integration with Cloud App Security is a feature in preview and available to all subscribers who have enabled preview features.

- **Azure ATP**   With Azure ATP integrated with Windows Defender ATP, you can use a single interface for both. To enable the integration, you turn on the Windows Defender ATP integration from the Azure ATP portal and turn on the Azure ATP integration from the Windows Defender ATP portal.

- **Office 365 Threat Intelligence**   Office 365 Threat Intelligence is a set of tools and reports that you can access in the Security & Compliance Center. We reviewed some of these in Chapter 6. Like other integrations, you must set up the integration on both sides—once in the Office 365 portal and once in the Windows Defender ATP portal.

- **Windows Server**   The exam won't cover Windows Server, so we'll just quickly mention that it is supported as a client. At the time of this writing, Windows Server 2019 is only supported as a preview feature. The mainstream product supports Windows Server 2012 R2, Windows Server 2016, and Windows Server version 1803. You must turn on server monitoring in the Windows Defender ATP portal and install the Microsoft Monitoring Agent (MMA) on each server that will be monitored.

- **Down-level Windows clients**   Windows 7 SP1 Enterprise, Windows 7 SP1 Pro, Windows 8.1 Enterprise, and Windows 8.1 Pro are supported. One of the key requirements for the down-level client support is that the clients require the Microsoft Monitoring Agent (MMA) to be installed. For organizations that have multiple client operating system versions, this down-level support enables Windows Defender ATP to be deployed to older clients until they are updated to the latest client operating system.

- **SIEM integration**   You can have a supported SIEM solution pull alerts from Windows Defender Security Center using a REST API. The two supported SIEM solutions for integration are Splunk and HP ArcSight. You must enable SIEM integration to start. Then, you configure your SIEM solution to pull the alerts. For organizations that want to centralize all monitoring related information, integrating with a SIEM enables that.

One technology that you don't see in the list of integrations is Microsoft ATA. Because it is an on-premises solution, ATA offers less integration with Microsoft's other cloud security offerings.

Understand Windows Defender ATP architecture

While Windows Defender ATP is a cloud service, you need to understand the components and visualize how everything works. Figure 2-25 shows Windows Defender ATP.

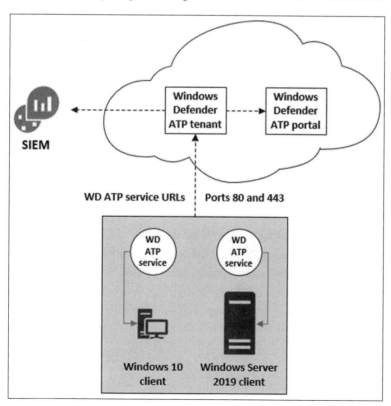

FIGURE 2-25 Windows Defender ATP architecture

The following is the environment shown in Figure 2-25.

- **Windows 10 client**   Windows 10 clients have Windows Defender ATP built in. What that really means is there is a service named Windows Defender Advanced Threat Protection Service. By default, it isn't running so as part of onboarding Windows 10 clients, you need to start the service.

- **Windows Server 2019 client**   Windows Defender ATP supports Windows server-based operating systems. There is nothing unique about a server-based client and you won't need to know anything about the server support for the exam.

- **SIEM**   A SIEM is shown in Figure 7-2. It is an optional integration with Windows Defender ATP. When integrated, the tenant can forward information to the SIEM solution. Optionally, you can pull information from the tenant using the REST API.

- **Windows Defender ATP tenant**   The tenant is a dedicated area for your organization's Windows Defender ATP, segregated from other customer tenants.

- **Windows Defender ATP portal**   The portal is the primary graphical interface to review your environment. Officially the portal is named "Windows Defender Security Center."

Earlier, we mentioned support for previous versions of Windows client devices, such as Windows 7 and Windows 8. One key difference between previous versions of Windows and modern versions is that the previous versions do not have the built-in Windows Defender Advanced Threat Protection Service. To have the previous version clients send data to Windows Defender ATP, you must deploy the Microsoft Monitoring Agent (MMA) to the devices.

Configure preferences

Although this title states "preferences," you should think of them as "settings." In Windows Defender ATP, there are some settings to control how the product functions, as well as integrations with other solutions. To get the most out of Windows Defender ATP, you should go through the settings based on your organization's needs and maximize the integration with other products.

Configure general settings in Windows Defender ATP

General settings are routinely configured as part of an implementation. In this section, we'll look at several general settings by describing what they are, what they do, and when you might use them.

- **Managing permissions**   There are two ways to manage permissions: basic permissions or role-based access.

  - **Basic permissions**   This is the default permissions model. Permissions are not granular with basic permissions. You can grant full access or read-only access. For full access, administrators must also be assigned to the Security Administrator Azure AD role. For read-only access, administrators must also be added to the Security Reader Azure AD role. For small environments, basic permissions might meet the requirements. In medium and large-sized organizations, you should use role-based access, which offers more granular permissions.

- **Role-based access** Permissions are more granular with role-based access. For example, you can granularly control which users or groups can take specific actions. You can create custom roles that directly align to how you operate and support Windows Defender ATP. Role-based access requires more overhead to design and maintain, but it is almost always worth the extra effort.

- **Configure cloud-delivered protection** You can turn this on or off. Turning it on provides protection enhanced from machine learning. Updates are delivered faster than typical on-premises implementations. Beyond just turning on cloud-delivered protection, you can also configure the protection level:

  - **High** This provides a robust level of protection. While this is the lowest strength setting, there is still a chance of it flagging legitimate files.

  - **High +** This provides more protection than High but has potential to impact performance on client devices. You should test this level before using it in production.

  - **Zero tolerance** This setting blocks all unknown executables, like a whitelisting of known executables. This protection level should be used with caution and/or with very specific scenarios.

- **Use the Windows Defender ATP APIs** You can build an app or integrate existing apps with Windows Defender ATP. This enables you to gain access to the Windows Defender ATP data and actions through your app. From there, you can build automation based on the data or send information to other apps or security systems in your organization. You need to create an app in Azure Active Directory, specify the WindowsDefender API, choose permissions based on your requirements (for example, you can use the permission to read alerts or run advanced queries), obtain the app Application ID, obtain an access token (you can use sample code to do that), and then use the API in your app.

EXAM TIP

A prerequisite to enabling role-based access is having an Azure administrator with the Global Administrator role or Security Administrator role Once you switch to role-based access, you cannot switch back.

Implement Windows Defender ATP policies

For this skill, we'll discuss implementing Windows Defender ATP at a high-level. While this objective specifically calls out "Policies," the exam objective domain (the blueprint for which skills are measured on an exam) was written very early in the development cycle of Windows

Defender ATP before all the features were known and before the wording was finalized. For the purposes of studying for the exam, we'll cover implementation and focus on the key implementation points.

Onboarding clients

There are several supported clients for Windows Defender ATP. We won't go through all of them. Instead, we'll focus on onboarding Windows 10 clients. For onboarding, you can use any of the following tools:

- **Microsoft Intune (or similar MDM)**   To use Intune, you need to have the clients enrolled. You can use an Intune profile to onboard clients. You use the WindowsDefenderATP.onboarding file as the onboard configuration package. You configure whether to share sample files and whether to send telemetry data to the service more frequently (good for high security environments).

- **System Center Configuration Manager (ConfigMgr)**   ConfigMgr has built-in support for configuring and managing Windows Defender ATP for clients. For older versions of ConfigMgr, you can create a policy, which deploys a package (the package being the Windows Defender ATP onboarding script).

- **Group Policy**   When you onboard using Group Policy, you deploy the onboarding script. In general, software distribution and/or script distribution through Group Policy is degraded when compared to ConfigMgr or Intune. The primary reason is the lack of reporting with Group Policy. You must generate your own reporting through PowerShell or other management tools. However, Group Policy is a better option than manually using the onboarding script.

- **Script**   Microsoft provides a script that you can use to onboard clients. This script is useful for small implementations, such as proof-of-concept deployments or trials. It isn't efficient for large-scale use. For large scale deployments, use one of the other tools.

Make sure that you understand the pros and cons of the various deployment methods. Table 2-10, describes some of the considerations of the deployment methods.

TABLE 2-10 Rating deployment methods for various scenarios

Deployment method	Good for PoC?	Good for small deployment?	Good for large deployments?
Intune	No	Yes	Yes
ConfigMgr	No	No	Yes
Group Policy	Reasonable	Reasonable	No
Script	Yes	Reasonable	No

The below bullets summarize and expand upon the data in Table 2-10:

- **Proof-of-concept (PoC) deployments**   With these deployments you want to move quickly without having to implement other technologies or wait on other teams to help configure their portions. For PoC deployments, using scripts or manual methods is often the fastest way to implement something. If you aren't sure that you will move forward with the solution, it is nice to be able to remove everything quickly too.

- **Small deployments** For these deployments, especially those that are permanent, it is beneficial to use existing deployment tools such as Intune. ConfigMgr is best for enterprise environments because of the complexity. Group Policy and scripts (or manual methods) are reasonable for small deployments.

- **Large deployments** For large deployments automation is important. You need to reduce administrative overhead as much as possible. Use existing tools, such as Config-Mgr, or Intune. Avoid the use of Group Policy for deploying software. Also avoid scripts for deployment.

EXAM TIP

Be familiar with the process to ensure an onboarded device is functional for Windows Defender ATP. You might want to test newly onboarded devices or test devices that have exhibited issues. Microsoft provides a PowerShell command that will be detected and is useful for testing. Run the following command:

```
powershell.exe -NoExit -ExecutionPolicy Bypass -WindowStyle Hidden
(New-Object System.Net.WebClient).DownloadFile('http://127.0.0.1/1.exe',
 'C:\test-WDATP-test\invoice.exe');Start-Process 'C:\test-WDATP-
test\invoice.exe'
```

Ensure that an alert appears in the portal. Also, you can use the online testing tools at *https://demo.wd.microsoft.com/?ocid=cx-wddocs-testground.*

Offboarding clients

Offboarding is a straight forward process and often mimics the onboarding process. Here are the high level-steps to offboarding Windows 10 clients:

1. Download the offboarding package from the Windows Defender Security Center site.

2. Deploy the offboarding script using your deployment method of choice (Group Policy, Intune, ConfigMgr). Optionally, you can run the offboarding script manually on one device at a time.

3. Validate that the clients are offboarded.

For the exam, be familiar with these key points about offboarding:

- The offboarding package expires 30 days after you download it. After that, it won't work.

- After offboarding clients, data from the clients will be available for six months.

- The offboarding script is valid for 30 days.

Troubleshooting issues in Windows Defender ATP

Troubleshooting questions are often a part of certification exams. There are good reasons for this. They often present real-world challenges to solve. Troubleshooting questions are fact-based and often lead to a single solution. One of the best ways to prepare for these questions is deploying the technologies in a non-prod environment (or in a production environment, if it aligns with your organization's needs) and working through the various issues you will encounter. For this exam, most of the technologies are available as a free trial. You sign up and you can download, install, and work with the products.

Windows Defender ATP has three possible health states:

- **Active**   Active is synonymous with healthy clients that are reporting into Windows Defender ATP without issue.

- **Misconfigured**   In this health state, clients might be reporting partial data or have an issue with portions of the communication to Windows Defender ATP. Action is usually required to get the health state to Active. You can verify connectivity to the Windows Defender ATP service URLs as one of your troubleshooting steps. Also, check your proxy service, if applicable. If data isn't coming in at all, ensure that the Windows 10 diagnostic data service (officially named "Connected User Experiences and Telemetry") is running and set to start automatically (while this is the default configuration for the service, you should check it as part of your troubleshooting).

- **Inactive**   Clients that do not report to Windows Defender ATP at all are considered inactive. If you take a client offline for more than seven days, it will be considered inactive. Other reasons for inactive clients are devices that had the operating system reinstalled or devices that were offboarded within the last seven days.

The Windows Event Viewer contains important troubleshooting information. After reviewing the health states and troubleshooting at that level, you should next open the Event Viewer on the problematic client. The path to the log is Applications and Services Logs\Microsoft\Windows\SENSE\Operational. You usually don't need to memorize event IDs for the exam, although it can't hurt to look through clients to be familiar with some of the typical events. Some of the key events that are logged in the Operational log are:

- A client onboarded correctly (event ID 11).
- A client did not onboard correctly (event ID 6, 10, 25, and 26).
- Windows Defender Advanced Threat Protection service did not start (event ID 3).

To review all of the potential events, see: *https://docs.microsoft.com/windows/security/threat-protection/windows-defender-atp/event-error-codes-windows-defender-advanced-threat-protection*.

Windows Defender ATP is an Azure cloud-based service. Sometimes, as part of your troubleshooting, you will need to ensure that the cloud service is running and operating normally. You can check the service health page in the portal to review the current status and review recent status (for example, to see if there were problems in the last few days).

Enable and configure security features of Windows 10 Enterprise

For this section, we are going to focus on two technologies that integrate with or enhance Windows Defender ATP. While Windows 10 has a myriad of security features, those are not in scope.

Understanding Windows Defender Antivirus

Windows Defender Antivirus (Windows Defender AV) is an anti-malware solution built into Windows 10 and Windows Server 2016 and later. The solution runs on mobile devices (Windows 10 Mobile), tablets, and laptop or desktop computers. The solution is free with the purchase of the Windows operating system, like other components such as the Edge browser and Internet Information Server (IIS).

Windows Defender Antivirus is improved when compared to the legacy version of Windows Defender. In early versions of Windows Defender, the application provided anti-spyware capabilities, but didn't detect or remove viruses. With the introduction of Windows 8, Microsoft expanded Windows Defender to include virus detection and removal. With the expansion of Microsoft's security offerings in the cloud, Windows Defender Antivirus has expanded the use and functionality of Windows Defender Antivirus' cloud integration. Some of the benefits of cloud integration include machine learning, artificial intelligence, and distributed resources.

By default, you have three primary features that are available to turn on or turn off:

- **Real-time protection**   Sometimes referred to as "always-on scanning," real-time protection protects your computer in real-time, as you perform your day-to-day computing tasks (opening files, visiting web sites, and installing applications).
- **Cloud-delivered protection**   By using the plethora of information coming from Microsoft's security offerings in the cloud, you can help protect computers against new threats. This feature is part of Microsoft's next generation technologies, which is being integrated into a variety of Microsoft offerings.
- **Automatic sample submission**   If Windows Defender Antivirus detects malware or potential malware, the file(s) will be sent to Microsoft for analysis. By submitting such files, you help to protect yourself and others from threats. You can, however, turn the feature off.
- Outside of the primary features, there are a couple of optional features and settings that you can use:
- **Exclusions**   If you have a file, folder, type of file (such as database files), or a process that you do not want to have Windows Defender Antivirus scan, you can mark it as excluded. In such a scenario, Windows Defender Antivirus will ignore the file, folder, file type, or process.
- **Notifications**   By default, Windows Defender Antivirus is configured to notify you about everything. This includes recent activity, scan results, threats, and files or activities that were blocked. Notifications are handled through the Windows Defender Security Center, which also handles notifications for items such as Windows Defender Firewall.

Understanding Windows Defender Exploit Guard

Windows Defender Exploit Guard (Windows Defender EG) is a new solution from Microsoft that provides intrusion prevention capabilities for your Windows 10 clients. The primary features of Windows Defender EG are:

- **Exploit protection**   This feature takes all of the features from the Enhanced Mitigation Experience Toolkit (EMET), which reached end of life on July 31, 2018. Additionally, there are new features not available with EMET. For example, EMET did not offer network protection or controlled folder access. Exploit protection relies on rules, which you configure to apply the level of protection you want.

- **Attack surface reduction**   Windows Defender Exploit guard offers attack surface reduction, albeit more limited than what you get with Windows Defender ATP. Like exploit protection, you enable protection by using rules.

- **Network protection**   The goal of network protection is to block network traffic that originates from your computers and tries to connect to destinations that have low reputations. Network protection is enhanced with Windows Defender ATP, because you get more detailed reporting and additional blocking capabilities. Network protection requires that Windows Defender AV real-time protection is enabled, and that cloud-delivered protection is enabled.

- **Controlled folder access**   This feature protects specific files, folders, and areas of memory from malware. This feature attempts to block unwanted changes to the specified files, folders, and areas of memory. This feature helps protect against ransomware attacks. Officially, controlled folder access is part of Windows Defender Exploit Guard, although it requires Windows Defender AV.

While you need Windows 10 E5 to gain access to all the features, portions of some of the Windows Defender EG features are available in Windows 10 Home, Windows 10 Professional, and Windows 10 E3. Table 2-11, shows the attack surface reduction rules available in Windows 10.

TABLE 2-11 Windows Defender Exploit Guard attack surface reduction rules in Windows 10

Block executable content from email client and webmail	Block all Office applications from creating child processes
Block Office applications from creating executable content	Block Office applications from injecting code into other processeseu-v20.events.data.microsoft.com winatp-gw-neu.microsoft.com winatp-gw-weu.microsoft.com
Block JavaScript or VBScript from launching downloaded executable content	Block execution of potentially obfuscated scripts
Block Win32 API calls from Office macro	Use advanced protection against ransomware
Block credential stealing from the Windows local security authority subsystem (lsass.exe)	Block process creations originating from PSExec and WMI commands
Block untrusted and unsigned processes that run from USB	

Note, Windows Defender EG requires all Windows Defender AV features. With Windows Defender ATP, there are additional attack surface reduction rules. For example, you can block Adobe Reader from creating child processes.

> **MORE INFO ATTACK SURFACE REDUCTION RULES IN WINDOWS DEFENDER ATP**
>
> If you are interested in comparing the attack surface reduction rules in Windows Defender ATP and comparing them against what is available in Windows 10, see: *https://docs.micro-soft.com/windows/security/threat-protection/windows-defender-exploit-guard/enable-attack-surface-reduction* (Windows Defender ATP rules) and: *https://docs.microsoft.com/windows/security/threat-protection/windows-defender-exploit-guard/attack-surface-reduction-rules-in-windows-10-enterprise-e3*.

Implementing Windows Defender Antivirus

Because Windows Defender AV is built into the endpoints, you will not need to deploy an agent as part of the implementation. Instead, you'll need to enable and/or enforce protection and configure the desired settings. You can manage Windows Defender AV with the following management tools:

- **Group Policy**   With Group Policy, you can enforce Windows Defender AV to be enabled and configure Windows Defender AV settings. If you rely only on Group Policy for management, the downside is that you will not have reporting available. Besides reporting, Group Policy provides a complete management solution for Windows Defender AV.

- **PowerShell** PowerShell is a useful tool for working with a single computer or a subset of computers. It isn't geared for day-to-day management of Windows Defender AV. It lacks a central console for configuration and reporting and it can be cumbersome to individually configure computers with PowerShell.

- **System Center Configuration Manager (ConfigMgr)** To manage Windows Defender AV with ConfigMgr, you need to have an Endpoint Protection Point site system role and enable Endpoint Protection with custom settings. In this scenario, you gain access to the reporting capabilities of Configuration Manager's Monitoring workspace, as well as email alerts. ConfigMgr provides a complete management solution for Windows Defender AV.

- **Windows Management Instrumentation (WMI)** Like PowerShell, WMI is useful for troubleshooting or temporarily working with a subset of computers. It isn't efficient enough for day-to-day management of Windows Defender AV. You can generate some reporting information on demand.

- **Microsoft Intune** You have complete control over Windows Defender AV from Intune. You can enforce it to be enabled, you can configure specific settings (such as whether to give end users access to the Windows Defender AV user interface), and you can access reporting in the Intune console.

Let's walk through the steps for enabling and configuring Windows Defender AV using Intune.

1. Sign into the Azure portal at *https://portal.azure.com*.

2. In the search bar, search for Intune and then click the **Intune service** in the search results.

3. From the Microsoft Intune workspace, click **Device Configuration** in the left pane.

4. In the right pane, click **Profiles**.

5. In the far-right pane, click **+Create Profile**.

6. Type a name and description for the profile, such as "Sales team profile" and "AV settings for the sales team."

7. In the Platform dropdown menu, select the Windows 10 and later platform.

8. In the Profile type dropdown menu, click **Device Restrictions** (which is where you can configure Windows Defender AV).

9. In the Device restrictions pane on the far right, scroll down to Windows Defender Antivirus and click it to bring up the available settings.

10. Configure the desired settings. For example, enable Real-time Monitoring And Behavior Monitoring. For the purposes of studying for the exam, consider enabling all features and testing the functionality from a client.

11. Click **OK** after configuring the settings.

12. Click **Create**. After creation, the profile will be displayed in the device configuration profiles, as shown in Figure 2-26.

FIGURE 2-26 Creating a profile in Intune

After you create a profile, you need to assign it to devices. Perform the following steps to assign a profile to devices.

1. From **Microsoft Intune**, click **Device Configuration** then click **Profiles**.

2. In the right pane, click the profile that you want to assign.

3. Click **Assignments**.

4. In the **Assign To** dropdown menu, click **All Devices**. Optionally, you can assign to all users or all users and all devices. Or, you can assign to an existing group.

5. Click **Save** to save the assignment.

Implementing Windows Defender Exploit Guard

With Windows Defender EG, you have some control over the configuration of each feature. You can use PowerShell and Group Policy to turn on, turn off, and manage Exploit Guard. In Figure 2-27, the GPO settings for Exploit Guard are shown.

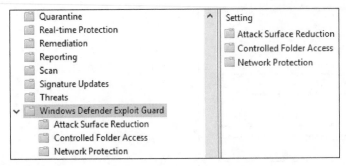

FIGURE 2-27 Windows Defender EG GPO settings

In Table 2-12 we outline the individual GPO settings and explain when they are used.

TABLE 2-12 Windows Defender Exploit Guard GPO settings

GPO setting	Exploit Guard feature	Description
Exclude files and paths from Attack Surface Reduction Rules	Attack surface reduction	Optional setting that you can use to exclude specific files and folder paths from attack surface reduction rules.
Configure Attack Surface Reduction rules	Attack surface reduction	Feature to enable attack surface reduction rules and configure their behavior (1 for block, 0 for off, 2 for audit only).
Configure allowed applications	Controlled folder access	Enable this setting to specify additional applications that should be trusted to modify or delete protected files and folders.
Configure Controlled folder access	Controlled folder access	Enable this setting to block or audit attempts to modify protected files or folders by untrusted applications. Optionally, you can just block, or audit writes to disk.
Configure protected folders	Controlled folder access	Enable this feature to protect additional folders outside of the default protected folders.
Prevent users and apps from accessing dangerous websites	Network protection	When enabled, blocks or audits apps that access unsafe domains that might be hosting malware.

You can implement controlled folder access using the following three methods:

- **PowerShell**   To turn on controlled folder access, run the `Set-MpPreference -Enable-ControlledFolderAccess Enabled` command. Optionally, you can use specify `AuditMode` instead of `Enabled` to test the feature first. Use PowerShell when you are working with one computer at a time or in a limited deployment scenario such as a proof-of-concept deployment. For larger implementations, use Group Policy.

- **Windows Security app**   Use the Windows Defender Security Center app. Click Virus & threat protection settings. Scroll down and click **Manage Controlled** folder access. Turn on controlled folder access by using the button. You might need to enter your administrative credentials at a User Account Control prompt, depending on your configuration. By default, system folders are protected and a few user-based folders, such as Documents, are also protected. You can add additional folders to be protected, if desired. In some scenarios, apps must modify files or folders that are protected. In many situations, this works without you having to take any action. However, sometimes you might have to add an app to the allowed app list for controlled folder access. Doing so enables the app to modify protected files and folders. Like PowerShell, individually configuring computers using the Windows Security app should be something you do for a small number of computers. For larger environments, use Group Policy.

- **Group Policy** For large implementations and for maximum control, you should use Group Policy to enable and configure controlled folder access. The path to the settings is Windows components/Windows Defender Antivirus/Windows Defender Exploit Guard/Controlled folder access. Figure 2-28 shows the settings in a GPO.

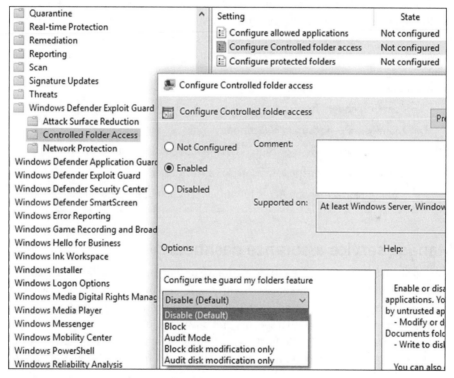

FIGURE 2-28 GPO settings for controlled folder access

Microsoft provides a Windows Defender Testground web site to test your Windows Defender implementations. You can test a myriad of features. Some feature testing requires signing in, some doesn't. Visit *https://demo.wd.microsoft.com/?ocid=cx-wddocs-testground* to test your implementation.

Skill 2.4: Manage security reports and alerts

Microsoft 365 includes several cloud services under its umbrella, each one enabled with security controls. As an Azure cloud administrator, it is important that you know what these controls are, how to configure alerts, and how to generate reports so that you can keep informed when an event occurs. In this chapter we are going to be working with a few different technologies dealing with Microsoft 365 security. This will include an introduction to service assurance and the various security assessment reports that Microsoft is making available to customers. We will also be onboarding Azure AD Identity Protection and exploring its capabilities. Finally, we will be exploring the event-based alerts available in the Office 365 Security & Compliance center.

This section covers how to:

- Manage service assurance dashboard
- Manage tracing and reporting on Azure AD Identity Protection
- Configure and manage Microsoft 365 security alerts
- Configure and manage Azure Identity Protection dashboard and alerts

---

Manage service assurance dashboard

In this skill section we review the service assurance dashboard in the Office 365 Security & Compliance Center. Service assurance was introduced to provide visibility into how Microsoft maintains the security, privacy, and compliance of customer data when using Microsoft cloud services. Customers that have strict security and privacy requirements, such as those defined by the General Data Protection Regulation (GDPR), can refer to the service assurance dashboard, reports, and documentation as a central location for retrieving relative information.

Plan for service assurance

Service assurance is a source of information for security, privacy, and compliance data. As you begin working with service assurance, these are a few planning considerations to keep in mind.

- **Licensing**   There are no additional licenses or subscriptions required to access service assurance. Customers that have an active Microsoft cloud service subscription, or are evaluating a Microsoft cloud service, will have access to service assurance.

- **Permissions** By default, all users with an Azure AD account have access to service assurance. If a user requires access to service assurance and it is not available in the Office 365 Security & Compliance Center, the default permissions have been altered. In this case the user will need to be granted the Service Assurance User role. To make this change, navigate to the Permissions page in the Office 365 Security & Compliance Center. Select Service Assurance User from the list of roles and update the membership.

- **Region and industry** The information provided by service assurance is based on your organizations region and industry. The first time you access the service assurance dashboard, you will be required to choose your region and industry.

Manage service assurance in the Office 365 Security & Compliance Center

As mentioned in the planning phase, the first step to managing service assurance is to configure your organization's region and industry settings. This will ensure the corresponding reports and documentation are relative to your needs. Follow these steps to configure the region and industry settings for your organization.

1. Sign-in to the Office 365 Security & Compliance Center at *https://protection.office.com*.

2. From the Navigation bar on the left, click **Service Assurance**.

3. Under Service Assurance, select **Settings**. If this is your first time accessing service assurance, you will automatically be redirected to the Settings page to define your Region and Industry.

4. On the Settings page, select the Region and Industry that apply to your organization. You can select multiple values for each property. Refer to Figure 2-29 for an example of the Region And Industry settings page.

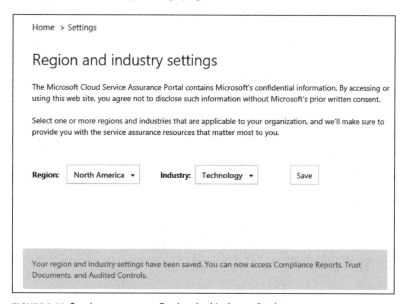

FIGURE 2-29 Service assurance – Region And Industry Settings

5. Click **Save**. This will apply your region and industry preferences for service assurance.

If at any time you need to update your Region And Industry Settings, you can do so on the Settings page under Service assurance. After completing this configuration, you can start navigating the various reports and documents available through service assurance. This list summarizes the content you have access to.

- **Dashboard**   The dashboard provides basic information about service assurance. This includes a What's New section for highlighting new features and capabilities, an Add Users' section for accessing user permissions, and an Onboarding Guide for granting access to Service Assurance for non-admins.

- **Compliance Reports**   The Compliance Reports page provides access to an independent third-party audit and GRC assessment reports for Microsoft cloud services. These reports are split into four groups.

  - **FedRAMP Reports**   This group contains reports from the Federal Risk and Authorization Management Program (FedRAMP). FedRAMP is a government-wide program that provides standardized assessments for cloud solutions.

  - **GRC Assessment Reports**   This group contains governance, risk, and compliance assessment reports for Microsoft Cloud Services.

  - **ISO Reports**   This group contains ISO information and security management related reports for Microsoft cloud services.

  - **SOC / SSAE 16 Reports**   This group contains Service Organization Controls (SOC) audit and assessment reports and other related reports for Microsoft cloud Services.

- **Trust Documents**   The Trust Documents page provides documentation and reports that outline how Microsoft protects your data in their cloud. This information is split into two groups.

  - **FAQ And White Papers**   The FAQ And White Papers page provides access to frequently asked questions and publications dealing with Microsoft cloud services security, privacy, and compliance.

  - **Risk Management Reports**   The Risk Management Reports page provides access to risk management reports that outline how Microsoft cloud services manages risks.

- **Compliance manager**   The compliance manager page links you to the Compliance Manager solution in the Service Trust Portal. Compliance Manager is a workflow-based risk assessment tool. It is designed to help customers review their data protection and compliance status, and then provide recommendations for improvement. This information is displayed using a compliance score. Figure 2-30 shows a screen capture of Compliance Manager.

This service is unavailable to the following subscribers: Office 365 operated by 21Vianet, Office 365 Germany, Office 365 U.S. Government Community High (GCC High), or Office 365 Department of Defense.

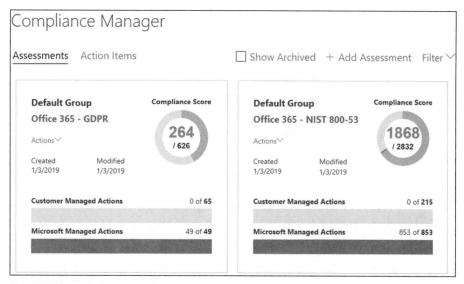

FIGURE 2-30 Service Trust Portal – Compliance Manager

- **Settings** Return to the Settings page to update your region and industry selections.

MORE INFO **COMPLIANCE MANAGER**

For more information about what Compliance Manager is and how to use it, visit: *https://docs.microsoft.com/en-us/office365/securitycompliance/meet-data-protection-and-regulatory-reqs-using-microsoft-cloud.*

EXAM TIP

Plan for exam items that test your knowledge of service assurance. For example, where can you find ISO information about Microsoft cloud services? Where can you evaluate your organization's risk assessment? What permissions do you need to access service assurance? Sign-in to the Office 365 Security & Compliance Center and explore each of the sections.

Manage tracing and reporting on Azure AD Identity Protection

Cloud-based identities are a high-profile target for attackers. As more services move to the cloud, gaining access to a compromised identity, regardless of privilege level, is a major concern. This level of access can enable an attacker to retrieve sensitive information. In this skill we will be working with Azure AD Identity Protection, a tool that Microsoft has developed to help discover compromised identities and enable automated actions when an issue is identified.

Plan for Azure AD Identity Protection

Azure AD Identity Protection is a service designed to be easily onboarded with your Azure AD tenant. This list contains the basic planning considerations that you will need to account for before onboarding Identity Protection.

- **Licensing**   Azure AD Identity Protection requires an Azure AD Premium P2 subscription. This is included as part of the Enterprise Mobility + Security E5 subscription.
- **Permissions**   There are three directory roles that can access Azure AD Identity Protection.
  - **Global administrator**   The global administrator role has full access to Identity Management. This includes onboarding the feature, configuring policies, remediating users, and resetting user passwords.
  - **Security administrator**   The security administrator role has access to onboard the feature and reset user passwords.
  - **Security reader**   The security reader role has read-only access to Identity Protection. With policies in place to automatically remediate issues, the security reader role may be sufficient for most security analysts.

Manage Azure AD Identity Protection

To begin managing Azure AD Identity Protection you first need to onboard the feature. This is accomplished through the Azure Marketplace. Follow these steps to onboard Azure AD Identity Protection with your Azure AD tenant.

1. Sign-in to the Microsoft Azure portal at *https://portal.azure.com*.
2. Click **Create a resource**.
3. On the New blade, type **Identity Protection** in the search field.
4. On the Marketplace blade, select **Azure AD Identity Protection**.
5. On the Azure AD Identity Protection blade, review the feature summary and click **Create**.
6. On the Azure AD Identity Protection blade, review the selected directory and summary. Click **Create**. You can access the Azure AD Identity Protection blade by clicking **All Services** and searching for Identity Protection.

   Now that you have onboarded the feature, open Azure AD Identity Protection in the Azure portal. The first blade you are presented with contains the Identity Protection dashboard, as shown in Figure 2-31. This dashboard provides a high-level view of your directory's Identity Protection wellness. From here you can drill down into individual reports to trace specific events.

FIGURE 2-31 Azure AD Identity Protection

The data provided through Identity Protection is grouped into three reports: Users Flagged For Risk, Risk Events, and Vulnerabilities. These reports can be accessed by clicking on the corresponding tiles in the dashboard, or by selecting them in the navigation bar under Investigate. The following list outlines what data you will find in each report when navigating from the dashboard view.

- **Users Flagged For Risk** This tile summarizes the number of user identities that are at risk. Clicking on the tile will take you to the list of users, as shown in Figure 2-32. This report includes the user's name, risk level, number of events, and last update time. Clicking on a specific user will display all the events for that user.

	USER	RISK LEVEL	RISK EVENTS	STATUS	LAST UPDATED (UTC)
	Ethan Rincon	High	1 risk event	At risk	1/3/2019 6:57 PM
	Jimmie Turman	High	1 risk event	At risk	1/3/2019 7:09 PM
	Roman Pilcher	Medium	1 risk event	At risk	1/3/2019 6:02 PM

FIGURE 2-32 Identity Protection – Users flagged for risk

- **Risk Events** This tile summarizes the number of events that have been flagged as "at risk" over a 90-day period. Clicking on the tile will take you to the list of events, as shown in Figure 2-33. This report includes the risk level, detection type, risk event type, number of closed events, and last update time. Clicking on a specific event will display all the associated records for that event type.

RISK LEVEL	DETECTION TYPE	RISK EVENT TYPE	RISK EVENTS CLOSED	LAST UPDATED (UTC)
Medium	Real-time	Sign-ins from anonymous IP addresses ❶	0 of 3	1/3/2019 6:57 PM

FIGURE 2-33 Identity Protection – Risk events

- **Vulnerabilities**   This tile summarizes the number of vulnerabilities detected by Identity Protection. Clicking on the tile will take you to the list of reported vulnerabilities. From there you can configure policies for automatic remediation, such as configuring a multi-factor authentication policy that requires MFA under certain risk types.

Configure and manage Microsoft 365 security alerts

In this skill section we work with alerts in the Office 365 Security & Compliance Center. The alerts available in this portal deal with user, administrator, and general Office 365 activity. These alerts are based on information contained in the Office 365 audit log. While you can review the audit logs to retrieve this information, creating an alert policy can ensure that you are notified about critical events. There are a handful of pre-defined alert policies that cover major events, such as a user account being elevated to Exchange administrator. New alert policies can also be created by an administrator to provide additional visibility around the Office 365 platform.

Plan for Office 365 alerts

Before you begin working with alerts in the Office 365 Security & Compliance Center, there are a few planning considerations that you need to be familiar with. These are the prerequisites for accessing managing Office 365 alerts.

- **Permissions**   The administrator that will be creating managing alerts must be granted the Organization Configuration role in the Office 365 Security & Compliance Center. This role is automatically granted to members of the Compliance Administrator and Organization Management role groups.
- **Audit logging**   Before you can start creating alerts, audit logging needs to be enabled for Office 365. Office 365 alerts are based on the information contained in the audit logs. To do this, navigate to the Office 365 Security & Compliance Center, select **Alerts**, then **Alert policies**. Select any one of the built-in alerts. On the alert policies settings you will be prompted to turn on auditing if it is not already enabled, as shown in Figure 2-34 In this example you can see two alerts at the top of the page. The first is prompting you to enable auditing, which is the option you need to select. The second is informing you that this is a default policy and it cannot be modified. This can be ignored for the purposes of this walkthrough.

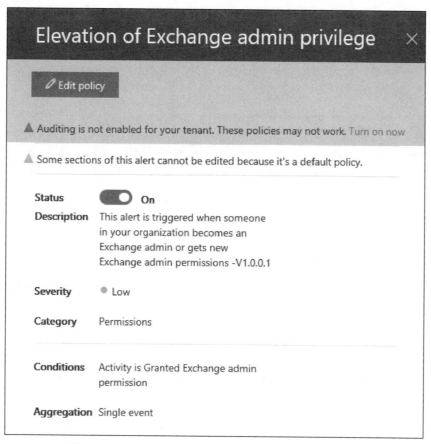

FIGURE 2-34 Office 365 Alerts – Enabling Audit Logs

Beyond these hard requirements, you should also create an action plan for implementation. This might include items such as who will be administering Office 365 alerts, who should be receiving notifications, and what items you need to create policies for.

Navigate Office 365 alerts

The alerts for Office 365 are visible in a few different formats, similar to the reports we saw with Azure AD Identity Protection. The first page we will look at is the Alerts dashboard. This can be accessed by signing-in to the Office 365 Security & Compliance Center, clicking Alerts, and selecting Dashboard. Refer to Figure 2-35 for an example of what to expect when you access the dashboard. There are a few different resources available in this view.

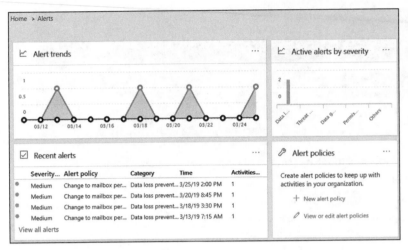

FIGURE 2-35 Office 365 Alerts Dashboard

- **Alert Trends** The Alert Trends tile shows recent activity by count for each of the different alert categories. Hovering your mouse cursor over the report tile will summarize event accounts for each category. This tile does not have a drilldown view.

- **Active Alerts By Severity** The Active Alerts By Severity tile provides summarizes active alerts by category and severity (low, medium, high). Hovering your mouse curse over the report tile will summarize the event counts by severity. This tile does not have a drilldown view.

- **Recent Alerts** The Recent Alerts tile provides a list of recent alerts, including Severity, Alert Policy, Category, Time, and Number Of Activities. Clicking on any of the events on this tile will bring up a blade with additional details about the event. From there you can see additional information about that specific event. You also have controls to resolve, suppress, or notify users about the alert.

- **Alert Policies** The Alert Policies tile provides helpful links to quickly create a new alert policy or manage the existing policies.

- **Other Alerts (not shown)** The Other Alerts tile provides helpful links to quickly create activity-based alerts, view restricted user accounts, and access advanced alert management.

It is worth noting that each of these tiles can also be pinned to the Office 365 Security & Compliance Center home page for quick reference. For situations where you need to browse all alerts, navigate to **Alerts**, then **View Alerts**. This page provides you with functionality to quickly filter all alerts, including those that have been resolved. Once you have isolated the alerts you need, you can also export them to CSV format from this page.

Configure Office 365 alert policies

The policy editor for Office 365 alerts enables you to create and manage additional custom alert policies. Through this interface you have access to all of the activities logged through auting. In the following example we will walk through creating a policy that generates an alert when a user's mailbox permissions are modified.

1. Sign-in to the Office 365 Security & Compliance Center at *https://protection.office.com*.

2. From the Navigation bar on the left, click **Alerts** and select **Alert Policies**.

3. On the Alert policies page, click **New Alert Policy**.

4. On the Name Your Alert page, fill in the following information and click **Next**.

    A. Name   Change to mailbox permissions.

    B. Description   Generate an alert when mailbox permissions are modified.

    C. Severity   Medium.

    D. Category   Data loss prevention.

5. On the Create alert settings page, fill in the following information and click **Next**.

    A. Activity Is   Granted mailbox permission.

    B. How Do You Want The Alert To Be Triggered?   Every time an activity matches the rule.

6. On the Set your recipients page, fill in the following information and click **Next**.

    A. Email Recipients   Your email address.

    B. Daily Notification Limit   No limit.

7. On the Review your settings page, review the proposed policy as shown in Figure 2-36. Select the option **Yes, Turn It On Right Away** and click **Finish**.

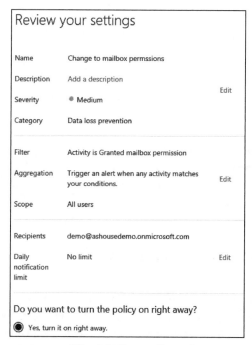

FIGURE 2-36 Office 365 Alerts – Alert Policy

Once the new alert policy has been applied you will start seeing associated events recorded in the Dashboard And Alerts page. The recipients that you configured in the policy will also begin receiving email notifications, as shown in Figure 2-37. These notifications will summarize each event and include a link that takes you back to the portal for further investigation.

Medium-severity alert: Change to mailbox permssions

 Office 365

A medium-severity alert has been triggered

⚠ **Change to mailbox permssions**

Severity: ● Medium
Time: 1/9/2019 7:15:00 AM (UTC)
Activity: AddMailboxPermission
User: eric@ashousedemo.onmicrosoft.com
Details: AddMailboxPermission. This alert is triggered whenever someone gets access to read your user's email.

View alert details

Thank you,
The Office 365 Team

FIGURE 2-37 Office 365 Email Alert

> **MORE INFO   MANAGING ACTIVITY ALERTS**
>
> For more information about activity alerts in Office 365, visit: *https://docs.microsoft.com/office365/securitycompliance/create-activity-alerts.*

Configure and manage Azure Identity Protection dashboard and alerts

Azure AD Identity protection was introduced earlier in this chapter as a monitoring and remediation solution for cloud-based identity protection. This feature adds an important layer to your cloud security defense. However, with large environments and multiple cloud applications, alerts, and visual indicators can help raise awareness for events that are most important. In this skill section we look at customizing your Azure AD dashboard to include Identity Protection, along with customizing the default alerts.

Configure the Azure AD Identity Protection dashboard

Azure administrators that need to keep an eye on Identity Protection can pin the different reporting tiles to their Azure dashboard. This is a useful configuration option when you want to see security relevance in parallel with other critical information. To accomplish this task, follow these steps.

1. Sign-in to the Microsoft Azure portal at: *https://portal.azure.com*.

2. Click **All Services**.

3. On the All Services blade, type **Identity Protection** and select **Azure AD Identity Protection** from the list of options.

4. On the Azure AD Identity Protection – Overview blade, move your mouse over the Risk Events tile and click the more options button. Click **Pin To Dashboard**, as shown in Figure 2-38. Repeat this step for the other tiles that you want to appear on the Azure dashboard.

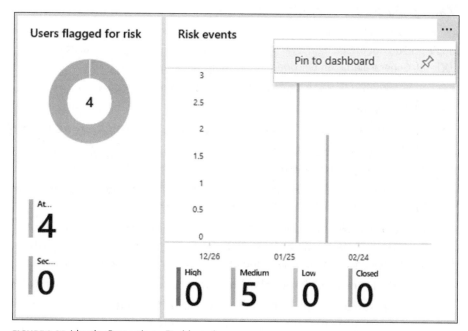

FIGURE 2-38 Identity Protection – Dashboard

5. Click **Microsoft Azure** in the top left corner to return to the Azure dashboard. The Identity Protection tile is now shown in line with the other tiles, as shown in Figure 2-39.

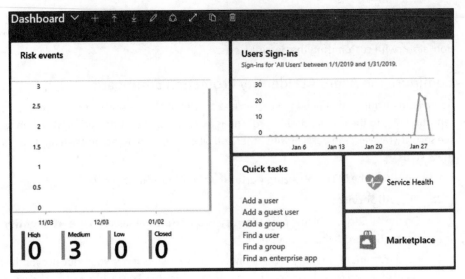

FIGURE 2-39 Identity Protection – Risk events

Manage Azure AD Identity Protection alerts

Azure AD Identity Protection includes two methods for sending alerts. Both methods are simple and do not offer a high level of customization. The fist is a general alert based on user risk level. General alerts can be configured by following these steps.

1. Sign-in to the Microsoft Azure portal at: *https://portal.azure.com*.

2. Click **All Services**.

3. On the All Services blade, type **Identity Protection** and select **Azure AD Identity Protection** from the list of options.

4. Under Settings, select **Alerts**.

5. On the Azure AD Identity Protection – Alerts blade, fill in the following information and click **Save**. Refer to Figure 8-12 for an example configuration.

    A. **Alert On User Risk Level At Or Above**   Set the user risk level. A low risk level is likely to generate more alerts and include less important events. A high risk level is likely to generate few alerts and include the most important events.

    B. **Emails Are Sent To The Following Users**   Select users from your Azure directory.

    C. **Add Additional Emails To Receive Alert Notifications**   Enter additional contacts that may not be in your Azure directory, as shown in Figure 2-40.

FIGURE 2-40 Identity Protection – Alerts

The second method for sending alerts is through the Weekly Digest. This option sends a weekly summary of new events to the included members. The summary email contains details and report links for the following categories:

- Users at risk
- Suspicious activities
- Detected vulnerabilities

To configure the weekly digest, follow these steps.

1. Sign-in to the Microsoft Azure portal at: *https://portal.azure.com*.
2. Click **All Services**.
3. On the All Services blade, type **Identity Protection** and select **Azure AD Identity Protection** from the list of options.
4. Under Settings, select **Weekly Digest**.
5. On the Azure AD Identity Protection – Weekly Digest blade, fill in the following information and click **Save**.
   A. **Weekly Email Digest** Set this switch to On.
   B. **Emails Are Sent To The Following Users** Select users from your Azure directory.

If you plan to enable both types of alerts, consider setting general alerts to Medium or High and relying on the weekly summary to address lower level risks.

Thought experiment

In this thought experiment, demonstrate your skills and knowledge of the topics covered in this chapter. You can find the answer to this thought experiment in the next section.

You are an IT administrator for Alpine Ski House, supporting 1,500 users across the United States, Europe, and Japan. Alpine Ski House has two on-premises data centers. Most of their IT infrastructure resides in the data centers. The company recently adopted a "cloud first" strategy and has been aggressively looking to expand their cloud presence. The users you support are running laptops with Windows 10, version 1809. The company recently adopted Office 365 and is working toward cloud-based solutions for their applications and services to improve the capabilities of their workforce. Today you know several users are using non-approved cloud apps for collaboration and file sharing. Your information security department would like to start exploring Microsoft Cloud App Security as a solution for monitoring and addressing security risks within Alpine Ski House. Your manager has requested that you lead the effort. You need to address the following items:

1. Your organization has an Office 365 Business Premium subscription. You need the full capabilities of Microsoft Cloud App Security. What additional licensing do you need to deploy Cloud App Security?

5. Your organization has two domains, one for the point-of-sale devices and one for general employees. How do you add these domains to your Cloud App Security portal so all devices on the network are shown as internal?

6. You are still waiting for approval to deploy a log collector on your network. What other method can you use to upload traffic logs for analysis?

7. You want to create a policy that will generate an alert when a single user performs an unusual number of downloads in a short period of time. What type of policy should you apply?

8. You are preparing to deploy an access policy for Microsoft Exchange Online. What prerequisites do you need to address before you can complete this task?

Separately, a new project from the management team is to deploy cloud-based solutions whenever they meet the project requirements. The project has a code name of "Sky High." As part of the project, the company decides to enhance the security of the environment in two ways:

- **Reduce and or eliminate phishing**   The company has had problems with phishing in the past. The company identified two key requirements: protecting specific individuals (such as high-ranking executives) and notifying users about potential phishing emails in Outlook.

- **Be notified about pass-the-hash and pass-the-ticket activity**   The company has heard about the dangerous of pass-the-hash and pass-the-ticket and wants to be notified about activity as soon as it occurs.

You need to choose solutions for the Microsoft Cloud App Security project and to address the company's goals of enhancing their security. What should you do?

Thought experiment answers

This section contains the solution to the thought experiment. Each answer explains why the answer choice is correct.

1. You will need to procure Cloud App Security licenses, obtainable through an EMS E5 subscription.

2. These domains can be added to the Cloud App Security portal by navigation to the **Settings** page and selecting **Organization** details. Enter your domains in the **Managed** domains field.

3. You can do a static log upload through snapshot reports. To complete this task, navigate to the Settings page and select Snapshot reports. Create a new snapshot report, select the matching data source, and upload the corresponding log files in the verified format.

4. You can create an activity policy to achieve this behavior. You can also use the built-in policy template: Mass Download By A Single User.

5. You will need an active Azure AD Premium P1 subscription to support Conditional Access policies. Then you will need to create a Conditional Access policy for Microsoft Exchange Online that has Use Conditional Access App Control enabled.

For the "Sky High" project, you need two solutions: one solution to address phishing and the other to address pass-the-hash and pass-the-ticket. To address phishing, you should implement ATP anti-phishing, which comes with Office 365 E5 or the Office 365 ATP add-on for other enterprise subscriptions. Potentially, use the anti-phishing capabilities of Office 365, although that would reduce the features. One key feature that would be missing is the ability to add specific users to protect (and this is something the company wants to use). For the pass-the-hash and pass-the-ticket solution, you could implement Microsoft ATA or Azure ATP. Both would notify you about pass-the-hash and pass-the-ticket. However, because the company has a specific mandate to deploy cloud-based solutions when they meet the requirements, you should implement Azure ATP in this scenario.

Chapter summary

- You should have a good understanding on how to navigate the various configuration settings in the Cloud App Security portal. Remember that there is a search field at the top of the settings page. This is helpful as you explore the various settings. Keep in mind that some settings are specific to certain elements in the portal. For example, file policies will require that you enable file monitoring.

- You should have a good understanding of each Cloud App Security policy type, what purpose they serve, and how to create them.

- You should be familiar with how Cloud App Security operates and what benefits it delivers to an organization.

- You should be familiar with how to navigate alerts in the Cloud App Security portal and how to dismiss or resolve alerts based on your findings.

- There are different data upload options available in the Cloud App Security portal, such as using a snapshot versus continues uploads. You should be familiar with setting up a data source and log collector in the Cloud App Security portal, providing continuous log uploads.

- Azure ATP is a cloud-based threat protection solution for your on-premises domain controllers.

- ATA is an on-premises threat protection solution for your on-premises domain controllers. The feature set is the same.

- Microsoft provides multiple ATP solutions. Azure ATP, Windows Defender ATP (for your client devices), and Office 365 ATP (focused around email protection).

- Azure ATP and ATA integrate with other key technologies including Azure Security Center, Windows Defender ATP, VPN solutions, and SIEM solutions (or syslog servers). Integrating with these other technologies enhances detection capabilities.

- ATA offers two types of agents. The ATA Gateway is deployed to a member server or standalone server (but not a domain controller) and requires port mirroring. The ATA Lightweight Gateway is installed on domain controllers and does not require port mirroring. For the highest performing scenario (number of packets captured per second), the ATA Gateway is the best choice.

- Office 365 has built-in anti-phishing protection. For additional anti-phishing features, you need to deploy Office 365 ATP which offers more granular control and additional settings.

- Office 365 has built-in anti-spam protection. Office 365 ATP does not offer any additional enhancements for anti-spam. There is a myriad of anti-spam settings to control how aggressive the anti-spam protection is, what happens when spam is detected, and how users are notified about spam or potentially malicious messages.

- Office 365 provides multiple policies to combat spam. Each policy has a role in the overall protection. There is an anti-spam policy (where you find most of the anti-spam settings), a connection filter policy (to whitelist or blacklist IPs), an outbound spam filter policy (only for outbound email messages), and a spoof intelligence policy (which you can use to decide what to do in a situation where a user or domain was spoofed).

- You should test your anti-malware protection by using the EICAR.TXT file and sending it through email. EICAR.TXT should be picked up as malware although it is benign. The primary purpose of testing is to validate the notifications and end user experience, in addition to the protection itself.

- Office 365 includes built-in protection against phishing. You can extend that by creating your own anti-phishing policies. You can extend that farther by obtaining ATP anti-phishing, which provides impersonation settings and advanced settings.

- Office 365 Threat Intelligence, included with Office 365 Enterprise E5, provides additional tools to help secure your environment. Three key tools in Threat Intelligence are attack simulators for spear phishing attacks, brute force password attacks, and password spray attacks.

- To troubleshoot email messages that might have been flagged as spam or as malware, you can use the Message Trace tool. The Message Trace tool can help you find out if an email messages was dropped and will also tell you why it was dropped.

- You can configure ATA to notify you via email about suspicious activities. Optionally, you can integrate ATA with your SIEM solution and have your SIEM solution notify you instead. This is helpful if you want to have a single place for all IT alerts.

- To maximize the information ATA gets and to enhance the detection capabilities, you should forward events 4776, 4732, 4733, 4728, 4729, 4756, 4757, and 7045 to ATA. This is only required when you use ATA Gateways (not ATA Lightweight Gateways).

- You can use the ATA Health Center to review alerts and other health information about your environment.

- You need to have Windows 10 Education or Enterprise E3 or E5 to obtain Windows Defender ATP for your Windows 10 devices.

- If you want to use Windows Defender ATP with Windows 7 or Windows 8.1, you need to turn on the preview feature, which enables the integration with down-level clients. This will likely be a permanent feature in future releases.

- All Windows Defender clients must be able to communicate with the Windows Defender ATP service URLs over port 80 and port 443. Use of a proxy server is supported.

- You can configure your SIEM solution to get alerts from Windows Defender Security Center through a REST API.

- For enterprise environments, you should use role-based access permissions. This enables you to adhere to the principle of least privilege, which ensures that administrators only have the minimum permissions needed to do their jobs.

- In high security environments, such as in government agencies, military settings, or high-risk private enterprises, you should look at cloud-delivered protection, an optional feature of Windows Defender ATP.

- If you want to ensure you have reporting when onboarding clients, use Intune or ConfigMgr for the onboarding process. Both have built-in reporting. Avoid Group Policy and scripts if reporting is required.

- Offboarding clients is like onboarding clients. You deploy an offboarding package through your preferred software distribution method. Data remains available for 6 months after onboarding.

- When troubleshooting Windows 10 devices, check the services named Connected User Experiences and Telemetry and the Windows Defender Advanced Threat Protection Service.

- Windows Defender Antivirus (Windows Defender AV) is a built-in anti-malware solution that provides real-time protection, cloud-delivered protection, and automatic sample submission.

- Windows Defender Exploit Guard is a new intrusion prevention solution for Windows 10 clients. It offers exploit protection, attack surface reduction, network protection, and controlled folder access.

- To gain access to all the Windows Defender Exploit Guard features, you need to be licensed for Windows 10 Enterprise E5.

- To understand the impacts of Exploit Guard, you can enable audit mode and review the auditing information after a few days.

- In skill 2.4 we reviewed the service assurance feature, including setup and navigation of the various documents and reports that Microsoft provides.

- You should be familiar with the prerequisites for setting up service assurance, including licensing, permissions, and configuring your region and industry.

- You should be familiar with each of the sections in service assurance and what information is available, specifically: compliance reports, trust documents, and the compliance manager.

- In skill 2.4 we introduced Azure AD Identity Protection. This skill covered prerequisites, onboarding, and navigation of the various reports.

- You should be familiar with the prerequisites for Identity Protection, in particular the Azure AD Premium P2 subscription requirement.

- You should be familiar with the Identity Protection dashboard and each of the reports and what information they provide. This includes users flagged for risk, risk events, and vulnerabilities.

- In skill 2.4 we explored the alerts available in the Office 365 Security and Compliance Center. This included a walkthrough of the alerts dashboard, drilldown reports, and configuration of alert policies.

- You should be familiar with the Alerts dashboard, how to pin tiles to the home page, and how to navigate the drilldown reports.

- You should be familiar with the default alert policies and what events they alert on.

- You should be familiar with creating custom alert policies and what controls are available.

- In skill 2.4 we reviewed how to configure the Identity Protection dashboard and configure alerts.

- You should be familiar with the steps to pin and unpin the Identity Protection tiles to the Azure dashboard.

- You should be familiar with the steps for configuring general alerts and the weekly digest email summary.

CHAPTER 3

Manage Microsoft 365 governance and compliance

This chapter looks at the key technologies for governance and compliance in Office 365. You should complete this chapter with a good understanding of which technologies are suitable based on a given scenario with specific requirements. You should also have a firm grasp of environment prerequisites, integration with other technologies, and common configurations. While focusing on five key technologies, you should familiarize yourself with complementary technologies to help solidify your knowledge for this area of the exam.

Skills covered in this chapter:

- Configure Data Loss Prevention (DLP)
- Implement Azure Information Protection
- Manage data governance
- Manage auditing
- Manage eDiscovery

Skill 3.1: Configure Data Loss Prevention (DLP)

Data Loss Prevention (DLP) is a technology made up of hardware and software to prevent, minimize, or protect against data loss or unauthorized access to data. Specific to Microsoft 365 and Office 365, DLP is a security feature to protect against data loss, data leakage, and unauthorized viewing of data in Exchange Online, SharePoint Online, and OneDrive for Business. In some cases, DLP is used to enable a company to meet compliance or government regulations. In other cases, DLP is used to enhance the security of an organization (from intellectual property loss, for example). DLP is one technology, and is intended to be layered with other security technologies such as data encryption, threat management, and anti-malware.

This is a hands-on skill section. Your goal should be to understand how to create, configure, and manage DLP policies with an emphasis on the configuration. Be prepared for questions related to different DLP policy settings. DLP policies are a key element of DLP, enabling you to implement protection mechanisms for your data. In this section, we will walk through how DLP works, then go through the creation of a DLP policy, and end by looking at configuring a DLP policy.

Understand how DLP works

Data Loss Prevention (DLP) is a technology that enables you to minimize the leakage of sensitive data. In Office 365, DLP is integrated with Exchange Online (and thus Outlook on the web and Outlook), SharePoint Online, and OneDrive for Business. Additionally, it helps protect information in the desktop versions of Excel, PowerPoint, and Word.

DLP relies on content analysis to detect information you have defined as sensitive. The content analysis includes the following methods:

- **Dictionary Matches**   DLP scans your dictionaries for matches (if you have any dictionaries). You can create optional dictionaries containing lists of sensitive information. A single dictionary supports up to 100,000 terms. For adding of a couple of keyword terms, you can opt to use keyword lists instead. Keyword lists are available as a way to manage smaller keyword lists.

- **Keyword Matches**   DLP scans for keywords that you define in keyword lists in sensitive information types. You do this by modifying a built-in sensitive information type.

- **Regular Expression Matches**   Sometimes, you need to protect company-specific sensitive information, such as internal project names or numbers. You can create a custom sensitive information type and use regular expressions to define the criteria. DLP will scan using the defined regular expressions.

- **Internal Functions**   DLP uses many internal functions to facilitate the built-in functionality. For example, one internal function is used to identify credit card information. The internal function `func_expiration_date` looks for date formats often used by credit cards such as 12/25 (for December of 2025).

By default, there are not any DLP policies. You need to create them. You can use the built-in templates to cover common use cases, such as protecting health information and financial information. Because these policies are used across multiple technologies, they must sync after creating them (or after modifying them). Figure 3-1 shows an overview of the sync process.

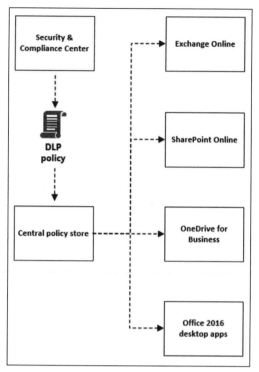

FIGURE 3-1 DLP policy sync process

The following list describes the DLP policy sync process.

1. You create a new DLP policy in the Security & Compliance Center. Note that all new policies are created there.

2. The DLP policy syncs to the central policy store.

3. From the central policy store, the DLP policy syncs to Exchange Online (and from there, Outlook on the web and Outlook), SharePoint Online, OneDrive for Business, and Office desktop apps (Word, Excel, PowerPoint).

4. After the syncing process completes, DLP begins to evaluate content in each of the services, based on the DLP policies.

> **NOTE   DLP SIDE-BY-SIDE**
>
> You might be wondering what happens if you have DLP policies in Exchange Online and in the Security & Compliance Center. In short, they work side-by-side. DLP policies in Exchange Online can only be used while DLP policies created in Security & Compliance Center are used across all integrated technologies. When the policies in Security & Compliance Center meet all of your needs, use it to simplify your environment. DLP policies in Exchange Online have additional email functionality that isn't available with policies created in the Security & Compliance Center.

DLP policies have the following characteristics:

- **Where to protect content** Use locations to configure where to protect content, such as Exchange Online, SharePoint Online, or OneDrive for Business.

- **When to protect content** Use conditions to configure when to protect content. For example, you might have a condition stating that a driver's license number must be shared with people outside of your organization. Conditions are stored in rules.

- **How to protect content** Use actions to configure what action should be taken when matching content is discovered. For example, you can configure an action to restrict access or notify a user. Actions are stored in rules.

Create DLP policies

You can create DLP policies from the Security & Compliance Center, or by using PowerShell. You should be familiar with both methods for the exam. Let's look at the steps for creating a new DLP policy in the portal.

1. Starting in the Security & Compliance Center, click the **+Create A Policy** button, as shown in Figure 3-2.

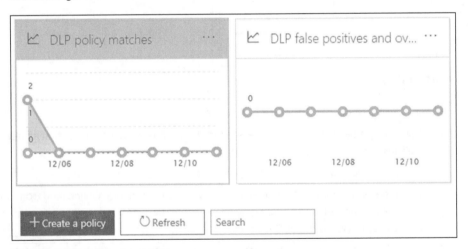

FIGURE 3-2 DLP policy sync process

2. A DLP wizard will present existing categories that have built-in templates, or you can choose to create a custom policy from scratch. For this example, click **Privacy,** click **U.S. Personally Identifiable Information (PII) Data**, and then click **Next** as shown in Figure 3-3.

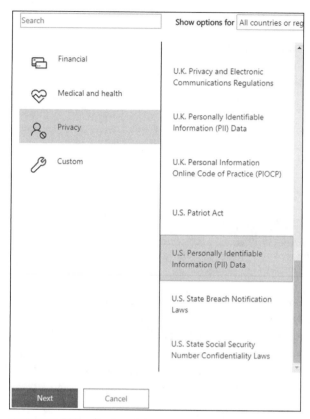

FIGURE 3-3 DLP policy templates

3. Type a name for the policy. Optionally, you can enter a description. For this demonstration, we'll use the default name. Click **Next**.

4. By default, all DLP policies will protect content in all supported locations (such as email, OneDrive and SharePoint). If you are creating a specific policy for a specific platform, you can opt to choose the specific services instead. For this demonstration, we want to protect content in all locations, so click **Next**.

5. In this template, there is specific information that the policy is configured to look for (and how aggressive it labels data by using a match accuracy number). You can click **Edit** to change that. By default, DLP will detect when content that contains personally identifiable data is shared with people outside your organization. You can opt to detect whenever data is shared only inside your organization. However, if you want to detect in all sharing scenarios, you need two policies. Alternatively, you can use advanced settings. With advanced settings, you can adjust the rules in the policy. This is useful if you want to add more conditions or exceptions to the configuration. Figure 3-4 shows the DLP policy content detected configuration.

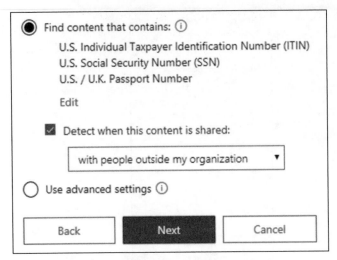

FIGURE 3-4 DLP policy content detection configuration

6. On the Notify Users When Content Matches The Policy Settings page, choose how users are notified when PII is detected. By default, a policy tip is shown to users, and users get an email notification. You can customize the tip and the email, if desired. You can also change the number of times sharing sensitive data must occur before detecting it as a violation. Finally, you can opt to restrict access to the data if there is PII or encrypt the data (such as with Azure Information Protection) Figure 3-5 shows the available options.

Notify users when content matches the policy settings

☑ Show policy tips to users and send them an email notification.
Tips appear to users in their apps (like Outlook, OneDrive, and SharePoint) and help them learn how can use the default tip or customize it to your liking. Learn more about notifications and tips

Customize the tip and email

Detect when a specific amount of sensitive info is being shared at one time

☑ Detect when content that's being shared contains:
At least [10] instances of the same sensitive info type.

  ☑ Send incident reports in email
  By default, you and your global admin will automatically receive the email.
  Choose what to include in the report and who receives it

  ☐ Restrict access or encrypt the content

  [Back] [Next] [Cancel]

FIGURE 3-5 DLP policy sync process

7. On the **Do You Want To Turn On The Policy Or Test Things Out First?** page, decide if you want to turn on the policy now, keep the policy off, or test it. By default, the policy will be in test mode. It is a good practice to test new policies first. For our demonstration, accept the default settings of test and then click **Next.**

8. On the **Review Your Settings** page, look at the settings to ensure they are correct and then click **Create.** Figure 3-6 shows the policy review page.

FIGURE 3-6 DLP policy settings review page

9. After creation, you will see the policy and status in the console. It can take up to an hour before the policy takes effect, as shown in Figure 3-7.

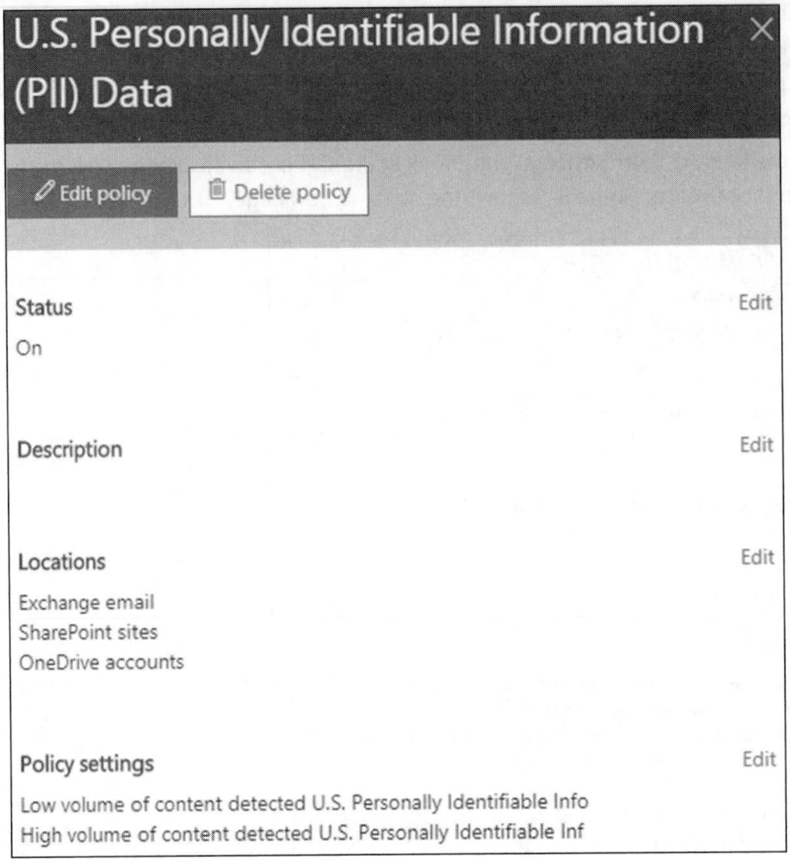

U.S. Personally Identifiable Information (PII) Data ✕

| ✏ Edit policy | 🗑 Delete policy |

Status   Edit
On

Description   Edit

Locations   Edit
Exchange email
SharePoint sites
OneDrive accounts

Policy settings   Edit
Low volume of content detected U.S. Personally Identifiable Info
High volume of content detected U.S. Personally Identifiable Inf

FIGURE 3-7 DLP policy overview

Next, let's review how to create a policy by using PowerShell. First, connect to the Security & Compliance Center. The following commands show you how to get connected. In your environment, follow these steps if you want to try some of the later commands in this chapter.

1. Open a PowerShell prompt.

2. Run the `$Credential = Get-Credential` command. In the credential window, enter your administrative credentials and then click **OK**. This stores the credentials in `$Credential` and can be reference in follow-on commands.

3. Run the `$Session = New-PSSession -ConfigurationName Microsoft.Exchange -ConnectionUri https://ps.compliance.protection.outlook.com/powershell-liveid/ -Credential $UserCredential -Authentication Basic -AllowRedirection` command. This command connects you to a remote PowerShell session for the **Security & Compliance Center.**

4. Run the `Import-PSSession $Session -DisableNameChecking` command. This command imports the cmdlets that you'll use to work with the Security & Compliance Center.

Next, you are ready to create a new DLP policy. Follow the next steps to create a new DLP policy.

1. After connecting PowerShell to the Security & Compliance Center, run the `New-DlpCompliancePolicy -Name "Sales"` command. This creates a new DLP policy named Sales. Because options were not specified, this policy is turned on, but isn't protecting any locations, so this policy isn't very usable.

2. Next, let's create a policy that protects all locations. Run the `New-DlpCompliancePolicy -Name "Legal" -ExchangeLocation All -SharePointLocation All -OneDriveLocation All -Mode Enable` command. Now, you have a blank policy that is protecting all locations, and you just need some rules.

3. Next, let's create a rule for our new Legal DLP policy. In this case, the rule will block the phrase "lorem ipsum" if it is shared with anybody outside the organization. Run the `New-DlpComplianceRule -Name "Block legalese" -Policy Legal -AccessScope NotInOrganization -BlockAccess $true -ContentPropertyContainsWords "lorem ipsum" -Disabled $false` command.

After creating a policy, the portal shows only limited information about it. You can use PowerShell to view additional information, which is useful in a troubleshooting scenario. For example, after policy creation, you might want to see if the policy was distributed successfully. To check the distribution status and results, run the `Get-DlpCompliancePolicy | select Name, DistributionStatus,DistributionResults -ExpandProperty DistributionResults` command. The following output shows an error with the distribution status.

```
Name                 : U.S. Personally Identifiable Information (PII) Data
DistributionStatus   : Error
DistributionResults  : {[OneDriveForBusiness]All:It's taking longer than expected
 to deploy the policy. It might take an additional 2 hours to update the final
 deployment status, so check back in a couple hours.}


Endpoint             : All
ObjectId             : e38407a8-5a9f-4c1d-b068-fca20b21baa0
ObjectType           : Scope
Workload             : OneDriveForBusiness
ResultCode           : PolicySyncTimeout
ResultMessage        : It's taking longer than expected to deploy the policy.
It might take an additional 2 hours to update the final deployment status,
so check back in a couple hours.
LastResultTime       : 12/3/2018 3:11:55 AM
AdditionalDiagnostics :
Severity             : Error
```

If you have more than one DLP policy, then policies are ordered, with each policy having an order number. The order number is shown when viewing policies in the portal. When getting information about policies from PowerShell, however, the term "priority" is used. An order of 3 is the same as a priority of 3. The first policy you create has an order or priority of 1. The second one has an order or priority of two, and so on. You can't change the order, and the lower the number, the higher the priority. When you have multiple policies that have conflicting rules, the most restrictive action is enforced. Here is an example of how priority works in action.

1. Rule 1 (priority / order 1), restricts access, allows user overrides
2. Rule 2 (priority / order 2), restricts access, notifies users, does not allow user overrides
3. Rule 2 (priority / order 3), notifies users, does not restrict access
4. Rule 4 (priority / order 4), restricts access, does not notify users
5. Rule 5 (priority / order 5), restricts access, notifies users, does not allow user overrides

If you send an email that matches all of the rules (rule 1, 2, 3 and 4), then Rule 2 is enforced. That's because Rule 2 is the most restrictive and highest priority. Note that Rule 2 and Rule 5 offer the same restrictions. Rule 2 is higher priority, so it ends up being the rule enforced.

Configure DLP policies

You can configure DLP policies when you create them or after you create them. Often, you'll configure DLP policies during creation and after creation (tweaking settings to enhance the outcome). In the configuration section, we first look at some key settings. After that, we'll walk through some of the policy settings.

Each policy can have three states.

- **Turned on**   When a policy is on, it evaluates content and takes actions, as configured.
- **Turned off**   When a policy is off, it does not evaluate content or take any action. Sometimes, administrators prefer to create policies with them being off, have the policies reviewed by a peer, and then turn them on during a maintenance window.
- **In test mode**   You can test a rule before turning it on by using test mode. Optionally, you can have policy tips shown in test mode. It is a good practice to use test mode, run DLP reports, and then make necessary tweaks before turning on a policy.

Rules can have two states:

- **Turned on**   By default, rules are turned on in a policy. Turning off rules is useful for troubleshooting.
- **Turned off**   If you are troubleshooting a policy or find an issue with a rule in a policy (too restrictive, for example), you can temporarily turn off a rule. After making changes, you can turn the rule back on.

Policies can protect information in three locations. Inside of each location, you have additional options, as follows:

- **Exchange Online**   You can specify specific distribution groups to be included for protection. You can also specify distribution groups to be excluded.
- **SharePoint Online**   You can specify specific SharePoint sites to be included or opt to exclude specific SharePoint sites.
- **OneDrive for Business**   For OneDrive for Business, you can include specific accounts or exclude specific accounts.

Next, we will review policy conditions in a rule. Figure 3-8 shows the conditions for content.

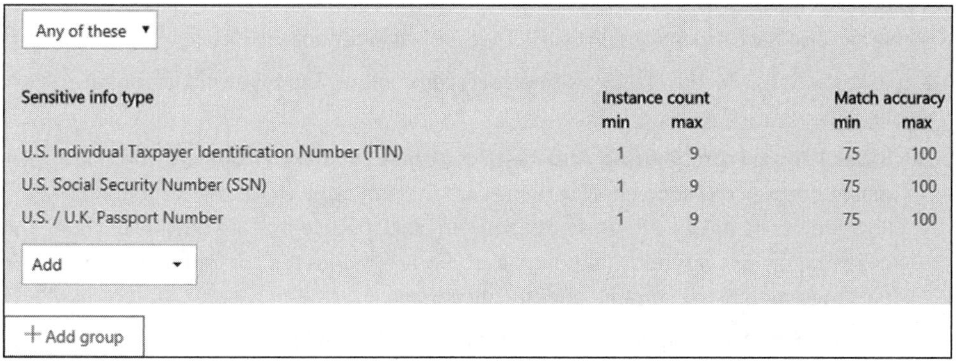

Any of these ▾					
Sensitive info type		Instance count		Match accuracy	
		min	max	min	max
U.S. Individual Taxpayer Identification Number (ITIN)		1	9	75	100
U.S. Social Security Number (SSN)		1	9	75	100
U.S. / U.K. Passport Number		1	9	75	100

Add ▾

+ Add group

FIGURE 3-8 DLP policy sync process

In this rule, there are three sensitive info types defined. This is a low volume rule and is intended to be triggered if there is between 1 and 9 instances of the sensitive info types, while falling between a match accuracy of 75 to 100. You can change the minimum and maximum instance counts and the minimum and maximum match accuracy numbers. For example, you could change the max instance count to 5 and handle everything above that in a high-volume rule.

As part of conditions, you can dictate whether a rule applies to content shared within your organization or outside of your organization. You can add conditions too. The list of conditions you can add is:

- **Sender IP Address Is** Use this condition to detect content sent from a specific IP address or range of IP addresses.

- **Any Email Attachment's Content Could Not Be Scanned** Use this condition to have the rule flag email with attachments that cannot be scanned.

- **Any Email Attachment's Content Didn't Complete Scanning** Use this condition to have the rule flag email with attachments that did not finish scanning.

- **Attachment Is Password Protected** Use this rule to message an attachment that is password protected (and thus, can't be opened to be scanned).

- **Recipient Domain Is** Use this condition to detect when content is sent to a specific domain (you can specify more than one domain too).

- **Attachment's File Extension Is** Use this condition to detect email messages with attachments that have a specific file extension (and you can specify multiple extensions so any match counts). For example, you might specify .exe as one file extension.

- **Document Property Is** Use this condition to match data that has document properties. Document properties are used in Windows Server File Classification Infrastructure (FCI), SharePoint, and other third-party systems. Some organizations already use document properties to classify content (for example, to classify sensitive data). In such organizations, it can be very efficient to reuse the document properties for DLP.

A rule can also have exceptions. In Skill 9.3, we look at exceptions in detail.

A rule has actions which dictate how to protect the content. The following actions are available:

- **Block People From Sharing And Restrict Access To Shared Content**   Blocking means people can't send email with the content, and can't access the content in SharePoint or OneDrive for Business. You can block people that are outside of your organization, or everybody (although everybody excludes the content owner, the last person to modify the content, and the site admin).

- **Encrypt Email Messages**   This action is only applicable to Exchange Online. This action encrypts email messages using Azure Information Protection.

Each rule has user notification settings. You can opt to notify users or not, based on your goals. It is a good practice to notify users because it helps them understand the sensitivity of the data and think through the proper data usage. Beyond notifying the user who sent, shared, or last modified the offending content, you can also email the SharePoint site owner, the owner of the OneDrive account or content, and additional people as designated by you. You can enable users to override a policy if they see a policy tip. However, this isn't a good practice when dealing with sensitive data, barring exceptions. This is because it adds risk to your organization by enabling users to bypass a DLP policy.

Design data retention policies in Microsoft 365

Data retention is an Office 365 feature that is part of data governance. You use data retention to ensure that important (or necessary) data is kept while unneeded data is not kept. This helps organizations manage their data and avoid accumulating vast amounts of data (such as by accumulating everything, forever). Note that this section covers "Design data retention policies in Microsoft 365" and "Plan information retention policies."

Understand how data retention policies work

Data retention works through policies. You can have one policy for everything or you can have a plethora of policies targeting specific users or types of content. If you don't have any policies, then you don't have DLP. Data retention policies have two primary duties:

- **To preserve content in its original form throughout the defined retention period**   While the original content is retained, it is not retained in its original location throughout the retention period. Preserving content is optional.

- **Delete content at the end of a retention period**   This is optional. You can choose to automatically delete content after a retention period or leave the content as is. To effectively manage their overall storage consumption, many organizations choose to automatically delete content after a retention period.

You can target content for retention based strictly on age. For example, your company might opt to keep everything for seven years. In such a scenario, the content of the data, who created it, or where it is stored, is irrelevant-all data must be kept for seven years. You have other options for targeting content. You can target events (new hire, employee terminations) or you can use labels. For example, you might use labels for files related to tax matters and tax forms. This enables you to retain specific types of data for a desired period.

A copy of the original content is made when content under retention is modified during the retention period. The storage location differs based on the location of the original content (see Figure 3-9).

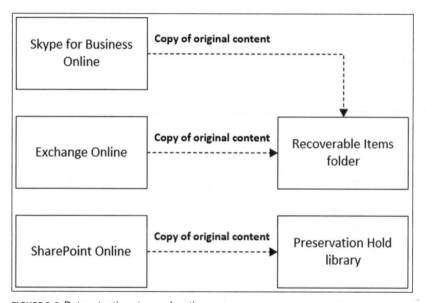

FIGURE 3-9 Data retention storage locations

In Figure 3-9, the diagram shows that original content in Skype is copied to the Recoverable Items folder, original content in Exchange Online is copied to the Recoverable Items folder, and original content in SharePoint Online is copied to the Preservation Hold library. Users continue to work with the original content in its original location. In fact, they aren't even aware of the copy process preserving an original copy of the data!

For data deletion, there is a series of steps that are followed based on the configuration. In Figure 3-10 we walk through the deletion process from a SharePoint Online perspective.

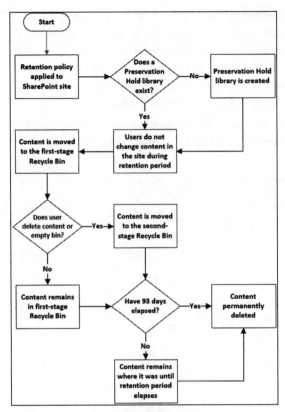

FIGURE 3-10 Data retention deletion flow chart

Below, we walk through the diagram in Figure 3-10.

1. **Retention Policy Applied To A SharePoint Site**. Note that all the steps in this walk-through are specific to SharePoint and OneDrive. Other steps are similar but have small differences.

2. **Does A Preservation Hold Library Exist**? A check is performed to find out. If one doesn't exist, it is created.

3. **Users Do Not Change Content In The Site During Retention Period**. In this case, content is moved to the first-stage Recycle Bin. While not shown in the diagram, if content is changed, a copy of the original content is copied to the Preservation Hold library.

4. **Content Is Moved To The First-Stage Recycle Bin**. This happens at the end of the retention period.

5. **Does User Delete Content Or Empty Bin**? If yes, the content is moved to the second-stage Recycle Bin. If no, content remains in the first-stage Recycle Bin.

6. **Have 93 Days Elapsed**? If yes, content is permanently deleted. If no, content remains where it was until the retention period elapses. Note that 93 days is how long content remains in the first-stage Recycle Bin, second-stage Recycle Bin, or in both bins (for example, spend time in each before permanent deletion).

Some organizations automatically delete data after a retention period. Other organizations prefer to review content prior to permanent deletion (to ensure that they don't lose something important). You can use the Disposition page in the Security & Compliance Center to review content prior to deletion. Note that disposition reviews require an Office 365 / Microsoft 365 Enterprise E5 subscription.

As part of the Office 365 preview program, you can try out the file plan manager. This tool enables you to manage your labels and policies throughout their lifecycle.

Create data retention policies in the portal

Data retention policies are the backbone of your data retention strategy. Without them, you don't have data retention. You should be familiar with creating policies from the portal and from PowerShell.

Your data retention policies can work with data in the following locations.

- **Exchange Email**   This location is specific to email. You can specify recipients for data retention or exclude specific recipients.

- **SharePoint Sites**   For SharePoint sites, you can choose specific sites or exclude specific sites.

- **OneDrive Accounts**   For OneDrive accounts, you can choose specific accounts or exclude specific accounts.

- **Office 365 groups**. This includes associated group mailbox, site, files, conversations, and OneNote data.

- **Skype for Business**   With Skype for Business, you select individual users for data retention. By selecting all individuals, you effective retain all Skype for Business data.

- **Exchange Public Folders**   You can retain your public folder data in Exchange by using this location.

- **Teams Channel Messages**   This location enables you to specify specific teams and exclude specific teams. You can select all teams too.

- **Teams Chats**   This location enables you to choose individual users or exclude specific users. Optionally, you can select all users to cover everything. Note that when you turn on either of the Teams location, you will not be able to specify other locations in the same policy.

Let's create a new data retention policy from the Security & Compliance Center.

1. Sign into the **Security & Compliance Center** then expand the **Data Governance** section.

2. Click **Retention** in the left pane.

3. In the right pane, click **+Create**.

4. On the **Name Your Policy** page, type a name for the policy. For our walk-through, use the name **Tax**. Then click **Next**.

5. On the **Decide If You Want To Retain Content, Delete It, Or Both** page, set the **Yes, I Want To Retain It** setting to **10** years. By default, the content will be retained based on the creation date. Optionally, you can base it on the last modified date. Under the **Do You Want Us To Delete It After This Time?** question, click the **Yes** radio button. This enables automatic deletion after the retention period. Then click **Next**.

6. On the **Choose Locations** page, click the **Apply Policy Only To Content In Exchange Email, Public Folders, Office 365 Groups, Onedrive, And Sharepoint Documents** radio button. Optionally, you can choose the location individually. Click **Next** to continue.

7. On the **Review Your Settings** page, look at the settings to ensure they match your desired settings. Then, click **Create This Policy**.

The policy is turned on by default. After creation, you will see the policy in the list of policies.

Create data retention policies by using PowerShell

If you are creating one or two policies, using the portal is enough. If, however, you are creating many policies, you should use PowerShell, which can save you time when working with many objects.

You can create, manage, and delete policies by using PowerShell. In the examples to follow, you must first connect to the Security & Compliance Center in PowerShell. The following command creates a new data retention policy named "IT" and only enforces the policy for the mailboxes of Brian Svidergol and Bob Clements.

```
New-RetentionCompliancePolicy -Name 'IT' -ExchangeLocation 'Brian Svidergol',
 'Bob Clements'
```

After you create a policy, you need to create rules. By default, new policies created by using PowerShell do not have any rules. So data is not retained. The following command creates a new retention rule in the IT policy named IT-5-years and retains data for 5 years (based on days).

```
New-RetentionComplianceRule -Name 'IT-5-years' -Policy 'IT' -RetentionDuration 1825
```

Because we didn't specify any conditions for the rule, all Exchange data will be retained for Brian Svidergol and Bob Clements. Optionally, you can specify the specific information to retain using a content search filter, or by specifying a sensitive information type. Also note that this policy retains data for 5 years, but it does not delete data after the retention period. The

`RetentionComplianceAction` optional parameter enables you to specify an action for a rule, such as Delete, Keep, or KeepAndDelete. If you specify Delete, then data is deleted after the retention period. Optionally, you can create a retention policy that just deletes data after the content is a specific age.

> **MORE INFO**
>
> To review all the available cmdlet parameters for New-RetentionComplianceRule, see: *https://docs.microsoft.com/en-us/powershell/module/exchange/policy-and-compliance-retention/new-retentioncompliancerule?view=exchange-ps.*

Manage DLP exceptions

So far, you've learned how DLP works and how a policy and a set of rules prevent or minimize data leakage. Next, we will look at exceptions. Exceptions are conditions that dictate when a DLP rule won't apply to content. For example, you might have a DLP rule to protect tax data. However, you might have an exception if a document has a specific property and value (for example, a property named Description with a value of Personal.

Understand DLP exceptions

Before you start implementing exceptions, you should have a good understanding of their capabilities. Thereafter, you should know how to create and modify exceptions. In a perfect world, you wouldn't need any exceptions and your DLP configuration would be simple and easy to work with. But, many times, exceptions are required to meet your goals. Even so, you should try to keep your configuration as simple as possible while also meeting your requirements.

The available exceptions are:

- **Except If Content Contains Sensitive Information** This exception enables you to specify sensitive information types or specific labels. In such scenarios, the content will not be subject to the rule.

- **Except If Content Is Shared** This exception enables you to specify content shared internally or externally and to ensure such content will not be subject to the rule.

- **Except If Sender IP Address Is** If you want to white list a specific IP address or IP address range, you can use this exception.

- **Except If Any Email Attachment Content Could Not Be Scanned** This exception applies if an email message has an attachment that cannot be scanned.

- **Except If Any Email Attachment Content Didn't Complete Scanning** This exception applies if an email message has an attachment that does not finish scanning.

- **Except If Attachment Is Password Protected** This exception applies if an email attachment has a password (and thus can't be scanned).

- **Except If A Recipient Domain Is** If you want to white list a domain, or multiple domains, you can use this exception. For example, imagine that you use DLP for external communication. You acquire a company, and after the acquisition closes, you need to ensure that email going to the acquired company's domain is not part of DLP.

- **Except If Attachment's File Extension Is**   If you want to white list specific file extensions for attachments, you can use this exception.

- **Except If Document Property Is**   Use this exception to check document properties for specific property values. In this scenario, you can exclude specific content based on the values.

Note that some settings are service specific. For example, when using an exception with recipient domain, it is limited to use with Exchange / email. As with most DLP settings, you should test them before you implement them in production. Otherwise, you might end up with undesirable behavior because it can be hard to understand the ramifications of an exception without seeing it work with production data.

Create DLP exceptions

You can create exceptions during your initial DLP rule creation. However, many times you'll find that you need to create exceptions after a policy and rule are deployed. You can do so by editing the rule in the portal. For example, in Figure 3-11 a rule is configured to protect email messages that contain IP addresses. Later, we added an exception for email sent to the contoso.com domain. This might be useful if you have a vendor or partner that handles your customer service department or tech support department and you will routinely send IP addresses to them via email (such as in trouble tickets or support email).

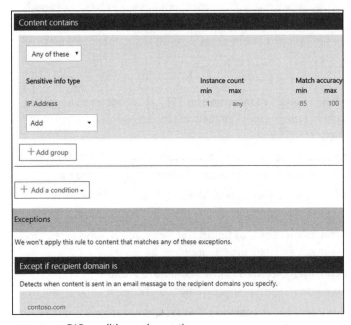

FIGURE 3-11 DLP condition and exception

When you create exceptions, always use test mode to understand the impacts of the exceptions on your detection behavior.

Monitor DLP policy matches

After you deploy DLP policies, you need a way to find out if they are working and how effective they are. You also need a way to pinpoint problems or unexpected behavior. Monitoring is an effective way to understand how DLP is functioning in your environment.

Use policy tips

Policy tips are small information messages displayed in a web page or in a client (such as Outlook). Often, tips are used to provide information to users. For example, if a user is sending an email message that violates a DLP policy, a policy tip can notify the user prior to the user sending the email. The user then has a chance to rectify the violation before sending the email. In Figure 3-12, a policy tip is shown in Outlook. In this scenario, Brian is sending Bob a message and there is a conflict with a DLP policy.

FIGURE 3-12 Policy tip in Outlook

In Figure 3-12, the policy tip is the default text. There are other default policy tips (such as when access to an item is blocked). Note that the default text does not indicate the DLP policy that was violated or provide much information for the user. Optionally, you can customize the text. Customization is per rule. In The customized tip configuration is shown in Figure 3-13.

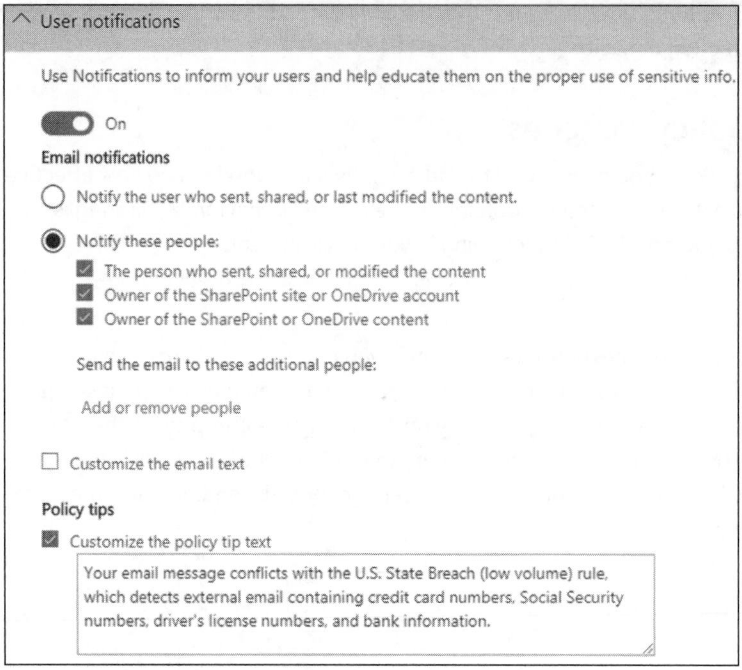

FIGURE 3-13 Customized policy tip

When you use policy tips, you have an option to enable users that have seen the policy tip to override the DLP policy. You can require them to report false positives or enter a business justification for the override.

Beyond modifying policy tips in the portal, you can also use PowerShell. For example, you can use the `Set-DlpComplianceRule` cmdlet with the `-NotifyPolicyTipCustomText` parameter to set the custom policy tip text in a rule.

Use incident reports

DLP incident reports show you DLP policy matches by date and service (Exchange / SharePoint / OneDrive for Business). You can view it in the Reports section of the Security & Compliance Center (on the dashboard). Figure 3-14 shows the DLP incidents report along with neighboring information. You can click the DLP incidents graph to go to the larger dedicated screen.

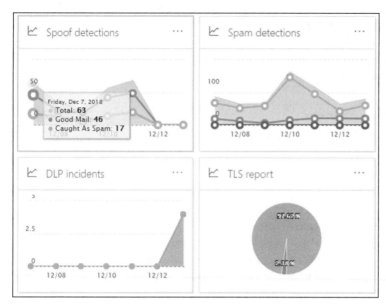

FIGURE 3-14 Reports dashboard

Once in the dedicated DLP Incident Report screen, you have additional options. Additionally, more information appears, such as the top insights and recommendations. Options to create a report schedule and request a report on demand are displayed in Figure 3-15.

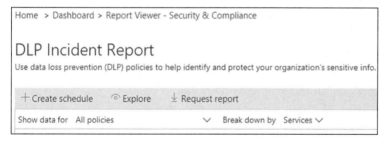

FIGURE 3-15 DLP Incident Report dedicated page

The Top Insights & Recommendations shows that some repeat users are contributing to DLP incidents in an organization, as shown in Figure 3-16.

FIGURE 3-16 DLP Incident top insights and recommendations

You can schedule DLP Incident reports to be emailed weekly or monthly. Additionally, you can request an ad-hoc report too, such as for the last 7 days.

Use DLP reports

Besides incident reports, you can use other reports to help you understand how your organization is complying with your DLP policies. The following reports are available in the Reports section of Security & Compliance Center:

- **DLP Policy Matches**   This report shows the number of policies that match in the last week. Although the default view is a graph, you can customize the output to view the data in a table. It also shows the breakdown of policy matches per service: Exchange, SharePoint, and OneDrive for Business.

- **DLP False Positive And Override**   If you enable users to report false positives and override a policy, this report will show you when and how often it is happening.

The DLP policy matches graph is shown in Figure 3-17.

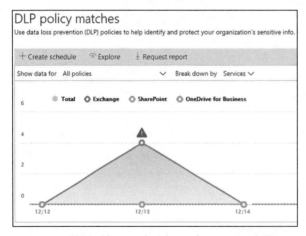

FIGURE 3-17 DLP Incident top insights and recommendations

Besides looking at the portal reports, you can also use PowerShell to obtain some report data. For example, you can run the `Get-DlpDetectionsReport` command to see a list of recent detections.

Manage DLP policy matches

For some customers, DLP will work right out of the box, without any customization. But for environments with complex needs, you will need to customize DLP to meet your goals. This section focuses on ensuring you are detecting the appropriate data with your policies.

Customize built-in sensitive information types

DLP comes with a plethora of sensitive information types. Many of them cover common types of sensitive information such as identification numbers, bank account information, and passport numbers. Some organizations can meet their goals by using the built-in sensitive information types. But many organizations need to augment the built-in sensitive information types. You have two options for augmenting the built-in sensitive information types:

- **Customize Built-In Sensitive Information Types**   When you customize the built-in sensitive information types, you alter the XML information that defines how rules detect information. If a rule is close to what you need, customizing is often a good choice.

- **Create Your Own Sensitive Information Types**   If the built-in sensitive information types don't cover everything you need, you can create your own sensitive information types. For example, imagine that you have a set of product code names that you use internally while products are still in development. You don't want those product names sent outside the organization. You can use a sensitive information type for that.

To customize built-in sensitive information types, you use PowerShell to export the sensitive information types to XML. The following PowerShell commands export the built-in rule package to D:\temp\DLPrules.xml. Note that you first must connect to Security & Compliance Center with PowerShell.

```
$DLPRules = Get-DlpSensitiveInformationTypeRulePackage
Set-Content -Path D:\temp\DLPrules.xml -Encoding Byte -Value
 $DLPRules.SerializedClassificationRuleCollection
```

After you have the XML file, open it in a text editor. Figure 3-18 shows a small snippet of the built-in rule package XML file. Notice the XML layout.

```
<Pattern confidenceLevel="75">
  <IdMatch idRef="Func_unformatted_ssn" />
  <Match idRef="Keyword_us_drivers_license" />
  <Any minMatches="1">
    <Match idRef="Keyword_district_of_columbia_drivers_license_name" />
    <Match idRef="Keyword_georgia_drivers_license_name" />
    <Match idRef="Keyword_iowa_drivers_license_name" />
    <Match idRef="Keyword_kansas_drivers_license_name" />
    <Match idRef="Keyword_massachusetts_drivers_license_name" />
    <Match idRef="Keyword_missouri_drivers_license_name" />
    <Match idRef="Keyword_montana_drivers_license_name" />
    <Match idRef="Keyword_oklahoma_drivers_license_name" />
    <Match idRef="Keyword_south_dakota_drivers_license_name" />
  </Any>
</Pattern>
```

FIGURE 3-18 DLP rule package exported to XML

You can alter the confidence level and the keyword matches, if desired. Or, for example, you can add another keyword.

Create new sensitive information types

To create a new sensitive information type, use the Security & Compliance Center and step through a wizard. You define a name, a description, and the requirements for matching. Figure 3-19 shows a snippet from the matching requirements.

FIGURE 3-19 DLP custom sensitive information type

In addition to defining the content and supporting element(s), you can also adjust the confidence level and how close in characters the content is from the supporting elements. In our example, we define 100 characters of proximity. So, if the name "Teewinot" is detected within 100 characters of "project" or "codename" or "code name", then our sensitive information type will be detected. Of course, you must use the sensitive information type in a rule to test it and ensure you are able to detect the content.

Create a custom dictionary

If you need to detect many different words, using keyword lists in sensitive information types is cumbersome. In such cases, you can create a keyword dictionary instead. A keyword dictionary can hold up to 100,000 words and you can have multiple dictionaries.

To create a custom dictionary, perform the following steps:

1. Create a text file containing all the words you want in the custom dictionary (with one word per line). The text file should be encoded in Unicode. Note that Notepad supports Unicode encoding. The screen capture below shows a valid file.

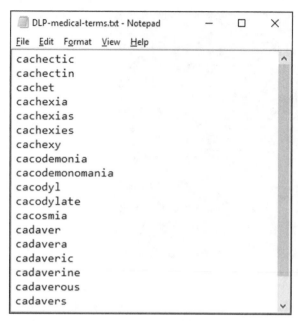

FIGURE 3-20 DLP custom dictionary file

2. Open a PowerShell prompt.

3. Run the `$Credential = Get-Credential` command. In the credential window, enter your administrative credentials and then click **OK**. This stores the credentials in $Credential and can be reference in follow-on commands.

4. Run the `$Session = New-PSSession -ConfigurationName Microsoft.Exchange -ConnectionUri https://ps.compliance.protection.outlook.com/powershell-liveid/ -Credential $UserCredential -Authentication Basic -AllowRedirection` command. This command connects you to a remote PowerShell session for the Security & Compliance Center.

5. Run the `Import-PSSession $Session -DisableNameChecking` command. This command imports the cmdlets that you'll use to work in the Security & Compliance Center.

6. In the PowerShell console, navigate to the location of the text file. Then run the `$File = Get-Content .\DLP-medical-terms.txt -Encoding Byte -ReadCount 0` command. Make sure to change the name of the file to match your file name.

7. Run the `New-DlpKeywordDictionary -Name DLP-medical-terms -Description 'medical language' -FileData $File` command to create the dictionary.

If successful, you'll see the custom dictionary properties such as those shown in Figure 3-21.

```
RunspaceId        : bae07a13-d0e6-47ea-9988-7d11629296d8
Identity          : 12536879-a160-4c35-aab9-6ea8e40baaeb
Name              : DLP-medical-terms
Description       : Foul language
KeywordDictionary : cachectic
                    cachectin
                    cachet
                    cachexia
                    cachexias
                    cachexies
                    cachexy
                    cacodemonia
                    cacodemonomania
                    cacodyl
                    cacodylate
                    cacosmia
                    cadaver
                    cadavera
                    cadaveric
                    cadaverine
                    cadaverous
                    cadavers

IsValid           : True
ObjectState       : Unchanged
```

FIGURE 3-21 PowerShell output after creating a custom dictionary

After you create a custom dictionary, you can use it in a custom sensitive information type (as a matching element or as part of a supporting element).

Document fingerprinting

Beyond just targeting keywords and using logic to detect outgoing data, you can also use document fingerprinting. For example, imagine that you work at employment placement company. Your company provides workers to large organizations on a contract basis. You have a policy that forbids sending out employment applications by email. With document fingerprinting, you can upload the blank employment application to DLP to have DLP fingerprint the document. This enables DLP to detect when the employment application is sent, even if it was filled out. Many file types are supported for fingerprinting including Office documents, .pdf files, text files, and image files.

EXAM TIP

You can only create a document fingerprint by using PowerShell.

To create a document fingerprint, perform the following steps.

1. Open a PowerShell prompt.

2. Run the $Credential = Get-Credential command. In the credential window, enter your administrative credentials and then click **OK**. This stores the credentials in $Credential and can be reference in follow-on commands.

3. Run the $Session = New-PSSession -ConfigurationName Microsoft.Exchange -ConnectionUri https://ps.compliance.protection.outlook.com/powershell-liveid/ -Credential $UserCredential -Authentication Basic -AllowRedirection command. This command connects you to a remote PowerShell session for the Security & Compliance Center.

4. Run the `Import-PSSession $Session -DisableNameChecking` command. This command imports the cmdlets that you'll use to work in the Security & Compliance Center.

5. Run the `$Doc = Get-Content 'D:\temp\application.docx' -Encoding byte -ReadCount 0` command, which reads the document into the $Doc variable.

6. Run the `$Fingerprint = New-DlpFingerprint -FileData $Doc -Description 'Employment Application'` command, which creates a new DLP fingerprint based on the document and stores it in the $Fingerprint variable.

7. Run the `New-DlpSensitiveInformationType -Name 'Employment Application' -Fingerprints $Fingerprint -Description The message has an employee application.'` command which creates a new DLP sensitive information type using the new fingerprint.

8. Run the `New-DlpComplianceRule -Name 'EmploymentApplicationRule' -Policy 'EmployeePIIPolicy' -ContentContainsSensitiveInformation @{Name='Employment Application'} -BlockAccess $True` command, which adds a new DLP rule to an existing DLP policy named EmployeePIIPolicy. The rule blocks access to offending data.

Skill 3.2: Implement Azure Information Protection

Azure Information Protection (AIP) is a technology that helps organizations protect data by using encryption, data classification, and labels. AIP is a Microsoft Azure cloud-based solution. Foundationally, it is built from Active Directory Rights Management Services (AD RMS) and some acquisitions that Microsoft made over the last few years. AIP provides everything that AD RMS provides, plus much more. While AD RMS is an on-premises service that is often restricted to internal use only, AIP is cloud-based and enables you to interoperate and share data with people at other organizations easily, even if they don't have AIP. This chapter starts with the planning concepts for AIP and ends with its implementation and configuration.

This skill section covers how to:

- Plan AIP solution
- Plan for deployment On-Prem rights management Connector
- Plan for Windows information Protection (WIP) implementation
- Plan for classification labeling
- Configure Information Rights Management (IRM) for Workloads
- Configure Super User
- Deploy AIP Clients
- Implement Azure Information Protection policies
- Implement AIP tenant key

Plan AIP solution

The first step in an AIP implementation project is to plan the implementation. To maximize your chances of a successful implementation, you need to uncover prerequisites, licensing, and integration information before you start the implementation.

Understand AIP prerequisites

While AIP is a cloud-based service, there are prerequisites that you must be able to meet before you can use AIP. Below are the key prerequisites:

- **Azure Active Directory (Azure AD)**   While many organizations have Azure AD for other reasons (for example Office 365 or other cloud-based apps), many organizations don't. Azure AD requires its own planning (for example, for Azure AD security, syncing from on-premises) but that isn't part of this exam.

- **Client computers**   AIP clients must run Windows 7 or later or macOS 10.8 (Mountain Lion) or later.

- **Mobile devices**   Android phones must run Android 4.4 or later while iOS devices must be running iOS 8.0 or higher.

- **On-premises applications**   To integrate Exchange Server with AIP, you need a minimum of Exchange Server 2010. For SharePoint, you need a minimum of SharePoint 2010. For integrating with Windows file servers (specifically, File Classification Infrastructure), you need servers that run Windows Server 2012 or later. You can protect data on Windows Server 2008 R2 by using PowerShell (but not by using a file management task like you can in Windows Server 2012 and later).

License AIP

In addition to meeting the prerequisites, you need to license AIP to use it. While you can consume AIP content without a license (such as if a licensed AIP protects data and sends it to you), you can't protect content. To protect content, you need a license. You have three options for AIP licensing:

- **Azure Information Protection Premium P1**   AIP P1 is included with Enterprise Mobility + Security E3 and Microsoft 365 E3.

- **Azure Information Protection Premium P2**   AIP P2 is included with Enterprise Mobility + Security E5 and Microsoft 365 E5.

- **Azure Information Protection for Office 365**   AIP for Office 365 is included with Office 365 Enterprise E3 or higher plans.

Table 3-1 shows the key feature differentiation between versions of AIP. Note that this is not an exhaustive list of features.

TABLE 3-1 AIP features

Feature	In AIP P1?	IN AIP P2?	In AIP O365?
On-premises connectors?	Yes	Yes	No
Track and revoke shared documents?	Yes	Yes	No
Automated classification?	No	Yes	No
Recommended classification?	No	Yes	No
Labeling?	No	Yes	No
Bring Your Own Key (BYOK)?	Yes	Yes	Yes
Hold Your Own Key (HYOK)?	No	Yes	No

Planning for AIP

Prior to deploying AIP, you need to plan for the implementation. Now that you understand the prerequisites, the licensing, and the features available, you need to figure out how your organization will use AIP and what you'll need to do to prepare your environment for AIP.

USERS AND GROUPS

Let's start by looking at Azure Active Directory. Earlier in this section, we noted that a prerequisite for AIP is to have a sync between your on-premises AD DS environment and Azure AD. To license users with AIP, they need to be in Azure AD. You can create users manually, however, a good practice is to sync users from AD DS instead, which reduces administrative overhead. Along with the users, you also need to account for AD DS groups. You can use groups for the delegation of administration, to control the use of AIP, or for document access. As part of your planning, you should figure out which users and groups need to be synced. In many organizations, you should sync your user accounts for your users, but not for your on-premises service accounts, or other non-human accounts.

LICENSING

After you have users and groups synced (or created) in Azure AD, you need to assign licenses. Each user that uses AIP must be licensed. You can individually assign licenses, however, this is tedious for organizations with more than a few users. You can also assign licenses to groups, such as AIP Users. This is effective, especially for large organizations. If you plan to do a phased implementation of AIP (such as where the IT department is the first department to use AIP), you can create multiple groups and use them for licensing.

AIP KEY

The AIP key is an import planning consideration. You can choose between the Microsoft-managed key (the default configuration) or bring your own key. We cover these considerations in Skill 10.9.

CONFIGURE CLASSIFICATION AND LABELING

Labels identify data based on the sensitivity of the data. For example, marketing materials used on your web site might be labeled Public, while documents outlining a product strategy for the future might be labeled Sensitive. When you apply a label to data, it can automatically encrypt data or adjust user access. Classification is the act of labeling data. For example, you might classify a Word document as Confidential (with Confidential being a label). You can manually classify data or use automatic classification. Additionally, you can opt for recommended classification tips. In this scenario, use conditions (such as "if a document contains XXXXX, then..."), and recommendations are displayed in supported applications (such as Microsoft Word). For example, Word might detect a condition in a document and then recommend that the document be labeled Confidential—users can accept that recommendation by clicking **Change Now** or opt to dismiss the recommendation by clicking **Dismiss**.

Some organizations have an existing use of classification and labeling. For example, if you use DLP, or if you are using AD RMS with on-premises file servers, you might use classification and labeling. For many organizations, classifying and labeling documents is a new concept. There is a default Azure Information Protection policy that provides some default labels, such as Confidential and Highly Confidential. You can build upon that, because most organizations will need more than the default labels.

As part of your classification and labeling strategy, you need to train end users on the proper labeling of data. At some point, you might also want to take advantage of advanced features, such as enforced labels, customization, and conditions.

- Enforced labels
- Customization
- Conditions.

We look at labeling in more detail later in this chapter.

Plan for deployment on-prem rights management connector

To integrate AIP with your on-premises applications, such as Exchange, SharePoint, or Windows file servers, you need to deploy the Rights Management Services (RMS) connector.

Understand RMS connector prerequisites

The RMS connector has a few key prerequisites that you need to be aware of before you begin your deployment. These prerequisites are more involved than typical prerequisites (such as having a certain patch installed) so be sure to understand these for the exam.

- **Directory sync between your on-premises Active Directory Domain Services (AD DS) environment and Azure Active Directory** Unless you are deploying this in a lab environment to study for the exam, you should avoid quickly configuring a sync, because there are important considerations to think through first. For example, do you want to sync all users (even service accounts)? Do you want to use federated authentication? How will you handle password sync?

- **Azure Rights Management must be activated** If you have a recent subscription, Azure Rights Management is activated by default. For older subscriptions with Exchange Online, Microsoft is retroactively activating Azure Rights Management. If you don't have Exchange Online and you have an older subscription that includes AIP, you will have to manually activate Azure Rights Management. You can do that from the Azure Portal. Figure 3-22 shows the message when it is activated.

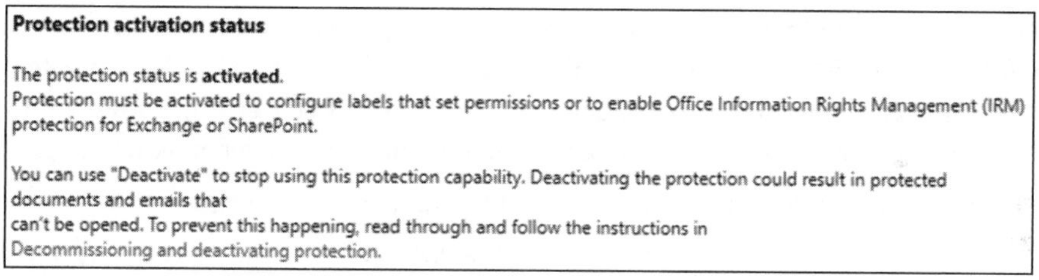

Protection activation status

The protection status is **activated**.
Protection must be activated to configure labels that set permissions or to enable Office Information Rights Management (IRM) protection for Exchange or SharePoint.

You can use "Deactivate" to stop using this protection capability. Deactivating the protection could result in protected documents and emails that
can't be opened. To prevent this happening, read through and follow the instructions in
Decommissioning and deactivating protection.

FIGURE 3-22 AIP activation status message

- **Deploy the RMS connector on a minimum of 2 servers** This is a prerequisite for high availability and for authorizing the servers. Note that you cannot install the connector on an Exchange server, SharePoint servers, or a file server that will use AIP. Additionally, do not install the connector on a domain controller.

Understand RMS connector planning considerations

After you deal with the RMS connector prerequisites, you should look at the planning considerations. These considerations enable you to deploy a supported environment, maximize the security of your deployment, and ensure a properly performing service.

During the installation of the RMS connector, you will be prompted to enter credentials for an account that has permissions to configure the RMS connector. There are three options that enable you to have enough rights to configure the RMS connector:

- **Azure Active Directory global administrator**   Of the three options to configure the RMS connector, this option is the least secure. A global administrator has more rights than necessary for the RMS connector configuration, so you should avoid using one.

- **Azure Rights Management global administrator**   An Azure Rights Management global administrator has less rights than an Azure global administrator, but still has more rights than necessary for configuring the RMS connector. If possible, avoid using an Azure Rights Management global administrator to configure the RMS connector.

- **Azure Rights Management connector administrator**   Of the three options, the Azure Rights Management connector administrator option is the best. It adheres to the principal of least privilege by only having the permissions required for the task at hand. You should use a connector administrator to configure the RMS connector.

After you have the connector installed, be sure to authorize servers that will use the connector. The servers will be your Exchange servers, SharePoint servers, and file servers. You can add servers individually or you can use groups. For example, you can use the Exchange Servers group to add all Exchange servers as allowed servers. For SharePoint and file servers, you can create groups.

Understand key RMS connector implementation details

The RMS connector is used to enable on-premises servers to use AIP. The connector itself is a service that you install on a Windows server, whether physical or virtual. You can even run it in a VM in Azure. The connector enables the on-premises servers to communicate with AIP, like how a proxy or relay server works. Earlier in this section, we covered the prerequisites and planning considerations. Now, we will look at some of the key implementation details.

Below are the high-level steps for the initial RMS connector installation and configuration.

1. On the first connector server, download the RMS connector from: *https://go.microsoft. com/fwlink/?LinkId=314106*.

2. Run the setup program (RMSConnectorSetup.exe).

3. Choose the Microsoft Rights Management connector on the computer option.

4. Agree to the license terms.

5. Enter your RMS connector admin account that has rights to configure the connector.

6. Click **Finish**.

7. Switch to the second connector server. Download the RMS connector from: *https://go.microsoft.com/fwlink/?LinkId=314106*.

8. Run the setup program (RMSConnectorSetup.exe).

9. Choose the Microsoft Rights Management connector on the computer option.

10. Agree to the license terms.

11. Enter your RMS connector admin account that has rights to configure the connector and complete the installation.

After the connector is installed, there are a couple of other steps:

- **Load balancing** Because you have more than one connector server, you need a way to enable your on-premises servers to connect to both connector servers. You do this by using load balancing. The load balancing system isn't relevant—you just need to balance the incoming requests across all of your connector servers. You should configure load balancing before you add any of your on-premises servers (otherwise, you might have to reconfigure the servers after you introduce load balancing).

- **Use HTTPS** You can use HTTP (default) or HTTPS. HTTPS is the best choice for organizations that want to maximize security. To use HTTPS, you need to have a certificate installed on each connector server. The certificate should use the virtual load balancing name, not the individual hostnames of the connector servers (although a certificate could include both).

Once you have load balancing in place and HTTPS configured, you can run the RMS Connector administration tool (from a connector server or by installing the administration tool by itself on a separate computer). From the tool, add your SharePoint, Exchange, and file servers that will use AIP.

EXAM TIP

The admin account you use to configure the RMS connector must not be configured to require multi-factor authentication, because the tool does not support it. Additionally, the account has some password restrictions whereby the password cannot contain certain special characters.

Plan for Windows Information Protection (WIP) implementation

Windows Information Protection (WIP) is a data protection technology focused on data residing on client computers running Windows 10. WIP combines mobile device management (MDM), AppLocker, and Encrypting File System (EFS). WIP isn't a direct competitor to AIP, but instead focuses on a different kind of protection, namely protecting local data on devices (whereas AIP is focused on protecting shared data or protecting data in Exchange, SharePoint, and on file servers).

Understand how WIP works

WIP relies on data encryption, through Encrypting File System (EFS), to encrypt corporate data based on your WIP MDM policies. These policies are MDM policies that dictate when and if corporate data is encrypted and when or if it can be accessed. WIP provides the following primary benefits:

- **Encrypt corporate data** By using EFS, corporate data is encrypted across all enrolled devices.

- **Wipe corporate data from devices** When users use their own devices, it can be challenging to manage the devices or ensure that corporate data isn't being lost on them. WIP provides the capability of wiping only corporate data on devices.

- **Enable personal devices to access corporate data** Some organizations prohibit the use of personal devices for accessing corporate data. With WIP, organizations can safely enable such access while providing data protection.

- **Specify the list of apps that can access corporate data** WIP enables you to specify a whitelist of applications that can access corporate data.

WIP relies on Windows 10 (version 1607 and later) and an MDM solution. At the time of this writing, the supported MDM solutions are Microsoft Intune and System Center Configuration Manager. You can also use a third-party MDM although you might not be able to take advantage of a GUI for the configuration (instead, you might have to use the EnterpriseDataProtection CSP.

WIP categorizes apps into two categories:

- **Enlightened apps** Enlightened apps can figure out the difference between corporate data and personal data.

- **Unenlightened apps** Unenlightened apps consider all data to be corporate data. These apps encrypt all data instead of just encrypting corporate data. You can convert an unenlightened app to an enlightened app by using code and the WIP API. Note that if an app is only intended to work with corporate data, you might not need to enlighten the app.

At the time of this writing, the following Microsoft apps are enlightened:

- Microsoft Edge
- Internet Explorer 11
- Microsoft People
- Mobile Office apps, including Word, Excel, PowerPoint, OneNote, Outlook Mail and Calendar
- Office 365 ProPlus apps, including Word, Excel, PowerPoint, OneNote, and Outlook
- OneDrive app
- OneDrive sync client (OneDrive.exe, the next generation sync client)
- Microsoft Photos
- Groove Music
- Notepad
- Microsoft Paint
- Microsoft Movies & TV

- Microsoft Messaging
- Microsoft Remote Desktop

WIP has some limitations that you should know about (this isn't an exhaustive list):

- **WIP is suited for single user devices**   If two or more people use the same computer, there might be app compatibility issues when using WIP. Instead, limit each device to a single user.

- **Sharing data with USB drives doesn't work**   If you use WIP, you can copy data to a USB drive and it stays encrypted. The data, however, is inaccessible on other devices or for other users. Instead, you should share files through your internal file servers or authorized cloud data repositories.

- **WIP is limited to a select set of apps**   WIP can't cover all use cases because it is limited to a specific set of apps. While you can add more apps, not all apps will support WIP integration.

Implement WIP

Before you start implementing exceptions, you should have a good understanding of their capabilities.

1.   From the Azure Portal, navigate to the Microsoft Intune app.

2.   Click **App Protection Policies** in the left pane and then click **+Create Policy** in the right pane, as shown in Figure 3-23.

FIGURE 3-23 Create Intune policy for WIP

3.   In the **Create Policy** blade, type a name for the policy, select the desired platform, and then choose the **With Enrollment State** option for the enrollment state. For the purposes of this walk-through, we are naming our policy **BYOD – WIP Policy**, choosing the **Windows 10** platform, and using **With Enrollment** as the enrollment state. Figure 3-24 shows the desired configuration

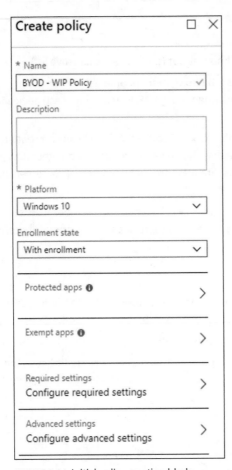

FIGURE 3-24 Initial policy creation blade

4. Click **Protected Apps**. Then click the **Add Apps** button. Next to **Word Mobile**, click the checkbox to the left and then click **OK**. Optionally, add additional apps. When finished, the list of protected apps will be displayed, as shown in Figure 3-25.

FIGURE 3-25 Protected apps list

5. Click **OK** to return to the **Create Policy** blade.

6. Click **Required Settings** in the left pane, click **Block** in the right pane, then click **OK**.

7. Click **Advanced Settings** in the left pane, click the **On** button under **Show The Enterprise Data Protection Icon**, then click **OK**.

8. Click **Create** to create the policy. After creation, the new policy will be displayed in the list of policies. Don't forget that you must assign the policy after creation! as shown in Figure 3-26

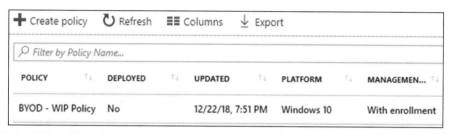

FIGURE 3-26 WIP policy list

While adding recommended apps is easy, adding desktop and store apps to the list of protected apps isn't as intuitive. In the steps below, we walk through the process of adding a desktop app (in this case, Microsoft Word).

1. On a computer that has the desired desktop app, open a **PowerShell** prompt.

2. Run the `Get-AppLockerFileInformation -Path 'C:\Program Files (x86)\Microsoft Office\root\Office16\WINWORD.EXE' | FL` command. Copy the publisher value to the clipboard.

3. In the Intune app in the Azure portal, click **App Protection Policies**. In the right pane, click the existing policy you created in the previous steps.

4. Click **Protected Apps** in the left pane and then click the **Add Apps** button in the right pane.

5. Click the dropdown menu at the top of the right pane and then click **Desktop Apps**.

6. In the text fields, enter the following information, as shown in Figure 3-27.

   A. Name   **Microsoft Word**

   B. Publisher   **Publisher value from PowerShell command output**

   C. Product name   **Microsoft Word**

   D. File **WINWORD.EXE**

   E. Min Version   **15.0**

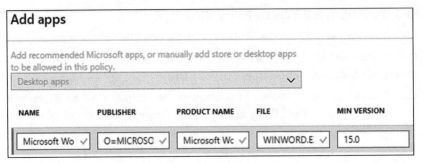

FIGURE 3-27 Add protected app to policy

7. Click **OK**.

When it comes to the policy, be aware of the following information:

- The filename for protected apps is the executable file of the application.

- The min version specifies the minimum app version. Be sure to account for the lowest version in use at your organization.

- There are four WIP modes you can use in a policy:

    - **Block**   Enterprise data is blocked from being copied or moved to an unprotected app.

    - **Allow Overrides**   Users are prompted if they try to copy or move data from a protected app to an unprotected app. They can override and perform the copy or move, but the action will be logged.

    - **Silent**   Users can copy or move data from protected apps to unprotected apps, but the actions are logged. Think of this as an auditing mode.

    - **Off**   Users can copy or move data from protected apps to unprotected apps, but the actions are not logged.

While we created a basic policy, there are additional options, advanced options, that you should be aware of. Below, we define and discuss the advanced options available in a policy. Each of the bulleted items represents an optional advanced setting.

- **Add Network Boundary**   Here, you can add boundaries for your enterprise data. These are locations from which clients can get enterprise data. For example, you can add cloud resources (such as SharePoint), protected domains, network domains, proxy servers, IPv4 or IPv6 ranges, and other resources.

- **Enterprise Proxy Servers List Is Authoritative (Do Not Auto-Detect)**   Windows auto detects proxy servers. Turn on this setting if you want to define an authoritative list of proxy servers.

- **Enterprise IP Ranges List Is Authoritative (Do Not Auto-Detect)**   Instead of having Windows auto detect IP address ranges, you can define them manually.

- **Data Protection**. You can upload an EFS Data Recovery Agent (DRA) certificate so that you can recover encrypted data. While this is optional, it is highly recommended.

Without a DRA, if anything happens to your EFS encryption key, your encrypted data is unrecoverable.

- **Prevent Corporate Data From Being Accessed By Apps When The Device Is Locked. Applies Only To Windows 10 Mobile**   This setting prevents data from being accessed while a device is locked.

- **Revoke Encryption Keys On Unenroll**   If a device un-enrolls from your policy, then the encryption keys are revoked. This is turned on by default.

- **Show The Enterprise Data Protection Icon**   The data protection icon enables users to know whether they are working with enterprise data or not. It is helpful for users, especially during the early stages of a WIP deployment.

- **Use Azure RMS For WIP**   Azure RMS can be used for WIP encryption, specifically to handle protecting data when it leaves a device. This is an enhancement that extends data protection compared to just using WIP by itself.

- **Allow Windows Search Indexer To Search Encrypted Items**   This is turned on by default and enables Windows Search to index encrypted items. In high security environments, you should turn this off.

- **Add Encrypted File Extensions**   You can add file extensions so that files with the extensions will be encrypted when copying to a file server in your corporate boundary.

> *MORE INFO*   **CREATE THE EFS DRA**
>
> You should familiarize yourself with the process of creating the EFS DRA. See *https://docs.microsoft.com/previous-versions/tn-archive/cc512680(v=technet.10)* for more information.

Plan for classification labeling

Labeling is critical to the success of your AIP implementation. Without the proper labeling, sensitive data might be unprotected or leaked outside of your organization. Too much complexity in your labeling is difficult to manage, thus confusing for users, and could lead to incorrect classifications (and in turn, potential leakage of sensitive data).

Understand label capabilities

Labels have capabilities, many of which are optional. At a minimum, labels provide a visual clue as to the sensitivity of the data. But you can configure other capabilities to enhance AIP labels. Below, we cover some of the key capabilities you should be familiar with for the exam.

- **A label can automatically protect a document or email message**   By default, a label does not protect data. You can turn on protection for a label. Or, you can have a label remove protection. Protection is applied by AIP. You can define the specific permissions for users and groups (for example, one group can have view/open/read permissions while another group can have view/open/read/edit/save). Additionally, you can opt to expire content and enable offline access. Figure 3-28 shows how the group Group1@svidergol.com has view rights.

FIGURE 3-28 AIP label protect permissions

■ **A label can mandate visual markings for a document** You can require a document header, a document footer, or a document watermark. In high security organizations, you can have a label apply all three visual markings. The document header option is turned on in Figure 3-29.

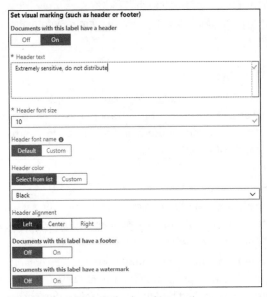

FIGURE 3-29 AIP label visual marking options

■ **A label can have conditions. Conditions require a P2 license** Conditions enable automatic classification. The available conditions are pulled directly from your configured sensitive information types, covered in Chapter 9 about DLP. For example, you can create a label that looks for Australia driver's license numbers in a document. Once a condition is added to a label, you can have the label applied automatically or have it recommended (which is the default setting), shown in Figure 3-30.

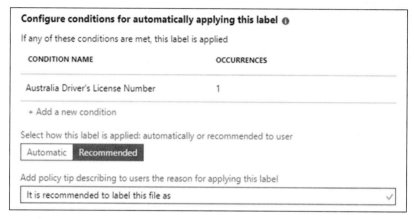

Configure conditions for automatically applying this label ⓘ

If any of these conditions are met, this label is applied

CONDITION NAME	OCCURRENCES
Australia Driver's License Number	1

+ Add a new condition

Select how this label is applied: automatically or recommended to user

| Automatic | Recommended |

Add policy tip describing to users the reason for applying this label

It is recommended to label this file as ✓

FIGURE 3-30 AIP label condition

- **Each label has a defined color** Colors help users associate sensitivity with color. For example, you might use yellow for minimally sensitivity data and red for highly sensitive data.

Create a new label

In this section, we will go through the step-by-step process to create a new AIP label in the Azure portal. For the purposes of this walk-through, we will create a policy to protect data automatically using the Yellow color.

Perform the following steps to create the label.

1. Use an administrative account to sign into the Microsoft Azure portal at: *https://portal. azure.com.*

2. Navigate to Azure Information Protection. You can search for it in the main search bar.

3. In the left pane of Azure Information Protection, click **Labels**.

4. In the right pane of Azure Information Protection, click **+Add A New Label**.

5. In the **Label** display name textbox, type **HR only**.

6. In the **Description** textbox, type **This Data Is Limited To HR Team Members Only**.

7. In the **Color** dropdown menu, click **Yellow**.

8. In the permissions for the label, click **Protect**.

9. Click the **Protection** context menu. In the **Protection** blade, click **+Add Permissions**. In the **Add Permissions** blade, click the **Reviewer** permissions. Then click **+Browse Directory**. In the **AAD Users And Groups** blade, click the HR associated group (in our environment Group1), and then click **Select**. Note that the group must be mail-enabled. Click **OK** to close the **Add Permissions** blade.

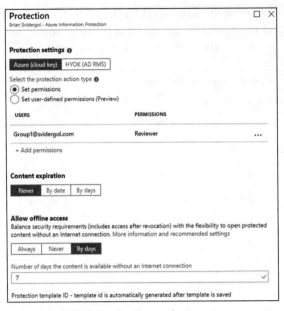

FIGURE 3-31 AIP label protection settings

10. Click **OK** to close the **Protection** blade.

11. In the **Label** blade, click **+Add A New Condition**.

12. In the **Condition** blade, click the **Privacy** industry. Then, navigate to and click the **USA Social Security Number (SSN)**. Then, click **Save**. In the **Save Settings** dialog box, click **OK**.

13. In the **Label** blade, below the new condition, click the **Automatic** label option. This ensures that any documents with a USA Social Security Number will automatically be labeled.

14. Click **Save**. In the Save settings dialog box, click **OK**.

After you create a label, it will be shown in the label list. Labels are listed along with whether the labels have visual markings and protection, as shown in Figure 3-32.

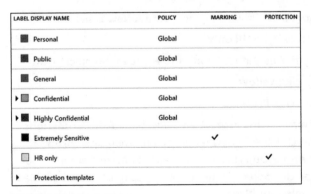

FIGURE 3-32 AIP label list

Configure Information Rights Management (IRM) for workloads

Azure Information Protection is functional when using it with Microsoft Office, but you can enhance the capabilities and take advantage of the benefits by extending the functionality to other supported applications. Earlier, we looked at integration with on-premises technologies such as file servers, Exchange Server, and SharePoint. In this section, we examine the process of integrating IRM with Office 365.

Understand supported integrations

AIP integrates with some Office 365 applications. You should be familiar with the applications and the integrations. Additionally, there are some specific implementation details that you should know for the exam.

Here are the supported integrations with Office 365:

- **Exchange Online** Integration with Exchange Online enables users to protect individual email messages. For example, you can prevent recipients from forwarding an email and protect attachments by encrypting attachments. Optionally, you can only enable the HR department to view specific attachments). On the backend, email administrators can use mail flow rules that automatically apply protection to email messages based on recipient, subject, or content, suchas with keywords or phrases. AIP is useful for DLP policies, because when something sensitive is being sent outbound it can automatically be protected with AIP.

- **SharePoint Online** Once SharePoint Online is integrated with AIP, admins can protect SharePoint lists and document libraries with IRM. As users download files, they will be protected based on the configured protection settings. When unprotected files are uploaded, they will be automatically protected upon download.

- **OneDrive for Business** After integration, users can configure their OneDrive for Business library for IRM. Note that OneDrive integration relies on the SharePoint Online integration with AIP. Optionally, admins can use PowerShell to configure IRM on behalf of users.

There are different capabilities offered with the integrations:

- **Protection** You need a subscription that includes Azure Information Protection to enable protection capabilities. All AIP levels (AIP for Office 365, AIP P1, and AIP P2) offer protection capabilities. AIP for Office 365 is included with Office 365 Enterprise E3 and above. AIP P1 is included with Microsoft 365 E3 and Microsoft Enterprise Mobility + Security E3. AIP P2 is included with Microsoft 365 and Enterprise Mobility + Security E5.

- **Classification and labeling** To enable classification and labeling, you need to have a subscription that includes AIP P1 or AIP P2. AIP for Office 365 does not include classification and labeling. Note that automatic labeling and classification is only included with AIP P2.

Integrate with Exchange Online

The integration of Exchange Online and AIP is quick and easy. For new tenants, the integration is automatic. You can use PowerShell to check whether Exchange Online is integrated with AIP. Run the following commands to connect to Exchange Online through PowerShell and check the IRM configuration.

```
$Creds = Get-Credential

$Session = New-PSSession -ConfigurationName Microsoft.Exchange
-ConnectionUri https://ps.outlook.com/powershell/ -Credential
$Creds -Authentication Basic -AllowRedirection

Import-PSSession $Session

Get-IRMConfiguration | FL *Azure*
```

If AzureRMSLicensingEnabled is True, then the integration is in place. If False, run the following command to enable the licensing:

```
Set-IRMConfiguration -AzureRMSLicensingEnabled $true
```

After integration, you can run a simple test to check the functionality. Run the following command to check functionality (change the sender email address to yours):

```
Test-IRMConfiguration -Sender brian@svidergol.com
```

If successful, the output will indicate the tests passed.

```
PS C:\Users\Brian> Test-IRMConfiguration -Sender brian@svidergol.com
Results : Acquiring RMS Templates ...
            - PASS: RMS Templates acquired.  Templates available:
      Confidential View Only, Confidential, Encrypt, Do Not Forward.
         Verifying encryption ...
            - PASS: Encryption verified successfully.
         Verifying decryption ...
            - PASS: Decryption verified successfully.
         Verifying IRM is enabled ...
            - PASS: IRM verified successfully.
         OVERALL RESULT: PASS
```

Once the licensing is in place, the integration is functional. Admins can configure backend mail flow rules that use IRM, and users can start protecting email and attachments.

Integrate with SharePoint Online and OneDrive for Business

Like Exchange Online, the integration with SharePoint Online and OneDrive for Business is quick and easy. Perform the following steps to enable the integration.

1. As an administrator, sign into *https://portal.office.com*.

2. In the left pane, click the **... Show More** button.

3. In the left pane, click **SharePoint** to open the SharePoint admin center.

4. In the SharePoint admin center, in the left pane, click **Settings**.

5. Scroll down to **Information Rights Management (IRM)**. Click the **Use The IRM Service Specified In Your Configuration** radio button.

6. Click the **Refresh IRM Settings**. The refresh can take up to an hour.

7. After the refresh, the integration is ready, and you can configure lists and document libraries for protection.

The SharePoint admin center IRM settings are displayed in Figure 3-33.

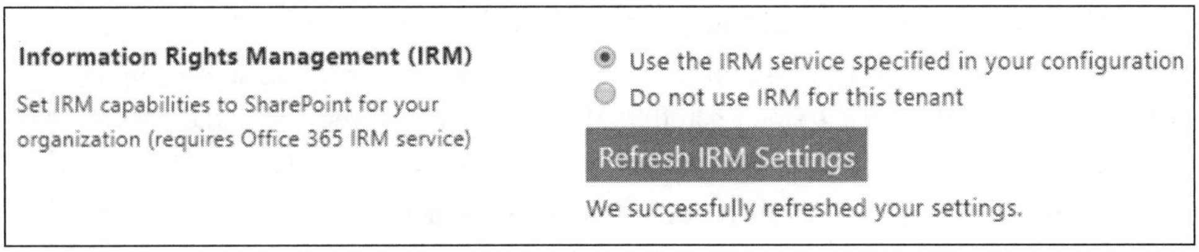

Information Rights Management (IRM)

Set IRM capabilities to SharePoint for your organization (requires Office 365 IRM service)

◉ Use the IRM service specified in your configuration
◯ Do not use IRM for this tenant

Refresh IRM Settings

We successfully refreshed your settings.

FIGURE 3-33 SharePoint Online IRM settings

After integration, admins can use IRM for a list of document library.

> **MORE INFO** **LEARN MORE ABOUT IRM FOR LISTS AND LIBRARIES**
>
> To learn more about configuring IRM for lists or libraries, see: *https://docs.microsoft.com/office365/securitycompliance/apply-irm-to-a-list-or-library*.

Configure Super User

For some customers, DLP will work right out of the box without any customization. But for environments with complex needs, you will need to customize DLP to meet your goals. This section focuses on ensuring you are detecting the appropriate data with your policies.

Understand the need for the Super User feature

Imagine that an employee uses AIP to protect all of his documents. He opts to protect them so that only he can view and edit the documents. Later, he leaves the company. You are stuck with the documents, but can't gain access to them. This isn't an ideal situation, especially if the documents are important for a project or other company business. The Super User feature enables you to gain access to the documents. Think of the Super User feature like you think of a data recovery agent with Encrypting File System (EFS). Or, think of the Super User feature like you think of a master key at a school. Teachers each have a key to their classroom. But the custodian or principal might have a master key that opens all locks at the school. Below are the primary uses of the Super User feature.

- **Gain access to any data encrypted with AIP**   This is useful when an employee leaves the company, or you want to replace existing policies with new policies.

- **Integrate AIP with Exchange Server or other apps and services**   Exchange Server and other apps and services sometimes need to inspect data that is protected (for example, with Exchange Server, it might be for DLP or archiving compliance).

- **You need to perform bulk decryption**   Imagine that your company is going through a legal fight with another company. During discovery, the judge orders your company to produce all documents created in the last 36 months. You can use bulk decryption to automate the decryption process so the data can be handed over for the trial.

Because the Super User feature enables assigned users to gain access to any encrypted document, you need to be extremely careful with it. The following recommendations will help you maximize the security of your environment once you enable the feature.

- **Do Not Assign Anybody As A Super User Until Necessary**   Think of this like you think of Schema Admins for Active Directory. You only assign it when needed and then remove it as soon as the admin is finished with their task.

- **In High Security Organizations, Leave Super User Disabled Until Needed**   By leaving it disabled, a malicious person would have to enable the service and add themselves prior to use. You can monitor the status of the Super User feature and alert when it is enabled with the goal of immediately disabling it or taking other actions.

- **Restrict Members Of Groups With Admin Access To AIP**   Global admins in Office 365 and admins assigned the Information Protection Administrator, or the Security Administrator role, can enable and disable the Super User feature. Additionally, they can add and remove users. Thus, it is important to severely limit members, and monitor,and alert on role membership changes.

By default, the Super User feature is disabled. In fact, you won't even see it mentioned in the Azure portal for AIP. In the next section, we walk through the process of enabling and configuring the Super User feature.

Enable and configure the Super User feature

You use PowerShell to enable the Super User feaure. Like other AIP cmdlets, you need to have the AADRM PowerShell module installed. See *https://docs.microsoft.com/azure/information-protection/install-powershell* for details on the module installation. Enabling the feature is quite simple—you run the following command:

```
Enable-AadrmSuperUserFeature
```

Alternatively, if you want to disable the feature, run the following command:

```
Disable-AadrmSuperUserFeature
```

When you are ready to assign a user named Brian with an email address of brian@alpineskihouse.com, run the following command:

```
Add-AadrmSuperUser -EmailAddress "brian@alpineskihouse.com"
```

Optionally, you can use the -ServicePrincipalId parameter to specify a service principal instead of a user account.

EXAM TIP
The Super User feature is automatically enabled if you configure the Rights Management Connector for Exchange Server.

Deploy AIP Clients

As part of your AIP deployment, you should deploy the AIP client on computers that will be used to protect data. In many organizations, the AIP client is deployed to all client computers. In other organizations, only a subset of users will use AIP. Thus, you need a way to selectively deploy clients too. The client isn't required for all use cases, but it enhances the user experience by making it easier to label and protect documents. For Office 201 users, the AIP client is mandatory.

Understand deployment options

The have a successful client deployment, you need to understand the client prerequisites. If some of your computers don't meet the prerequisites, you can upgrade or replace them prior to your AIP client deployment. Below are the operating system prerequisites for computers.

The following computer operating systems support the Azure Rights Management service:

- Windows 7 (x86, x64)
- Windows 8 (x86, x64)
- Windows 8.1 (x86, x64)
- Windows 10 (x86, x64)
- macOS: Minimum version of macOS 10.8 (Mountain Lion)

Mobile devices must be one of the following versions (or newer):

- **Windows Phone**   Windows Phone 8.1
- **Android phones and tablets**   Minimum version of Android 4.4
- **iPhone and iPad**   Minimum version of iOS 8.0
- **Windows tablets**   Windows 10 Mobile and Windows 8.1 RT

Below are the deployment options. Note that these options are like any typical deployment options you would use for deploying software.

- **System Center Configuration Manager**   In this scenario, you can deploy the client using System Center Configuration Manager. This deployment works like any other MSI-based deployment. Microsoft provides the .MSI file for the client. If your company already has and uses System Center Configuration Manager, this is your best option.

- **Intune**   In this scenario, you use Intune to deploy to clients. This is effective, especially when all your client computers are managed by Intune. If your company already has and uses Intune, this is your best option.

- **Group Policy**   In this scenario, you create a new GPO and use the built-in software deployment functionality of Group Policy. While this can be effective at smaller organizations, it doesn't have as much functionality as Intune or System Center Configuration Manager.

- **Manual installation**   In a manual installation, you download the .exe installation file and copy it to a client. Then, you run it and follow the installation wizard until the client is installed. This is effective for troubleshooting or testing a couple of clients prior to a larger proof-of-concept or similar deployment.

For the exam, you should be aware of the pros and cons of each deployment method. You are not, however, expected to be experts at each method. Table 3-2 contains some of the pros and cons for the deployment methods.

TABLE 3-2   Client Deployment Method Comparison

Deployment method	Minimizes admin hours?	Reduces human error?	Effective for very large installs?	Built-in reports?	Effective for single computer install?
System Center Configuration Manager	Yes	Yes	Yes	Yes	No
Intune	Yes	Yes	Yes	Yes	No
Group Policy	Yes	Yes	No	No	No
Manual installation	No	No	No	No	Yes

Install the client

The installation of the client will vary based on your deployment method. We have already covered app deployment with Intune in the skill titled "Plan for devices and apps" (specifically in the "Plan app deployment" section). Here, we will show the manual installation method. Note that the manual installation method is simple, but there are a couple of key points to be knowledgeable about for the exam.

Prior to your manual installation, you need to download the client. You can download the client from: *https://www.microsoft.com/download/details.aspx?id=53018*. There are two files available:

- **AzInfoProtection.exe**   This is the file to download if you want to perform a manual installation.

- **AzInfoProtection_for_central_deployment.msi** This is the file to download if you want to deploy the client using a software deployment tool, such as Intune.

To install the client, perform the following steps.

1. To proceed with a manual installation, perform the following steps:Download the .exe installation file to the client computer.

2. Double-click the installation file named **AzInfoProtection.exe**.

3. In the **Microsoft Azure Information Protection** window, click the **I Agree** button, as shown in Figure 3-34.

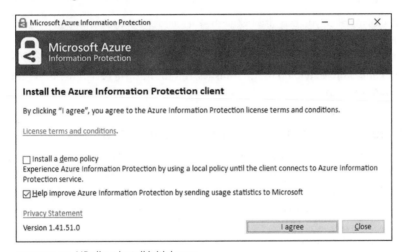

FIGURE 3-34 AIP client install initial page

4. After the installation completes, a message indicating success will be displayed. Click **Close** to close the installation wizard, as shown in Figure 3-35.

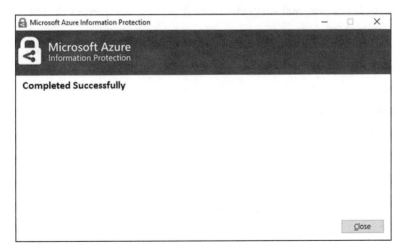

FIGURE 3-35 AIP client install last page

- There are only two options in the installation wizard. You should be familiar with both for the exam.

- **Install A Demo Policy** If your client computer can't connect to the internet or you do not have AIP, you can install a demo policy to experience how the AIP client functions. Note that if the client connects to the Internet later, the demo policy will be replaced with your AIP policy.

- **Help Improve Azure Information Protection By Sending Usage Statistics To Microsoft**. Select this option if you want to send anonymous usage statistics to Microsoft to help improve the product. For high security organizations, it is common to disable this option.

Besides the GUI installer, you can also install the AIP client from the command line. For example, to deploy the AIP client with the default installation options (which sends usage statistics to Microsoft), run the `AzInfoProtection.exe /quiet` command. To install the client in the background and disable sending usage statistics, run the `AzInfoProtection.exe /quiet / AllowTelemetry=0` command.

Implement Azure Information Protection policies

AIP comes with a single default policy named Global. It applies to all users and contains some default labels (such as Public and Confidential) as well as some optional settings, most of which are turned off. While the default policy and settings might work for some organizations, many organizations will have to add additional policies and customize the Global policy.

Update the Global policy

In this section, we will review the Global policy and make some adjustments, which will apply to all users.

1. Sign into the Azure portal at: *https://portal.azure.com*.

2. Navigate to **Azure Information Protection** in the portal. You can search for it if you don't have it pinned.

3. From the Azure Information Protection panel, click **Policies** in the left pane. You will see a **Global** policy and any custom policies (if you have any). Figure 3-36, below, shows two policies.

FIGURE 3-36 Existing AIP policies

4. Click the **Global** policy.

5. Scroll down to the default settings and adjust the desired settings. Click **Save** when finished, as shown in Figure 3-37.

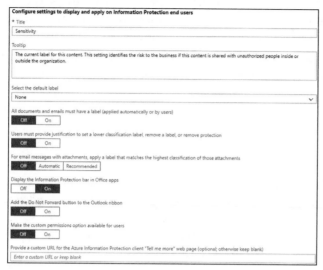

FIGURE 3-37 Default settings in AIP Global policy

Below are the primary end user settings in the Global policy with a description of their usage.

- **All Documents And Emails Must Have A Label (Applied Automatically Or By Users)** This setting is turned off by default. If you turn it on, users will be prompted to label a document or email when they save a document or send an email. Optionally, you can automatically label a document or email based on a condition or automatically assign a default label.

- **Users Must Provide Justification To Set A Lower Classification Label, Remove A Label, Or Remove Protection** This setting is turned off by default. If you turn it on and a user tries to lower the label classification, remove protection, or remove a label, they will be prompted to provide an explanation. The explanation is saved to the local event log. The Applications and Services Logs / Azure Information Protection log is the name of the log. It is usually not captured by log archiving or SIEM solutions, so be sure to consider capturing this log as part of your AIP deployment.

- **For Email Messages With Attachments, Apply A Label That Matches The Highest Classification Of Those Attachments** This setting is turned off by default. You can configure it for Automatic or Recommended instead. When set to automatic, labels are automatically applied. When set to Recommended, users will be prompted to choose a label.

- **Display The Information Protection Bar In Office Apps** This setting is turned on by default. When turned on, users can select a label from the bar in Office apps or from the Protect button. If this setting is turned off, users must select labels only from the Protect button. Turning this setting off degrades the end user experience slightly, especially in a new AIP deployment.

- **Add The Do Not Forward Button To The Outlook Ribbon** This setting is turned off by default. If you turn it on, a Do Not Forward button is added to the Protection group in Outlook. This setting does not impact whether a user can use the Do Not Forward functionality, but instead just dictates from where they can use it.

- **Make The Custom Permissions Options Available For Users** This setting is turned off by default. When turned off, users cannot customize the protection settings or remove protection. When turned on, users can customize the protection settings and remove protection, if desired. In a high-security organization, this setting should be turned off.

Create and configure a scoped policy

It is a good practice to minimize the changes to the Global policy. Instead, create custom policies. Many organizations opt to use scoped policies, where each policy is scoped to a department. For example, the HR department might have their own scoped policies. In a scoped policy, you can implement departmental settings that override the Global policy settings. In the steps below, we create a new scoped policy.

1. Sign into the Azure portal at: *https://portal.azure.com*.

2. Navigate to **Azure Information Protection** in the portal. You can search for it if you don't have it pinned.

3. From the **Azure Information Protection** panel, click **Policies** in the left pane. You will see a Global policy and custom policies (if you have any).

4. Click **+Add A New Policy** in the right pane.

5. In the **Policy** blade, type a name for the policy. For example: HR data. Then, type a description for the policy.

6. Click **Select Which Users Or Groups Get This Policy. Groups Must Be Email-Enabled**. In the AAD Users and Groups pane, navigate to an email-enabled group, click it, then click **OK**. The group will be displayed below the name and description, as shown below in Figure 3-38.

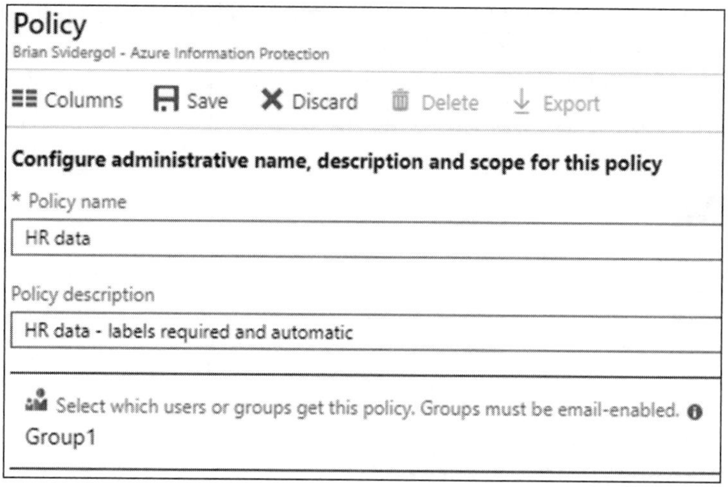

Policy

Brian Svidergol - Azure Information Protection

≡≡ Columns   **🖫 Save**   **✕ Discard**   🗑 Delete   ↓ Export

Configure administrative name, description and scope for this policy

* Policy name

| HR data |

Policy description

| HR data - labels required and automatic |

👥 Select which users or groups get this policy. Groups must be email-enabled. ❶

Group1

FIGURE 3-38 New scoped policy configuration settings

7. Click the **On** button for the setting titled **All Documents And Emails Must Have A Label (Applied Automatically Or By Users)**.

8. Click the **Automatic** button for the setting titled **For Email Messages With Attachments, Apply A Label That Matches The Highest Classification Of Those Attachments**.

9. In the top of the right pane, click **Save**. In the dialog box, click **OK** to confirm the save and publish the new policy.

When you have multiple policies, they are applied in order. The last policy in the list is applied. Users will see labels from the Global policy and any sublabels configured. When using scoped policies, it is a good practice to use sub-labels. This enables departments to have more precise labels instead of the default labels such as Public and Confidential. Here we create a new sub-label for the Confidential label.

1. In the **Azure Information Protection** blade, click **Labels** in the left pane.

2. In the right pane, to the right of the **Confidential** label, click the ellipsis (**...**). From the context menu, click **Add A Sub-Label**.

3. In the **Sub-Label** blade, type a name for the sub-label such as **HR PII** and type a description such as **HR PII data – automatic headers**. Figure 3-39 shows the sub-label.

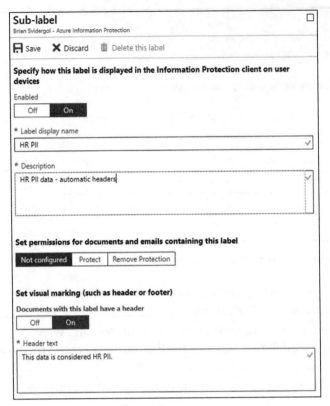

Sub-label
Brian Svidergol - Azure Information Protection

💾 Save   ✕ Discard   🗑 Delete this label

Specify how this label is displayed in the Information Protection client on user devices

Enabled

| Off | **On** |

* Label display name

| HR PII | ✓ |

* Description

| HR PII data - automatic headers| | ✓ |

Set permissions for documents and emails containing this label

| **Not configured** | Protect | Remove Protection |

Set visual marking (such as header or footer)

Documents with this label have a header

| Off | **On** |

* Header text

| This data is considered HR PII. | ✓ |

FIGURE 3-39 New sub-label with headers

4. Click **Save**. In the confirmation dialog box, click **OK** to confirm the save and publish the sub-label.

5. The sub-label will now be displayed if you expand the Confidential label. Note that the sub-label is created but not tied to a policy, as shown in Figure 3-40.

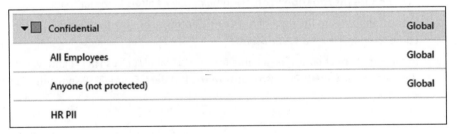

▼ ☐ Confidential	Global
All Employees	Global
Anyone (not protected)	Global
HR PII	

FIGURE 3-40 Confidential label showing sub-labels

6. In the left pane, click **Policies**.

7. In the right pane, click **Global**.

8. In the **Policy: Global** pane, click **Add Or Remove Labels**.

9. In the **Policy: Add Or Remove Labels** pane, click the **HR PII** label so that it has a checkmark next to it (like the default labels). Then click **OK**.

10. Click **Save** in the **Policy: Global** blade.

11. In the **Policies** blade, click the **HR Data** policy (or the custom policy you want to use for the sub-label).

12. In the **Policy: HR data** blade, click the **Select The Default Label** dropdown menu, click **Confidential\HR PII**, then click **Save**.

> **MORE INFO** **LEARN MORE ABOUT POLICY SETTINGS AND LABELS**
>
> To learn more about policy settings and creating new labels, see the tutorial at:
> *https://docs.microsoft.com/azure/information-protection/infoprotect-quick-start-tutorial.*

After you have policies, labels, and clients, the next task organizations often take on is protecting data. Microsoft offers an Azure Information Protection scanner. The scanner runs as a service on a Windows server and can scan and protect local files on the server, UNC paths, and on-premises SharePoint libraries and sites.

> **MORE INFO** **AIP SCANNER**
>
> For more information about the AIP scanner, see:
> *https://docs.microsoft.com/azure/information-protection/deploy-aip-scanner.*

Implement AIP tenant key

AIP relies on a tenant key. A tenant key, by default, is a Microsoft-managed key that you don't have to manage. Optionally, you can use a customer-managed key using Bring Your Own Key (BYOK).

Understand the key options

The tenant key is the root key that is tied to your Azure Information Protection tenant. Other keys used by AIP are chained to the root key (like a web server certificate is chained to a root certificate). You have two options to consider for your tenant key:

- **Managed By Microsoft** With this option, which is the default option, Microsoft generates the tenant key and manages the tenant key. This is the simplest option and is often appropriate for smaller organizations or organizations.

- **Bring Your Own Key (BYOK)** With this option, you create the key. You also manage the key. This is the most complex option and is often used by large organizations or organizations that place a heavy emphasis on security.

Each key option has its pros and cons. You should familiarize yourself with these so that you can opt for the right key option based on a given scenario. Table 3-3 shows the differences between the keys.

TABLE 3-3 Tenant key pros and cons

Tenant key attribute	Applicable to Managed by Microsoft keys?	Applicable to BYOK?
Quick, easy, automatic creation	Yes	No
Low administrative overhead	Yes	No
Low cost	Yes	No
Compatible with on-premises HSM?	No	Yes
Offers complete control over the key?	No	Yes

If you opt to use the BYOK approach, you have two options:

- **Create A Key In Azure Key Vault**   In this scenario, you create the key in Azure Key Vault, andou manage the key. This is the simpler solution, but doesn't offer the same level of protection and confidence that the HSM offers.

- **Create A Key In Your On-Premises HSM**   If you have an on-premises HSM, you can create your key with it then transfer it to Azure Key Vault. This option has the most administrative overhead and cost, but it also provides the best security (and is often required to meet certain compliance requirements).

EXAM TIP

You must have Azure Key Vault Premium to use an HSM-protected key. HSM-protected keys cost money every month, so cost is a key consideration when planning for HSM-protected keys.

Perform key management tasks

There are five key management tasks. Some are relevant to Microsoft-managed keys, some are relevant to BYOK, and some are relevant to both.

- **Revoke Your Key**   Revoking a key render is unusable. You do this if the key has been breached or if there have been other security incidents.

- **Rekey Your Key**   When you rekey a key, you archive the existing key and get a new key. Rekeying is a good practice so that keys do not remain valid indefinitely. Think of rekeying as as you would think of changing a password.

- **Backup And Recover Your Key**   The tenant key is important. It should be backed up and recoverable from backup. Otherwise, in the event of a disaster, you might not be able to get to your protected data.

- **Export Your Key** Exporting your key creates a copy of the key. You can use it for backup and recovery too.
- **Respond To A Breach** If there is a breach or similar security incident, you need to be able to quickly respond. In many scenarios, the response is to rekey your key.

In Table 3-4 we look at the management tasks and their applicability to each key option.

TABLE 3-4 Applicability of key management tasks

Key task	Applicable to Managed by Microsoft keys?	Applicable to BYOK?
Revoke your key	No, Microsoft handles this (such as when you cancel your AIP)	Yes
Rekey your key	Yes	Yes
Backup and recover your key	No, Microsoft is responsible for backup and recovery of the key	Yes, can backup and recovery by using HSM. Can also backup in Azure Key Vault (Backup-AzureKeyVaultKey) but can't use it outside of Azure Key Vault
Export your key	Yes, by contact Microsoft Customer Support Services	No, not from Key Vault because the key becomes non-recoverable once transferred to Azure Key Vault
Respond to a breach	Yes	Yes

> **MORE INFO STEPS TO IMPORT HSM-PROTECTED KEYS**
>
> To learn more about HSM-protected keys and the details of the import process, see: *https://docs.microsoft.com/azure/key-vault/key-vault-hsm-protected-keys#prerequisites-for-byok.*

Skill 3.3: Manage data governance

Organizations need to manage their data by keeping it while it is needed, deleting it when it is no longer needed, and **labeling it to enable** any special handling requirements. These data management tasks are often referred to as "data governance". In Office 365, data is spread across multiple services, so your **data governance** must be viable across the services. Historically, data governance has been delivered in each individual service, such as Exchange Online. Now, data governance is moving toward a centralized service, which can be implemented across all Office 365 services. In this chapter, we will look at the built-in data governance features in Office 365.

Configure information retention

Office 365 retention applies to your SharePoint content, email content, and Skype/Teams content. To retain data, you need to configure retention policies. The policies will be based on your company requirements and which services you use. For the exam, you should be familiar with the capabilities across all the services and understand the limitations of the built-in retention capabilities.

Understand information retention prerequisites

Retaining information is sometimes a requirement for compliance or legal reasons. Other times, it is merely a way to help employees work more efficiently. Imagine searching for a document in your organization. Instead of searching through only the last year of documents, you might have to search every document ever produced (for example, in a company that indefinitely keeps all data). That's not efficient. In many organizations, data is retained based on compliance, legal, and efficiency reasons. Sometimes, we also run across organizations that maintain data "just in case" or "because they aren't sure if they will need it sometime in the future." This often points to immature information retention policies or a non-existent information retention strategy.

The exam covers two ways to retain data. One way is using information retention policies. The other is using retention labels. There are differences between them:

- **Information retention policies**   Retention policies are used to retain data for a specific period of time, delete data after retention (optional), or just delete data when it is a certain age. You choose the location(s) for the policy, including Exchange Online, SharePoint Online, and OneDrive. We look at all of the locations later in this section.

- **Retention labels**   Retention labels are displayed in apps such as Outlook and OneDrive. Users can opt to use them to retain data or delete data. One downside is that users are choosing which labels to use and whether to use labels. To avoid that, you can apply labels automatically based on conditions you dictate (this requires an E5 license). Labels can be used across Exchange, SharePoint, OneDrive, and Office 365 groups, but not across other services such as Teams, which is supported by retention policies.

Beyond retention policies and labels, we will also cover built-in features for managing data, such as the In-Place Hold in Exchange Online, and the SharePoint Recycle Bin. Some of these built-in features are deprecated or are no longer being developed in favor of using retention labels and retention policies. Before you implement information retention, you should have a good understand of the prerequisites, capabilities, and the limitations of the Office 365 capabilities related to information retention.

PREREQUISITES

- To use retention policies for Exchange Online mailbox data, mailboxes must be tied to an Exchange Online Plan 2 license, an Office 365 E3 or Office 365 E5 license, or a Microsoft 365 E3 or E5 license. Anything less than that requires a separate Exchange Online Archiving license.

- To use retention policies with SharePoint Online (by way of the preservation hold library), you need SharePoint Online Plan 2, Office 365 E3 or E5, or Microsoft 365 E3 or E5.

RETENTION POLICIES CAPABILITIES

Retention policies work across several areas of Office 365. While our focus is on the major services of Office 365 (Exchange Online, SharePoint Online, or OneDrive for Business), you should be familiar with the applicable locations for the smaller services. The following services are supported locations for retention policies.

- **Exchange email**   With Exchange email, you target mailboxes. While you can use a distribution group or a mail-enabled security group as a target, the groups are expanded at the time of use and not dynamic. That means, if you add Group1 to a retention policy and it contains 9 members, only those 9 members will be the target of the retention policy, even if you add 10 more people to the group 3 months later. Beyond including mailboxes, you can also exclude mailboxes.

- **SharePoint sites**   For SharePoint Online, you can target the site level. You just need the site URL or you can select the site from the list of sites.

- **OneDrive accounts**   For OneDrive, you can add accounts individually. You can use the account URL, or you can select a site from the list of sites.

- **Office 365 groups**   Office 365 groups can be targets of retention policies. You can search for a group or select groups from the list of groups.

- **Skype for Business**   For new policies, this is off by default. If you enable it, you can choose individual users.

- **Exchange public folders**   For new policies, this is off by default. You can enable this, which automatically retains all public folders.

- **Teams channel messages**   For Teams, you can target channel messages for select teams and exclude specific teams.

- **Teams chats**   For chats in Teams, you can include or exclude individual users.

Retention labels have a capability of starting the retention period at the time of labeling, while retention policies start the retention based on the age of the content or last modification date. Additionally, after a retention period, labels can kick off a disposition review, which requires SharePoint or OneDrive documents that must be reviewed before they can be deleted.

LIMITATIONS

Microsoft is rapidly enhancing its services. As such, the limitations listed here exist at the time of this writing and at the time of the original exam development. Typically, the exam will reference limitations, especially when they are long term limitations (or permanent limitations). For short term limitations, the exam often avoids those. Be aware of the following limitations for the exam:

- When you create a retention policy for Teams (Teams channel messages or Teams chats), all other retention locations are turned off. To retain Teams data, you must have a dedicated retention policy.

- Teams retention does not support advanced retention. Therefore, you cannot create a retention policy to apply to data that meets specific conditions.

- Advanced retention does not apply to Skype for Business or Exchange Online public folders. That's because public folders and Skype for Business do not support sensitive information types (which is one of the options for advanced retention).

- Retention labels are not valid for Teams channel messages, Teams chats, or Skype for Business.

- Only one retention label can be applied at a time.

Configure information retention labels

There are two types of labels you can use: sensitivity labels and retention labels. These cannot be used interchangeably. If you want to use a label for retention, it must be a retention label. In this section, we will go through the retention label creation process and describe the options available.

1. Sign in as an administrator to the Security & Compliance admin center at: *https://protection.office.com*.

2. In the left pane, expand **Classifications** and then click **Labels**.

3. By default, you will see a list of your existing sensitivity labels. Click the **Retention** tab near the top of the right pane (see Figure 3-41).

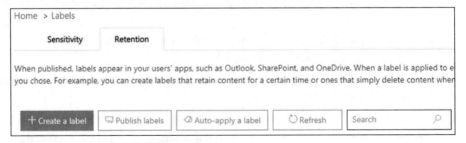

FIGURE 3-41 Retention labels in the admin center

4. Click **+Create A Label**.

5. On the **Name Your Label** page, type a name for the label. For this walk through, we will use **Tax data - 7 years**. Optionally, you can add a description for admins and a

description for users. Both are recommended. While you might know what the label is, others might not, and the label usage might not be obvious say three years from now. Click **Next**.

6. On the **Label Settings** page, click the **Retention** button to turn on retention. Without retention being turned on, you cannot use the label for retention! Maintain the default setting of retaining content for seven years and leaving content as is when the retention period expires. Optionally, you can retain content forever or for a different period. After the retention period ends, you have the option to automatically delete the retained content or trigger a disposition review (reviewers get an email to review the data). Additionally, you can use a retention label to delete old data, even if the data was not retained by a retention policy. The last option on this page enables you to use the label to classify the content as a record. Content classified as a record cannot be edited, deleted, or have the retention label edited or removed. Click **Next**.

7. On the **Review Your Settings** page, click **Create This Label**.

8. On the **Tax Data – 7 Years** workspace, click **Close**.

Now that you have a retention label, you can use it to retain data! Of course, the label must first become available for use. Remember, you create labels from the Security & Compliance Center. After that, labels need to sync to the applicable services such as Exchange Online and SharePoint Online. For SharePoint and OneDrive, the sync might take up to one day. For Exchange Online, the sync might take up to seven days.

> *MORE INFO* **DIGGING INTO RETENTION LABELS**
>
> To find out more detail about the label sync process and timing, along with other details of how labels work, see: *https://docs.microsoft.com/office365/securitycompliance/labels*.

Monitor data governance

After you implement data governance, you need a way to find out if it is effective. You must also find the usage rates, and see whether any gaps exist in your implementation. On the data governance dashboard, you can review key data governance data at a glance:

- Top five labels
- Labels trend over the past 90 days
- Top label users/policies
- Risky labels activity
- How labels were applied

The data governance data is available for up to 90 days. Thus, if you need to maintain data longer, you should plan to capture the data before it becomes unavailable.

UNDERSTAND SUPERVISION

One option for monitoring data governance is to use supervision policies, which enable you to capture organizational communications that can then be examined. Supervision is often used for individual employees, or to monitor communications between specific groups in your organization. During the communication examination, an examiner classifies items as Compliant, Non-Compliant, Questionable, or Resolved. The examination takes place in Outlook on the web (via an add-in) or in the Outlook desktop app (also via an add-in).

Plan for Microsoft 365 backup

While many administrators are familiar with backing up their data when the data is on-premises, they are not familiar with backups in the public cloud. Many of the on-premises backup solutions don't work for cloud-based services or feel like quickly developed add-ons that lack critical features. In this section, we will look at the planning concepts for backing up data in Microsoft 365/Office 365.

Understand backup capabilities and limitations

Built-in backup capabilities provide basic recovery of data in specific scenarios. Many organizations use the built-in capabilities in Office 365. However, some organizations enhance and/or extend the built-in capabilities with third-party tools to meet all of the requirements for their disaster recovery and business continuity needs. In this section, we will outline the capabilities and limitations, separating Exchange from SharePoint and OneDrive.

EXCHANGE ONLINE

Microsoft uses Database Availability Groups (DAGs) to protect the Exchange Online service. Your data is stored in multiple data centers that are geographically dispersed. These backups, however, are used in case of a service outage. You still need a way to maintain your data. Backup capabilities for Exchange Online are focused on email data and public folder data. This is like what you find with Exchange Server on-premises. Outside of email, key data also exists in Active Directory (if you are syncing users and groups from on-premises), or in Azure Active Directory if your users and groups are in Azure Active Directory, but not in an on-premises Active Directory environment. Below are the key capabilities:

- **Recovering deleted items** Deleted items are stored in the Deleted Items folder and are recoverable by users. Once permanently deleted, the items are stored in Recoverable Items/Deletions for 14 days by default, although you can extend to a maximum of 30 days. Administrators can recover permanently deleted items.

- **Archiving email data forever** In Office 365, you can create archive mailboxes for users. Archive mailboxes store older email data, configurable based on time or size. Initially, the archive mailbox had a maximum size of 100 GB, although you could call Microsoft to increase the size. Today, archive mailboxes have an unlimited size. They also automatically increase in size, as needed, although this is an optional feature. A minimum license of Exchange Online Plan 2, an Exchange Online Archiving license, or an Office 365 E3/Microsoft 365 E3 is required for unlimited archiving.

- **Maintaining email for legal purposes** During a lawsuit or similar legal matter, organizations are often required to preserve email data specifically related to the matter. Organizations have relied on Office 365 features such as In-Place Hold and Litigation Hold for maintaining email data. An In-Place Hold enables you to granularly hold specific data, such as data based on a query for keywords or similar. When a Litigation Hold is placed on a mailbox, all mailbox data is maintained, and you can't choose otherwise, including archive mailbox data, if it exists. You can also use an In-Place Hold for public folders, but you can't use a Litigation Hold for public folders. Note that items on hold do not count against a mailbox quota.

> **MORE INFO IN-PLACE HOLD IS GOING AWAY**
>
> The In-Place Hold feature is deprecated. Microsoft is officially transitioning to Litigation Hold and retention policies. The exam is unlikely to call out the deprecation of In-Place Hold, so you should plan to be familiar with the technology.

Below are the key limitations of the backup features in Exchange Online:

- **Restoring mailboxes to a point in time** Imagine that a mailbox becomes flooded with malware, spam, or has some type of corruption. Restoring to a point in time enables you to go back to the point just before the corruption started. This capability is commonly found in on-premises solutions for Exchange Server. It is not, however, offered with Exchange Online.

- **Archive mailboxes have limits in some plans** Archive mailboxes are limited to 50 GB for Office 365 Business Essentials, Office 365 Business Premium, and Office 365 Enterprise E1. See: *https://docs.microsoft.com/us/office365/servicedescriptions/exchange-online-service-description/exchange-online-limits#mailbox-storage-limits* for more information and capabilities tied to the different plans.

SharePoint Online and OneDrive for Business

In SharePoint Online, Microsoft backs up the environment every 12 hours and retains that data for 14 days. Additionally, you have SharePoint Online available in two geographically dispersed datacenters. This is helpful from a SharePoint Online service perspective. But you still need a way to maintain your own data. Below are the key capabilities for maintaining data:

- **SharePoint document versioning** With document versioning, each time a document is updated, a new version is created. You can store up to 50,000 major versions (such as 1.0, 2.0) and 511 minor versions (such as 2.1, 2.2). Versioning is configurable–you can turn it off, set it to only create major versions, or set it to configure major and minor versions. Versions take up space in your tenant. For example, if you have 5 MB Excel file and it has 10 versions, then it takes up 50 MB in your tenant.

- **The SharePoint site's Recycle Bin keeps data for 93 days** After 93 days, the data is permanently deleted.

- **The SharePoint site collection Recycle Bin maintains data for up to 93 days** The time is based on how much time the data spent in the site's Recycle Bin. For example, if data is kept in the site's Recycle Bin for 40 days, and then deleted, it will be stored in the site collection Recycle Bin for 43 days. Data is maintained for up to 93 days, no matter which Recycle Bin is used.

- **OneDrive offers the OneDrive Files Restores feature** This feature enables users to restore data from up to 30 days ago.

- **OneDrive offers a Recycle Bin** The Recycle Bin maintains data for up to 93 days.

Remember the Microsoft backups we talked about at the beginning of this section? You can request a restore from those backups.You can, however, only request a restore of an entire site collection or sub-site with all of its content. Consider this as a last resort if you are unable to get the data elsewhere. This is because the restores can take up to a few days.

Back up Exchange Online data

In this section, we will walk through some of the configuration items for maintaining your Exchange Online data. This isn't traditional "backup" whereby you use software to make backup copies of your Exchange databases. Exchange Online offers retention policies and retention tags. These are service-specific, and only apply to Exchange Online. Policies and labels in the Security & Compliance Center protect content across services and are the recommended method to use.

CONFIGURING HOW LONG TO RETAIN DELETED ITEMS

You need to use Exchange Online PowerShell to work with the settings for retaining deleted items in your mailbox, . By default, deleted items are maintained for 14 days. You can change the period, although 30 is the maximum number of days. Run the commands below to connect to Exchange Online PowerShell.

```
$Creds = Get-Credential
$Session = New-PSSession -ConfigurationName Microsoft.Exchange
-ConnectionUri https://outlook.office365.com/powershell-liveid/
-Credential $Creds -Authentication Basic -AllowRedirection
Import-PSSession $Session -DisableNameChecking
```

The following command looks at the retention settings for Brian Svidergol's mailbox:

```
Get-Mailbox -Identity "Brian Svidergol" | select RetainDeletedItemsFor
```

To individually set Brian's mailbox to retain deleted items for 30 days, run the following command:

```
Set-Mailbox -Identity "Brian Svidergol" -RetainDeletedItemsFor 30
```

If you want to set all mailboxes to retain data for 21 days, run the following command:

```
Get-Mailbox -ResultSize unlimited -Filter {(RecipientTypeDetails -eq
'UserMailbox')} | Set-Mailbox -RetainDeletedItemsFor 21
```

CREATE ARCHIVE MAILBOXES

By default, archive mailboxes are not created for new mailboxes. To use mailbox archiving, you need to create archive mailboxes. Perform the following steps to create an archive mailbox.

9. Sign in as an administrator to: *https://protection.office.com*.

10. In the left pane, expand **Data Governance** and then click **Archive**.

11. In the right pane, a list of your mailboxes will be displayed along with whether there is an associated archive mailbox, which is shown as **Enabled** if a mailbox has an archive mailbox or **Disabled** if it doesn't). Click a mailbox that you want to configure for archiving.

12. On the right side, click **Enable**. A popup warning will warn you that items older than two years will be moved to the archive mailbox. This is based on the archiving policy, which is configured for two years. Click **Yes** to continue.

You can also use PowerShell to enable archiving and view the current archiving configuration. First, connect to Exchange Online PowerShell:

```
$Creds = Get-Credential
$Session = New-PSSession -ConfigurationName Microsoft.Exchange
-ConnectionUri https://outlook.office365.com/powershell-liveid/
-Credential $Creds -Authentication Basic -AllowRedirection
Import-PSSession $Session -DisableNameChecking
```

To check **All Mailbox For Their Current Archiving Status,** run the following command.

```
Get-Mailbox -Filter {ArchiveStatus -Eq "None" -AND RecipientTypeDetails
-eq "UserMailbox"} | Select Name,*ArchiveSt*
```

To enable archiving for a single mailbox (Brian's mailbox, in this example), run the following command:

```
Enable-Mailbox -Identity "Brian Svidergol" -Archive
```

To enable archiving for all user mailboxes, run the following command:

```
Get-Mailbox -Filter {ArchiveStatus -Eq "None" -AND RecipientTypeDetails
-eq "UserMailbox"} | Enable-Mailbox -Archive
```

Backup SharePoint Online and OneDrive for Business data

In this section, we will walk through some of the configuration items for maintaining your SharePoint Online and OneDrive for Business data. This isn't a traditional backup, whereby you use software to back up your SharePoint databases but provides data retention and recoverability.

CONFIGURE DOCUMENT VERSIONING

In this section, we will configure the SharePoint Online document versioning. Perform the following steps to modify document versioning settings.

1. Sign in as an administrator to the SharePoint site that you want to configure.

2. In the upper right corner, click the gear icon to display the dropdown menu. Click **Library Settings,** as shown in Figure 3-42.

FIGURE 3-42 SharePoint site library settings

3. On the library settings page, click **Versioning Settings**, as shown in Figure 3-43.

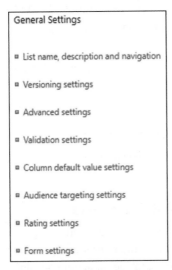

FIGURE 3-43 SharePoint library versioning settings

4. On the Versioning Settings page, you can configure several versioning settings:

   A. **Require Content Approval For Submitted Items**   This is off by default. When enabled, items that are new or edited remain in a draft state until approved. This setting can slow down the content publishing process, but is useful in highly regulated or high security environments.

B. Create Major Versions   This is enabled by default. This ensures modifications are saved to a major version, such as version 1, version 2, and so on.

C. Create Major And Minor (Draft) Versions   This is disabled by default. If enabled, documents have a major and minor version when changed. For example, 1.1, 1.2, and so on.

D. Keep The Following Number Of Major Versions   By default, 500 major versions are kept. You can increase the number to the maximum of 50,000.

E. Keep Drafts For The Following Number Of Major Versions   This disabled by default. If you enable content approval, then you can also configure versioning for drafts.

F. Draft Item Security   This is disabled by default. The settings are not available until you require content approval. You can configure drafts so that only the users that can edit the drafts can read them, and any users can read them, or only approvers and the author can read them. This is useful for highly regulated industries or high-security organizations.

G. Require Check Out   This is disabled by default. If you enable it, users must check-out a file before editing it. When checked out, other users cannot edit the document.

5. After you configure the desired versioning settings, click **OK** to save them.

EXAM TIP

If you plan to use document co-authoring, you must disable the option of requiring check-out. Otherwise, people cannot co-author a document. Requiring checkout limits one person at a time from editing a document.

CONFIGURE ONEDRIVE DATA RETENTION FOR DELETED USERS

By default, OneDrive content is retained based on the SharePoint retention settings. For deleted users, OneDrive keeps the user data 30 days. Perform the following steps to adjust the retention period for deleted users:

1. Sign in as an administrator to the OneDrive admin center at: *https://admin.onedrive.com/*.

2. In the left pane, click **Storage**.

3. On the **Storage** page, update the days to retain files for deleted users. The default is 30 days. The maximum is 10 years (3650 days). Note that the days are counted from the time the user is deleted. Enter the desired number of days in the textbox and then click **Save**.

When users are deleted, access to the OneDrive content is automatically enabled for the user's manager (if configured). This is controlled in the SharePoint settings with a feature named Enable Access Delegation, which is enabled by default. Optionally, you can manually designate a secondary owner, which is useful if the user doesn't have a manager. Managers will be notified by email with instructions to access the deleted user's data.

Plan for restoring deleted content

As an administrator, you can restore deleted content in SharePoint Online, OneDrive for Business, and in Exchange Online. This section looks at the details of the restore process for SharePoint Online, OneDrive for Business, and Exchange Online.

Restore deleted data in Exchange Online

You can restore deleted items by using Outlook and Outlook on the web. In this section, we will look at the options in the Outlook desktop app, which provides the same functionality as Outlook on the web.

RESTORING DELETED DATA IN OUTLOOK

To restore deleted items in Outlook, perform the following steps.

1. Launch Outlook.
2. In the left pane, click **Deleted Items**.
3. In the list of deleted items, drag and drop items from Deleted Items to the desired location, such as Inbox. This restores them.
4. If you don't see any items in the Deleted Items folder, click the **Recover Items Recently Removed From The Folder** hyperlink at the top of the Deleted Items folder.
5. In the **Recover Deleted Items** window, select the items you want to restore. You can multi-select using the CTRL button, and left-click on multiple items, and then click **OK**. Note that you can also permanently delete items in this window, if desired.

RESTORING PURGED ITEMS IN EXCHANGE ADMIN CENTER

Purged items are items that a user deleted and then purged using the Recover Deleted Items tool. Once items are purged, only an administrator can recover them, if they are still recoverable. As an administrator, you can use the In-place eDiscovery & Hold functionality to recover items. This functionality is partially built into the content search feature in the Security & Compliance Center. To restore purged items, perform the following steps:

1. Sign into the Exchange admin center as an administrator.
2. Ensure that you are a member of the Discovery Management role. If you aren't, add yourself, sign out, then sign back in.
3. In the left pane, click **Compliance Management**.
4. On the In-place eDiscovery & Hold page, click + to start a search.
5. In the **New In-Place eDiscovery & Hold** window, type a name for the search, such as **Recovering Purged Items** and then click **Next**.

6. Click the **+** icon to specify the mailbox to search. Click the mailbox in the list of mailboxes, clickA**add**, and then click **OK**. Click **Next**.

7. On the **Search Query** page, click **Next** to maintain the default to search all content.

8. On the **In-Place Hold Settings** page, maintain the default option not to place results on hold. Click **Finish**. The search operation will start. Click **Close** in the save window.

9. In the list of searches, click the search you just ran. Then, click the magnifying glass (search) icon. In the dropdown menu, click **Copy** search results.

10. In the **Copy Search Results** window, on the **Recovering Purged Items** page, deselect the **Enable De-Duplication** option.

11. Click **Browse**, click the **Discovery Search Mailbox,** click **OK**, and then click **Copy**, as shown in Figure 3-44.

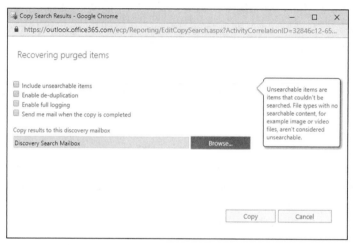

FIGURE 3-44 Exchange Online copying search results

12. If a warning is displayed notifying you about an empty search returning all results, click **OK**.

13. Once the search is complete, highlight the search, and then click **[Open]** in the right pane.

14. A new tab will open Outlook on the web for the Discovery Search Mailbox. Expand the **Recoverable Items** folder and then click **Purges**. In the right pane, items that are recoverable in the Purges folder will be displayed. Once you confirm that the data you want to restore is displayed, go back to the Exchange admin center browser tab.

15. Click to highlight the search results, then click the down arrow icon (download icon). If prompted to download and install the eDiscovery PST Export Tool, proceed to download and install it.

16. In the **eDiscovery PST Export Tool** window, click **Browse**, specify a location to save the .PST file, and then click **Start**. Once downloaded, the .PST file can be provided to the

end user, or an administrator can import the items into the user's mailbox to complete the recovery operation.

Restore deleted data in SharePoint Online

You can restore data from the SharePoint Online site Recycle Bin or from the site collection Recycle Bin after data has been deleted from the site Recycle Bin.

To restore data from a site's recycle bin, perform the following steps:

1. Sign in as an administrator to the SharePoint site from which you want to restore deleted items.
2. In the left pane, click **Recycle Bin**.
3. On the **Recycle Bin** page, a list of deleted items will be displayed. Click the item you want to restore, then click the **Restore** button.

To restore data from a site collection's Recycle Bin, perform the following high-level steps:

4. Sign in as an administrator to the SharePoint admin center.
5. Go to site collections.
6. In the list of site collections, click the site collection that has the data you want to restore and then go to the site collection's Recycle Bin.
7. Restore the desired data.

Restore deleted data in OneDrive for Business

For OneDrive for Business, there are a few scenarios where you need to restore data. One is when data was deleted. Another is when a user was deleted. A third is when you need to restore OneDrive data to a specific date, such as if all data was accidentally deleted.

RESTORE ONEDRIVE DATA FROM THE RECYCLE BIN

To restore items that were deleted from your OneDrive, but are still in the Recycle Bin, perform the following steps.

1. Sign in to OneDrive in a browser. The URL is: *https://<SiteName>-my.sharepoint. com* where *<SiteName>* represents your individual site name. This will redirect to *https://<SiteName>-my.sharepoint.com/personal/<User_UPN-with_underscores>/_ layouts/15/onedrive.aspx*, where *<SiteName>* is the individual site name and *<User_UPN_with_underscores>* is the user's UPN with underscores (such as brian_ svidergol_com for brian@svidergol.com).
2. In the left pane, click **Recycle Bin**.
3. In the right pane, files in the Recycle Bin will be displayed. Click the file that you want to restore and then click **Restore**.

RESTORE DELETED USER'S ONEDRIVE

If a user was recently deleted (within the last 30 days, by default), you can restore the user and all of the OneDrive data by using the Microsoft 365 admin center. At a high level, go to the admin center, and restore the user from the deleted users area. If a user was deleted too long in the past and the user doesn't show up in the deleted users area, you can use PowerShell to restore the user.

For our example, we will use a fictitious name of Kari Tran with our Alpine Ski House organization. To connect to SharePoint Online via PowerShell as Kari, run the following commands:

```
$adminUPN=kari@alpineskihouse.com
$orgName="karitran"
$userCredential = Get-Credential -UserName $adminUPN -Message "Type the password."
Connect-SPOService -Url https://$orgName-admin.sharepoint.com
-Credential $userCredential
```

To restore the deleted user with OneDrive content, perform the following steps:

1. From the PowerShell prompt, run the `Get-SPODeletedSite -IncludeOnlyPersonalSite | FT url` command. If the site appears in the output, you can restore it.

2. Obtain the site URL. You can review existing my site URLs by running the `Get-SPOSite -IncludePersonalSite $true -Limit all -Filter "Url -like '-my.sharepoint.com/ personal/" |select Url` command. Substitute Kari's UPN at the end of the URL along with your tenant name at the beginning of the URL.

3. Run the `Restore-SPODeletedSite -Identity <URL_of_deleted_site>` where <URL_of_ deleted_site> is the deleted user's my site URL you obtained in step #2.

RESTORE ONEDRIVE TO A PREVIOUS DATE

Another option to restore OneDrive data is to restore OneDrive to a previous date. This is handy if you need to restore all of the data, such as after a malware infestation, or a large amount of data when clicking individual files, since to restore them would be too time con-suming. This feature, called Files Restore, is limited to restoring data that is available in version history, the Recycle Bin or the site collection Recycle Bin. Perform the following steps to restore your OneDrive to a previous date:

1. Sign into your OneDrive site in a browser.

2. In the upper right side of the page, click the gear icon (Settings icon) and then click **OneDrive** (Restore your OneDrive) in the menu.

3. On the **Restore your OneDrive** page, select a date from the dropdown menu and then click **Restore**.

Skill 3.4: Manage auditing

Historically, auditing has been a decentralized feature available in each of the Office 365 services. You individually configure each service for auditing and individually search each service for items. Microsoft is moving to a more centralized approach by approaching data governance with a centralized solution. Today, while you can individually configure services for auditing, you can search the audit logs across all services from the same place. We will look at the auditing feature and configuration in this chapter.

> **This skill section covers how to:**
> - Configure audit log retention
> - Configure audit policy
> - Monitor Unified Audit Logs

Configure audit log retention

Office 365 audits many activities by default. From an administrative perspective, there isn't much to do to configure audit log retention. In this section, we will look at default and additional auditing you can enable.

Understand prerequisites

While auditing is enabled by default, you might need to look at licensing, permissions, or settings before you start looking at the audit logs. The following items represent the key prerequisites you need to know about:

- **Permissions**   To have complete control over the auditing settings, you need to be assigned the Organization Management role, Compliance Management role, or a Global Administrator in Office 365. While there are other roles, they can't turn auditing on or off. For searching and viewing audit logs, you can use the View-Only Audit Logs role or the Audit Logs role.

- **Licensing**   The Office 365 E3 license offers up to 90 days of audit log retention. The Office 365 E5 license offers up to 365 days of audit log retention. You can, however, use any Office 365 subscription, plus add on the Office 365 Advanced Compliance license, to get up to 365 days of audit log retention. Today, you can get the Office 365 Advanced Compliance bundled with Azure Information Protection in a package named Information Protection & Compliance. Expect package names and offerings to change. For the exam, just be aware of the Office 365 Advanced Compliance add-on to gain additional days of retention.

Understand default auditing

Office 365 audits several areas across various services by default. For some organizations, the default auditing is enough to meet company requirements. The following activities are audited by default:

- Admin activity in Azure Active Directory
- Admin activity in Exchange Online
- Admin activity in SharePoint Online
- User activity in SharePoint Online and OneDrive for Business
- User and admin activity in Dynamics 365
- User and admin activity in Microsoft Flow
- User and admin activity in Microsoft Stream
- User and admin activity in Microsoft Teams
- User and admin activity in Power BI
- User and admin activity in Sway
- User and admin activity in Yammer
- eDiscovery activities in the Office 365 Security & Compliance Center

Some activities are not audited by default, including the following:

- **User activity in Exchange Online**   These are activities, such as creating mailbox items, purging messages, and updating mailbox permissions. While the audit log search interface enables you to search for these activities, you won't receive results by default.
- **SharePoint site-specific auditing**   These are items such as editing items, deleting or restoring items, and searching site content.

For these activities, you need to enable additional auditing to capture the activities. We go through the steps to enable the auditing next.

Configure additional auditing

While a ton of information is available with default auditing, you sometimes need to capture more information. In this section, we'll look at two popular places where you can increase the auditing: Exchange Online (capturing user mailbox activity) and SharePoint Online (capturing site-specific events).

TURNING MAILBOX LOGGING ON OR OFF

With logging on, you will find a host of activities being logged (assuming you have activity in the services). If you try to search for mailbox activities, however, you won't find anything. That's because you must turn on auditing at the mailbox level for mailbox audit information. To enable auditing for Brian Svidergol's mailbox, run the following command:

```
Set-Mailbox 'Brian Svidergol' -AuditEnabled $True
```

To set all mailboxes to have auditing, run the following command:

```
Get-Mailbox -ResultSize Unlimited -Filter {RecipientTypeDetails
-eq "UserMailbox"} | Set-Mailbox -AuditEnabled $True
```

TURNING SHAREPOINT SITE-SPECIFIC AUDITING ON

To turn on additional auditing for a SharePoint site, perform the following steps.

1. Navigate to the SharePoint site in your browser and sign in as a site administrator.

2. In the upper right-hand corner, click the gear icon, and then click **Site Settings** in the dropdown menu.

3. On the **Site Settings** page, click **Site Collection Audit Settings** under Site Collection Administration.

4. On the **Configure Audit Settings** page, click the checkboxes next to the events you want to audit. Figure 3-45 shows how to enable the editing of items, along with editing content types and columns. Note that checking in and checking out of items is audited by default.

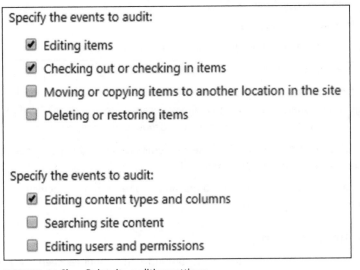

FIGURE 3-45 SharePoint site auditing settings

5. After clicking the checkboxes, click **OK** to save the auditing settings.

Configure audit policy

The exam blueprint was written before some of the Office 365 features were finalized and available. As such, we have seen a few areas of the exam blueprint that call out something that doesn't make sense with the product today. This skill, "Configure audit policy," is one area that doesn't make sense today. This is because auditing is enabled by default and it covers the vast majority of auditing. There is almost nothing to configure! In the previous section, and in the next section, we cover the content for auditing, which covers the couple of items that might appear in this skill.

Monitor unified audit logs

Prior to a unified audit log, admins needed to search logs in each service. For example, the admin might search in the Exchange Online logs and then search through the SharePoint Online logs. With a unified audit log, admins can search in one place: the Security & Compliance Center. Auditing is turned on by default, but you need to have permissions to search the logs before you can begin searching. In this chapter, we will look at an overview of the unified audit log and walk through various search scenarios.

Prepare to use the unified audit logs

Before you start using the unified audit logs, you need to look at the prerequisites and ensure that audit logging is enabled. While we mentioned that audit logging is enabled by default, that may not always be the case. And, it can be disabled.

TURNING UNIFIED LOGGING ON OR OFF

Our first task is to check if logging is enabled. To do that, perform the following steps:

1. Run the following PowerShell script to connect to Exchange Online.

    ```
    $Creds = Get-Credential
    $Session = New-PSSession -ConfigurationName Microsoft.Exchange
    -ConnectionUri https://outlook.office365.com/powershell-liveid/
    -Credential $Creds -Authentication Basic -AllowRedirection
    Import-PSSession $Session -DisableNameChecking
    ```

2. From the PowerShell prompt, run the `Get-AdminAuditLogConfig | FL *unified*` command. It will output True or False for the logging being enabled. And, it will show the date the admin audit log was first enabled (if applicable).

3. If logging is not enabled and you want to enable it, run the `Set-AdminAuditLogConfig -UnifiedAuditLogIngestionEnabled $true` command.

4. If logging is enabled and you want to disable it, run the `Set-AdminAuditLogConfig -UnifiedAuditLogIngestionEnabled $false` command.

EXAM TIP

Watch out for troubleshooting scenarios on the exam whereby you aren't getting the data you expect in the audit logs, or aren't getting audit data at all. Scan through the answers to see if you find anything related to turning on auditing or anything related to adjusting permissions. If so, you might have found your answer!

Perform searches using the unified audit logs

The unified audit logs are available for searching in the Security & Compliance portal or through PowerShell. You can search for all activities, very specific activities, or for activities in a specific service, such as Exchange Online.

The following steps walk you through the search in the portal.

1. Navigate to the Security & Compliance portal at *https://protection.office.com*.

2. Sign in as an administrator.

3. In the left pane, expand the **Search & Investigation** menu.

4. In the left pane, under **Search & Investigation**, click **Audit Log Search**.

5. Choose the activities you want to search for. You can pick predefined activities, such as Checked Out File, you can search for items matching a keyword, or you can search for all activities.

6. Specify the dates. You can choose a start date and an end date. If you are licensed with E3 or equivalent, audit logs are retained for 90 days. If you are licensed for E5 or equivalent, audit logs are retained for 365 days (currently, as part of a preview, but likely to go to general availability soon).

7. Specify the User(s) that you want to include in the search. You can specify one user, multiple users, or all users (by leaving the field blank).

8. Specify the file, folder, or site that you want to search for. This is optional and is relevant for some services. The screen capture below shows a search for all activities for January 28, 2019 to January 29, 2019, for any user, without a specific file, folder, or site. Figure 3-46 shows the search interface.

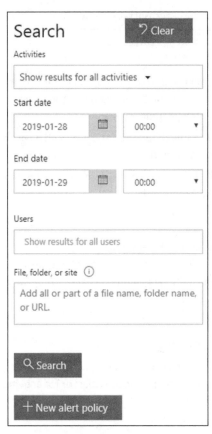

FIGURE 3-46 Unified audit log search interface

9. Click **Search**. The results will be displayed in the right pane. You can click on an entry to bring up the details for that entry.

Besides using the portal to search the log, you can also use PowerShell. PowerShell provides additional flexibility for finding specific data, outputting that date, or for piping the output to other commands. To search for all activities from January 28, 2019 to January 29, 2019 for brian@svidergol.com, run the following command:

```
Search-UnifiedAuditLog -StartDate 1/28/2019 -EndDate 1/29/2019
-UserIds brian@svidergol.com
```

If you run a command like the command above, the first thing you might notice is that much of the data is lumped together in the output, like this:

```
AuditData    : {"CreationTime":"2019-01-28T01:25:19","Id":"3078a622-0467-44ea
-8946-6dcde800ce50","Operation":"UserLoggedIn","OrganizationId":"1ae53066
-382a-4c22-9648-acfdd0f39613","RecordType":15,"ResultStatus":"Succeeded","UserKey":
"40037FDE82450E58@svidergol.com","UserType":0,"Version":1,"Workload":
"AzureActiveDirectory","ClientIP":"70.187.130.195","ObjectId":"Unknown","UserId":
"brian@svidergol.com","AzureActiveDirectoryEventType":1,"ExtendedProperties":
[{"Name":"UserAgent","Value":"Microsoft Office\/16.0 (Windows NT 10.0;Microsoft
Outlook 16.0.10730;Pro)"},{"Name":"UserAuthenticationMethod","Value":"1"},{"Name":
"RequestType","Value":"OrgIdWsTrust2:process"},{"Name":"ResultStatusDetail",
"Value":"Success"}],"Actor":[{"ID":"7bcd445a-08b9-4783-ae05-818c64128dc4",
"Type":0},{"ID":"brian@svidergol.com","Type":5},{"ID":"10037FFE81450D58",
"Type":3}],"ActorContextId":"1ae53046-382a-4c12-9548-cfdd0f39613","ActorIpAddress":
"10.9.8.7","InterSystemsId":"e2a90c0a-cb5f-461d-9e3a-1be0ac17a092","IntraSystemId"
:"492b133e-136b-456f-a181-aa722e3c4600","Target":[{"ID":"Unknown","Type":0}],
"TargetContextId":"1ae53066-392a-4c22-9648-acfdd0f39613","ApplicationId":
"00000002-0000-0ff1-ce00-000000000000"}
```

It is difficult to read and parse (such as by using a script). Luckily, there is a formatting parameter. To run the same command, but output with formatting, run the following command:

```
Search-UnifiedAuditLog -StartDate 1/28/2019 -EndDate 1/29/2019
-UserIds brian@svidergol.com -Formatted
```

With this command, the data comes back formatted and easy to read and parse. The output below is truncated but shows the difference:

```
AuditData   : {
                 "CreationTime": "2019-01-28T23:36:22",
                 "Id": "64519b52-4a90-46f8-4c8b-08d68566980",
                 "Operation": "MailboxLogin",
                 "OrganizationId": "1ae5316-382a-4c22-9648-acfd40f3r613",
                 "RecordType": "ExchangeItem",
                 "ResultStatus": "Succeeded",
                 "UserKey": "10037FFD31450D58",
```

Sometimes, you might want to use PowerShell to search for events that include specific IP addresses. In the following example, we search for events between January 28, 2019 and January 29, 2019 for user brian@svidergol.com with free text of 10.9.8.7.

```
Search-UnifiedAuditLog -StartDate 1/28/2019 -EndDate 1/29/2019 -UserIds brian@svidergol.
```

```
com -IPAddresses '10.9.8.7'
```

You can also exclude the user to find out all of the activities, including 10.9.8.7:

```
Search-UnifiedAuditLog -StartDate 1/28/2019 -EndDate 1/29/2019 -IPAddresses '10.9.8.7'
-Formatted
```

There are additional parameters that you might find useful, such as -Freetext, to search for free text in events.

> **MORE INFO**   **DEEP DIVE INTO SEARCH-UNIFIEDAUDITLOG**
>
> To find out more detail about the Search-UnifiedAuditLog, including all of the additional filtering you can do, see: *https://docs.microsoft.com/powershell/module/exchange/policy-and-compliance-audit/search-unifiedauditlog?view=exchange-ps*.

Skill 3.5: Manage eDiscovery

Electronic Discovery (eDiscovery) is a way to identify, preserve, and produce data. Often, eDiscovery is related to data pertinent to litigation, government investigations, or civil incidents. Office 365 offers eDiscovery features and makes these features available in the Security and Compliance Center. In this chapter, we will look at working with the eDiscovery features and help you understand their requirements and basic operational tasks.

> **This skill section covers how to:**
> - Search content by using Security and Compliance Center
> - Plan for in-place and legal hold
> - Configure eDiscovery

Search content by using the Security and Compliance Center

The content search tool enables administrators to quickly search for content across various services in Office 365. This is often the first step an administrator will take before creating an eDiscovery case (a topic covered later in this chapter). Content search and eDiscovery will generate the same results, but offer different capabilities, such as exporting reports or assigning an in-place hold. The results can include data from email messages, Skype for Business conversations, documents in SharePoint Online or OneDrive for Business, Microsoft Teams, and Office 365 Groups. In this skill we will review the prerequisites for content search and how to use the tool.

Understand prerequisites

In this section, we will look at the prerequisites for working with content search and eDiscovery. Both tools are part of the eDiscovery solution, so licensing and permissions are similar. For prerequisites, we will look at the licensing considerations and the permissions required to perform various tasks. You must understand these components clearly for the exam.

LICENSING

The licensing options for content search are tied to eDiscovery. As you move up in licensing, you unlock more eDiscovery features. When you look at licensing, you want to acquire the license that provides all of the features you require, but not more. To do this, you must understand the features and limitations of the eDiscovery licensing. Below are the key license types that include eDiscovery functionality. Note that Office 365 enterprise plans are functionally equivalent to Office 365 government plans. Thus, E1 is the same as G1, E3 is the same as G3, and E5 is the same as G5.

- **Office 365 E1 / Office 365 F1 / Office 365 Business Essentials / Office 365 Business Premium** The E1 license is the lowest license that provides some eDiscovery capabilities. With an E1 license, you can perform searches across Office 365 services. You can also search across multiple mailboxes or sites in a single search. You cannot use content holds or export results from the searches.
- **Office 365 E3** With an E3 license, you get all of the functionality from E1. Additionally, you can export data from the search, and you can use content holds. You can also use eDiscovery cases, which enables you to organize and segment searches.
- **Office 365 E5** With an E5 license, you get all the functionality from E3. Additionally, you gain access to the Advanced eDiscovery feature, which uses cloud-based analytics to provide analysis of your searches. Advanced eDiscovery provides a more efficient eDiscovery process, potentially reducing costs.

EXAM TIP

If you have Office 365 E3 and want to use Advanced eDiscovery, you can purchase the Advanced Compliance add-on instead of upgrading to the E5 license. Users that are targeted by Advanced eDiscovery must have an E5 license! Thus, this is something you can do for some admins, but not across your entire user population.

PERMISSIONS

To enable administrators to perform eDiscovery or content searches, you need to assign the necessary permissions. By default, nobody has permissions, even your existing Office 365 administrators. The Security & Compliance Center provides several built-in role groups. One such role group, eDiscovery Manager, has two role groups inside of it. You assign these to administrators that need to work with eDiscovery.

- **eDiscovery Manager**   An eDiscovery Manager can create, view, and edit cases that they have access to. By default, they only have access to cases that they create. You can add users or groups to this role group.

- **eDiscovery Administrator**   An eDiscovery Administrator can view and edit all cases. By default, they only have access to cases that they create. They can, however, add themselves to any other case. You can only add users, not groups, to this role group.

The eDiscovery Manager role group is assigned roles. The roles give the permissions needed to perform eDiscovery tasks. The default roles for the eDiscovery Manager role group are:

- **Export**   With this permission, you can export data from a search.

- **RMS Decrypt**   You can decrypt RMS-protected content so that you can export the data from a search.

- **Review**   This permission enables you to work with the advanced eDiscovery features, such as analyzing results.

- **Preview**   You can view the list of items returned from a search.

- **Compliance Search**   You can search across multiple mailboxes.

- **Case Management**   You can create, edit, and delete eDiscovery cases. You can also adjust permissions for cases you own.

- **Hold**   This permission enables you to place a hold on content.

You can edit the roles included in the role group, however, this isn't necessary unless you have a specific requirement to enable more functionality or restrict some eDiscovery tasks.

Besides eDiscovery role groups, there are roles that can perform some eDiscovery tasks:

- **Reviewer**   A reviewer can use advanced eDiscovery functions for existing cases that they are a member of.

- **Organization Management**   Role members can create, edit, and delete eDiscovery cases, search across multiple mailboxes, place content on hold, and perform search and purge tasks (perform a search then delete data in bulk based on that search).

- **Compliance Administrator**   A compliance admin can create, edit, and delete eDiscovery cases, search across multiple mailboxes, and place content on hold.

Work with content search

You can use the content search tool to quickly search your Office 365 services for material matching targeted criteria. The results can be used to determine scope, impact, and next steps in the event additional action is required, such as a legal hold. Search queries can be saved for reuse and search results can be exported for offline review.

In the steps below, we create a search query for a fictitious company named Alpine Ski House. The legal department needs to know if any documents were shared in the last 30 days related to Project 1080.

1. Sign in as an administrator to the Security & Compliance Center at: *https://protection. office.com.*

2. In the left pane, expand **Search**and then click **Content Search**.

3. On the Content search page, click **+Guided Search**. This option provides a guided experience for creating a new search query. Once you are comfortable with creating a query, you can click **+New search** and create your own queries.

4. On the **New Search** flyout, for **Name Your Search**, type a name for your new search query. In our example, we will name the search query **Project 1080**. Type a description, if desired. A description should be provided to help differentiate between search queries. Click **Next**.

5. On the **Choose Locations** tab, click the **All Locations** radio button. This enables your search to find data across Office 365 services. If you intend to only search a specific service, such as Exchange Online, you can opt to specify that location instead. Click **Next**.

6. On the **Create Query** tab, in the **Keywords** field, enter the following keywords: **project; project 1080; 1080**.

7. Below the search query, click **+Add Conditions**. In the **Add Conditions** flyout, click the checkboxes for **Date** and **File Type**, and then click **Add**. In the date section, configure the dates desired. In our example, we'll configure the date representing the last 30 days. In the file type section enter the following file types: **docx; xlsx; pptx; pdf**.

8. Click **Finish**. You will be brought back to the searches page and the query will automatically run. Any results from the query will be displayed in the main window.

Administrators can update search queries and save their changes from the search results page for the specific query. For example, if there are too many results returned for the Project 1080 query, you can open the results for that search query and update the list of keywords or add additional conditions.

Results for search queries can also be exported. The export options for content search are accessible from the search flyout. In Figure 3-47 we have selected the Project 1080 search and clicked More, revealing options to export results or export reports.

FIGURE 3-47 Content Search - Export

- **Export Results**   This export option outputs a copy of all discovered results. Exchange content can be exported as a PST file or as individual emails. Individual messages and SharePoint content can be exported as a compressed ZIP file.

- **Export Report**   This export option outputs a report in CSV format. The report contains properties such as sender, recipient, attachments, and date received.

Plan for in-place and legal hold

At any point your organization may be required to preserve content in Office 365. With eDiscovery this is accomplished by placing the content on an in-place hold. An administrator can place content on hold across all Office 365 services. Content holds offer granular controls leveraging the same query interface seen in content search and eDiscovery. In this skill we are going to look at how holds work and how to configure them in the Security & Compliance Center.

How holds work

Holds focus on preserving data. Sometimes, holds are for a defined period. Other times holds are indefinite (or the hold requirements are not finalized yet). Holds are invisible to users and cannot be bypassed. Holds are available for the following areas:

- **Exchange Online mailboxes**   You can place holds on mailboxes. While you can target groups too, the mailboxes that are members are placed on hold, not the actual group.

- **Exchange Online public folders** You can place holds on public folders. You cannot, however, specify individual public folders. Instead, you have to place a hold on all public folders if you want to hold items in any of the folders.

- **SharePoint Online sites** You can choose individual SharePoint Online sites to hold data. You just need the URL for the sites you want to target for holds.

When you place holds on mailboxes, the data is preserved by using the Recoverable Items folder, which isn't viewable with the default view in Outlook. The Recoverable Items folder also holds permanently deleted items, such as when users delete items from the Deleted Items folder. A dedicated subfolder named DiscoveryHold is used to store held items. For the exam, be sure to know some of the details around holds, such as:

- Items in the Recoverable Items folder don't count toward a user's mailbox quota. Instead, the Recoverable Items folder has its own quota, which defaults to 30 GB.

- When a hold is placed on a mailbox, the quota for the Recoverable Items folder is automatically increased to 100 GB. You can enable the archive mailbox and use auto-expanding archiving if you need more space.

- A minimum license of Exchange Online Plan 2 or Office 365 E3 is required for a mailbox to be placed on hold.

- Deleting a mailbox on hold will convert it to an inactive mailbox. Inactive mailboxes can no longer receive messages and are not listed in the global address list. The contents of the mailbox will be retained for the duration of the hold.

MORE INFO **WORKING WITH OFFICE 365 HOLDS**

To find out more about the details around holds, read through: *https://docs.microsoft.com/ exchange/security-and-compliance/in-place-and-litigation-holds.*

Configuring holds

The following steps show the process to create a hold for all email items for one mailbox. Note that the prerequisite is having an existing case created and a search defined.

1. From your existing case, click the **Holds** tab.

2. On the **Holds** tab, click **+Create**.

3. On the Create A New Hold flyout, type a name for the hold. For example, type **Holding Brian's email per divestiture**. Click **Next**.

4. On the **Choose Locations** tab, click **Choose Users, Groups, Or Teams**. Then, click **Choose Users, Groups, Or Teams**. In the search textbox, type the name of the person you are targeting for the hold. A search will be performed dynamically. If not, click the magnifying glass (search) icon. In the results, click the checkbox next to the target mailbox and then click **Choose**. Click **Done** and then click **Next** to continue.

5. On the **Create Query** tab, type a keyword or list of keywords, such as a configuration referred to as a Query-Based Hold. Or, if you want to hold everything, do not enter

anything. This is referred to as an Indefinite Hold. Optionally, add conditions. Then click **Next**.

6.   On the **Review Your Settings** tab, click **Create This Hold**. Refer to Figure 3-48 for an example of the hold status flyout. In this example a hold has been applied to two mailboxes in the marketing department for a duration of 90 days.

FIGURE 3-48 eDiscovery – Hold Details

7.   On the flyout, click **Close**.

> **MORE INFO   MANAGING CONTENT HOLDS**
>
> To find out more about configuring and managing holds, read through: *https://docs.microsoft.com/office365/securitycompliance/ediscovery-cases#step-4-place-content-locations-on-hold.*

Configure eDiscovery

Earlier in this chapter we introduced you to content search, which enabled you to quickly run search queries against your Office 365 services. In this skill we will be working with eDiscovery. The eDiscovery tool extends the capabilities of content search. With eDiscovery, administrators can create cases for ongoing events. Cases offer an extra layer of permissions, enabling you to control who has access to a case and what level of access they have. We will also be working with advanced eDiscovery, an enhancement that enables additional analysis of the eDiscovery results.

Work with eDiscovery cases

You can use eDiscovery cases to organize your eDiscovery searches, preserve content, and export data from your searches. Cases help to organize your eDiscovery work. You create and manage cases from the Security & Compliance Center.

In the steps below, we create and configure an eDiscovery case based on a fictitious company named Alpine Ski House that needs to uncover information about a broken ski lift in the last 3 months.

1. Sign in as an administrator to the Security & Compliance Center at *https://protection. office.com*.

2. In the left pane, expand **eDiscovery** and then click **eDiscovery**.

3. On the eDiscovery page, click **+Create A Case**.

4. On the **New Case** flyout, type a name for the case. In our example, we will name the case **Broken Ski Lift**. Type a description, if desired. If you work with many cases, you should provide a description to help others differentiate between cases. Click **Save**.

5. In the list of cases, click **Open** next to your case.

6. On the case page, click **Searches** and then click **+New Search**.

7. On the **Search Query** page, type keywords for your search. In our case, we will search for *ski lift*, *lift*, and *broken*.

8. In the **Locations** section, click the **All Locations** radio button. This enables your search to find data across Office 365 services. If you intend to only search a specific service, such as Exchange Online, you can opt to specify that location instead.

9. Below the search query, click **+Add Conditions**. In the **Add Conditions** flyout, click the **Date** checkbox and then click **Add**. In the date section, configure the dates desired. In our example, we'll configure the date representing the last 90 days. You can add multiple conditions. Often, you need to so that you can reduce the total amount of items returned in a search.

10. Click **Save & Run**. On the **Save Search** flyout, type a name for the search. In our example, we will use the name **Broken Ski Lift**. Optionally, type a description. In a complex case, you will have multiple searches. By using descriptive names and descriptions, you can minimize duplicate searches. Click **Save**. The search begins immediately. A preview of the results will be displayed.

ADJUSTING AND EXPORTING

After previewing the results, you can adjust your search query, similar to a content search. For example, you can add more conditions, change the locations, or add more keywords. To export the results from a search, perform the following steps:

1. Click the **More** button and then click **Export Results** in the dropdown menu.

2. In the Export results flyout, configure the export options:

    A. **Output Options**. You can export all items that are in a usable format, all items regardless if in a usable format, or just items that are in an unusable format.

B. **Export Exchange Content Options**. You can export all Exchange content in a single PST file for each mailbox where data was found, in a single PST file for all messages found, one PST file with a single folder for all messages found, or individual messages.

C. **De-Duplication**. Optionally, you can enable de-duplication. For example, if your search found results in 53 mailboxes, you can use de-duplication so that you don't get the same message from all 53 mailboxes (instead, you get a single message).

3. After configuring your export options, click **Export**.

4. Click the **Exports tab**. Completed exports will be displayed. Click the export you just ran. In the flyout, copy the export key. The export key is sensitive so protect it like a password or secret. It can be used by anybody to download the search results.

5. Click **Download Results**. Note that you must use Microsoft Edge or Internet Explorer to perform the download. If this is your first time downloading results, you will be prompted to install the Microsoft Office 365 eDiscovery Export Tool, because the tool is required to download results. Click **Install** to proceed. In the eDiscovery Export Tool pop-up box, paste the export key, browse to the location that you want to save the data to, and then click **Start**. When the status shows that the process is complete, click **Close**.

6. The exported data will be saved to a folder. Inside, you will find a summary CSV file along with the data, separated by folders for each service where data was found.

USING ADVANCED FEATURES

By default, the Core eDiscovery functionality is used when working with eDiscovery cases. You can switch to Advanced eDiscovery to unlock additional functionality, however, such as analyzing your search results. As discussed earlier, you need to have the right licensing for the advanced functionality. Perform the following steps to analyze your search:

1. After performing a search, while viewing the preview results, click **Prepare For Advanced eDiscovery.**

2. In the **Prepare For Advanced eDiscovery** flyout, click **Prepare**.

3. To view the progress, click the **Exports** tab, and then click the name of your search. A flyout will show you the current progress. To update the progress, close the flyout and open it again.

4. After preparation, the initial setup is complete. Next, you need to run a processing job. Click the **Prepare** tab. In the **Setup** screen, highlight the source search and then click **Process**. Upon completion, you will see a high-level graphical representation of the total number of files and errors.

5. Click the **Express Analysis** tab, click the search you are working with, then click the **Express Analysis** button. By default, the results are downloaded to the local computer, but can optionally be sent to Azure blob storage. The analysis takes time, so for most searches, you need to let it run and move onto other tasks while you wait.

After the analysis runs, you can view the Results page to see pivot tables and charts summarizing the analysis. Some of the information delivered includes:

- Total amount of data, such as email and documents.

- Breakdown of the data, such as documents, emails, or attachments.

- Breakdown of duplicate data. For example, you might find that 58% of the data analyzed is duplicative, as shown in Figure 3-49.

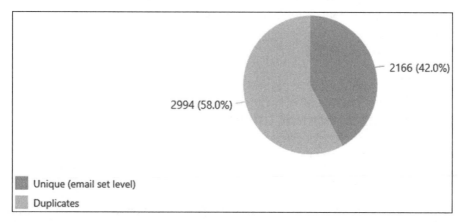

- Summary of errors in the analysis, if any.

MORE INFO **EXPRESS ANALYSIS SETTINGS**

To find out more about the options when you run an Express Analysis, see: *https://protection.office.com/?ContentOnly=1#/ediscovery/AED/64bbf6df-1ab1-45af-83a8-f0acfde661e2?l1=ExpressAnalysis&l2=TaskStatus&l3=&l4=.*

Thought experiment

You are the systems administrator for Alpine Ski House. Alpine Ski House runs several skiing and outdoor activity locations throughout the world. The company has an on-premises environment with two data centers. The company has Active Directory Domain Services on-premises, along with some internal servers, and Windows 10 clients. For email and collaboration, the company uses Office 365. Soon, the company will start using OneDrive for Business to store data that is currently stored on on-premises file servers. The company recently created a dedicated IT team to handle IT security. The new team is responsible for compliance, data loss prevention, backups, and data governance.

The new team reviewed the existing implementation for data in Office 365 and found the following:

- The company is using Exchange Online retention tags and retention policies.

- The company is not using Information Rights Management (IRM) with SharePoint Online.
- The company is not retaining SharePoint data.
- The company is not using OneDrive for Business.

The security management team has drafted new requirements for the organization:

- The company must centralize the configuration of retention to ensure that retention settings are the same across as many Office 365 services as possible.
- The data in some SharePoint Online libraries must be encrypted, even if users do not opt to encrypt the data.

You need to reconfigure the environment to meet the new requirements.

Thought experiment answer

In this scenario, there are multiple requirements. We will look at solutions for one requirement at a time.

The first requirement is to centralize the configuration of retention. The company currently uses retention, but it is configured in Exchange Online. That retention configuration cannot be used outside of Exchange Online. To centralize the retention configuration, you need to configure retention in the Security & Compliance Center. In this scenario, you should configure retention to apply to Exchange Online, SharePoint Online, and OneDrive. This will ensure you meet the requirement to retain data across as many services as possible.

The second requirement is to encrypt SharePoint data in libraries. To meet this requirement, you need to enable Information Rights Management (IRM) which enables the use of encryption throughout SharePoint Online. Thereafter, you need to configure document libraries with IRM settings to ensure that documents are encrypted. This ensures you meet the requirement to encrypt data even if users do not opt to encrypt their files.

Chapter summary

- DLP uses dictionary matches, keyword matches, regular expression matches, and internal functions to detect sensitive data in DLP rules.
- DLP has a central policy store which is the place where policies and rules are initially created and stored. From the central policy store, replication is used to replicate policies to Exchange Online, SharePoint Online, OneDrive for Business, and Office 2016 desktop apps.
- DLP offers a wide array of built-in DLP policies covering financial companies, medical and health companies, and privacy settings applicable to just about all organizations.
- DLP offers a test mode for policies. In test mode, you can see whether the policy does what you expect before you turn it on for your production environment.

- Data retention policies can be used to retain data for a specified period. For example, you can retain data for five years. Users cannot bypass data retention policies.

- Data retention policies can be used to delete data, once the data reaches a specified age. For example, all data older than seven years can be automatically deleted. You can combine policies to retain data with policies to delete data.

- Data retention for Exchange Online stores copies of original content in the Recoverable Items folder while SharePoint Online stores copies of original content in the Preservation Hold library.

- You can use PowerShell to create, manage, and delete policies for DLP or data retention.

- AIP has 3 versions that you can license: Azure AIP for Office 365 (least features), Azure AIP P1 (standard features), and Azure AIP P2 (most features).

- AIP has a prerequisite of Azure AD. Additionally, a sync between your on-premises AD DS and Azure AD is required so that you can license your users.

- The RMS Connector enables integration between AIP and on-premises versions of SharePoint, Exchange, and file servers running Windows Server.

- WIP is a data protection technology that complements AIP and is focused on protecting data on client computers that run Windows 10.

- With WIP, an enlightened app is an app that can differentiate between personal data and corporate or organizational data.

- Labels in AIP help users easily see the sensitivity of data (such as with visual markings) and can automatically protect data based on the data as well as conditions.

- The Super User feature of AIP enables you to view and remove the protection on any protected content. This is helpful in a scenario where a user that protected data is no longer with the organization, but left behind protected data.

- Some applications, such as Exchange Server, need to be AIP Super Admins to fully function. This enables applications to inspect the data and ascertain whether an action is required. For example, Exchange Server can inspect an outgoing email address and see if it must be blocked or protected before sending it.

- To deploy the AIP client, you can use a manual installation method, Intune, System Center Configuration Manager, or Group Policy. Each deployment method has pros and cons.

- AIP provides a built-in policy. You can create new policies and scope the policies to specific departments or people. This is useful if some departments have different protection requirements than others.

- By default, AIP uses a tenant key that is managed by Microsoft. For high security organizations, you can use the Bring Your Own Key (BYOK) option, whereby you create and manage the key.

- Retention policies enable you to retain data, delete data, or both. You can retain data across multiple Office 365 locations.

- Retention labels enable users to retain data, by putting a label on their content. Labels can also be applied automatically, which strengthens your retention.

- Exchange Online has multiple data recovery methods built-in, including saving deleted items, archiving email with archive mailboxes, and holds (legal and in-place).

- SharePoint Online stores data for SharePoint and OneDrive. There are two Recycle Bins (site level and site collection level) that maintain deleted data for up to a total of 93 days.

- SharePoint Online and OneDrive for Business offer document versioning. With document versioning, documents have a version number associated with them. When documents are changed, a new version number is created. Users can go back to previous versions, if needed.

- By default, OneDrive for Business keeps deleted user data for 30 days. You can configure the service to maintain deleted user data for up to a maximum of 3650 days.

- An administrator can restore email items out of the Purged items folder. However, users can only restore deleted items that are in the Deleted Items folder or in Recoverable Items recently deleted from the Deleted Items folder.

- For some operations in Exchange Online and SharePoint Online, you must use PowerShell. Each service has a specific method to connect to PowerShell.

- Your Office 365 licensing dictates how long your audit logs are retained. For some subscriptions, you get up to 90 days of logs, while other subscriptions provide up to 365 days.

- Most admin activity is logged by default. Many user activities are also logged by default. User activity for Exchange Online is not logged by default, and some SharePoint site-specific information is not logged by default.

- You can search the unified audit logs by using the Security & Compliance Center or by using PowerShell.

- You can disable audit logging altogether, although this isn't recommended due to the lack of information that will be available for investigating security incidents.

- Unified audit logs cover Azure Active Directory, Exchange Online, SharePoint Online, OneDrive for Business, Dynamics 365, Microsoft Flow, Microsoft Stream, Microsoft Teams, Power BI, Sway, Yammer, and eDiscovery activities in the Security & Compliance Center.

- You can use the built-in reports in Security & Compliance Center to get an overview of your DLP incidents, DLP policy matches, and DLP overrides.

- Content search and eDiscovery will deliver the same results and leverage the same search query format. Content searches should be used for quick scenarios, while eDiscovery should be used for case tracking and in-place holds.

- To organize your searches, preserve content, and export data, you can use eDiscovery cases. Cases are especially beneficial if you have multiple administrators and perform many searches.

- You can enable more eDiscovery features by upgrading your Office 365 licenses. Office 365 E1 provides search capabilities, Office 365 E3 provides search, export, and holds. Office 365 E5 provides search, export, holds, and advanced eDiscovery features such as analysis.

- An eDiscovery Manager can work with cases that they create or are given access to. An eDiscovery Administrator can gain access to any case.

Index

Private Store, 60
Protect, 245, 255
PROTECTED, 261
Protected Apps, 240-241
protection, 245-247

Q

Quotes, 64

R

Raise Alerts Only For Suspicious Activities
        Occurring After Date, 131
Ready To Upgrade, 112
Recent Alerts, 194
Recover Items Recently Removed From The Folder, 272
Recovering Purged Items, 273
Register Your Domain, 95
Registration URLs, 10
Regular Expression Matches, 206
Release Preview Ring, 93
Remove Other Versions Of Office (MSI) From End User
        Devices, 73
Report Name, 142
Require Content Approval For Submitted Items, 270
Required Settings, 241
Restriction Type, 25
Retention, 220
Retention Policy Applied To A SharePoint Site, 218
Review, 284
Review In Progress, 111-112
Review Known Driver Issues, 112
Review Low-Risk Apps And Drivers, 112
Review Your Settings, 211, 220, 265, 288
Reviewer, 245, 284
Revoke Encryption Keys On Unenroll, 243
Risk Management Reports, 188

S

Save, 28, 52, 84, 124, 164, 166, 183, 188, 198-199, 246, 255,
        257-259, 271, 289
Save Copies Of Org Data, 86
Save Search, 289
Save Settings, 136
Screen Capture And Google Assistant, 87

Script, 176
Search Query, 273, 289
Select, 11-13, 20, 27, 41-43, 52, 82, 84, 86, 89, 105, 127, 129,
        144, 187, 192, 195, 198-199, 245, 254
Select Apps, 41
Select Groups, 27
Select Groups To Include, 52
Select Minimum PIN Length, 87
Send Alert As Email, 126
Send Org Data To Other Apps, 86
Service Assurance, 187
Servicing Channel Support Servicing Channel New Re-
        leases End, 94
Servicing Plan, 107
Session Policy, 133
Settings, 6, 65, 67, 69, 86-89, 108, 124, 130-131, 141-144,
        158, 187-189, 201, 246, 249, 275
Share Web Content With Policy Managed Browsers, 87
Show The Enterprise Data Protection Icon, 241, 243
Silent, 242
Site Collection Audit Settings, 278
Site Settings, 278
Software Library workspace, 106
Source, 144
Spam properties, 158
State Does Not Equal Approved, 133
Supported Apps, 135
Supported Platforms, 67
System Security, 50-51

T

Target operating system, 108
Target To All App Types, 86
Target Version To Be Evaluated, 108
Teams Chats, 219
Telemetry, 108
Test Now, 137
This Data Is Limited To HR Team Members Only, 245
Threat Detection, 132
Threat Management, 165
Troubleshooting And Support, 56

U

Uninstall, 74
Update Channel, 73